THE
2002 ANNUAL:
Volume 1
Training

(The Thirty-Eighth Annual)

JOSSEY-BASS/PFEIFFER
A Wiley Company
www.pfeiffer.com

THE
2002 ANNUAL:
Volume 1
Training
(The Thirty-Eighth Annual)

Edited by Elaine Biech

JOSSEY-BASS/PFEIFFER
A Wiley Company
www.pfeiffer.com

Published by

JOSSEY-BASS/PFEIFFER

A Wiley Company
989 Market Street
San Francisco, CA 94103-1741
415.433.1740; Fax 415. 433.0499
800.274.4434; Fax 800.569.0443

| www.pfeiffer.com |

Looseleaf ISBN: 0-7879-5965-0
Paperback ISBN: 0-7879-5963-4
ISSN 1046-333X

Acquiring Editor: Josh Blatter
Director of Development: Kathleen Dolan Davies
Developmental Editors: Susan Rachmeler and Rebecca Taff
Senior Production Editor: Dawn Kilgore
Manufacturing Manager: Becky Carreño

Printing 10   9   8   7   6   5   4   3   2   1

PREFACE

Welcome to *The 2002 Annual: Volume 1, Training*. This year represents the thirty-first year the *Annuals* have been published. Through the years, trainers, consultants, and performance-improvement technologists have turned to the *Annuals* as a resource for experiential learning activities and instruments, a reference for cutting-edge articles, and a source of inspiration as they design their own materials. This year's *Annuals* will continue to provide that same support.

The *Annuals* have been published as a set of two since 1995: Volume 1, Training, and Volume 2, Consulting. The materials in the training volume focus on skill building and knowledge enhancement. The training volume also features articles that enhance the skills and professional development of trainers. The consulting volume materials focus on intervention techniques and organizational systems. The consulting volume also features articles that enhance the skills and professional development of consultants. As you might imagine, it can be difficult in some cases to place materials strictly in one volume or the other. As a fellow practitioner, I encourage you to examine both volumes to find the materials that will meet your needs.

As we look toward 2002, we see that many organizations are re-establishing the training departments that they outsourced in the 1990s or increasing the size of training departments that they previously downsized.

The consultants we speak with are busier than ever, as organizations continue to implement new initiatives with a short supply of employees. These situations require more and more productivity from you as a trainer or consultant, so make the *Annuals* your companions as you meet the needs of your employer or client.

To ensure that you receive the most from all the *Annuals,* be sure that you have a *Reference Guide to Handbooks and Annuals* to help you identify all the resources available to you. The *Reference Guide* is a giant index that helps you locate just what you need based on topics and key words.

The *Annual* series has been valuable to the training and consulting professions for the past thirty-one years for several reasons. First, and most important, the *Annuals* provide you with a variety of materials that cover many topics—from the basics to cutting-edge issues. They are focused on what you as a trainer or consultant require in order to improve your own competencies in areas such as facilitating skills, team building, consulting techniques, and opening and closing techniques. The *Annuals* also provide content for you to use to design materials or to develop strategy for your internal or external clients.

Second, the *Annuals* are valuable because the materials are applicable to varying circumstances. You will find instruments for individuals, teams, and organizations; experiential learning activities to round out workshops, team building, or consulting assignments; and articles to assign as pre-reading, to read to increase your knowledge base, or to use as reference materials in your writing tasks.

Third, the *Annuals* are ready when you are. All of the materials contained in them may be duplicated for educational and training purposes. If you need to adapt or modify the materials to tailor them for your audience's needs, go right ahead. We only request that the credit statement found on the copyright page be included on all copies. In addition, if you intend to reproduce the materials in publications for sale or if you wish to use the materials on a large-scale basis (more than one hundred copies in one year), please contact us for prior written permission. Our liberal copyright policy makes it easy and fast for you to use the materials to do your job. Please call us if you have any questions.

While the *2002 Annuals* are the newest in the series, you will benefit from having the entire series for your use. They are available in paperback, as a three-ring notebook—and the Pfeiffer Library is available on CD-ROM.

The *Annuals* have always been a valuable resource to the profession. The key is that the materials come from professionals like you who work in the field as trainers, consultants, facilitators, educators, and performance-improvement technologists. This ensures that the materials have been tried and perfected in real-life settings with actual participants and clients, to meet real-world needs. To this end, we encourage you to submit materials to be considered for publication in the *Annual*. At your request, we will provide a copy of the guidelines for preparing your materials. We are interested in receiving experiential learning activities (group learning activities based on the five stages of the experiential learning cycle: experiencing, publishing, processing, generalizing, and applying); inventories, questionnaires, and surveys (both paper-and-pencil as well as electronic rating scales); and presentation and discussion resources (articles that may include theory related to practical application). Contact the Jossey-Bass/Pfeiffer Editorial Department at the address listed on the copyright page for copies of our guidelines for contributors or contact me directly at Box 657, Portage, WI 53901; on email at Elaine@ebbweb.com; or call our office at 608/742–5005. We welcome your comments, ideas, and contributions.

Thank you to the dedicated people at Jossey-Bass/Pfeiffer who produced the *2002 Annuals*: Josh Blatter, Kathleen Dolan Davies, Dawn Kilgore, Susan Rachmeler, Samya Sattar, and Rebecca Taff. Thank you to Beth Drake of ebb associates inc, who organized this huge task and ensured that all the deadlines were met.

Most important, thank you to our authors, who have once again shared their ideas, techniques, and materials so that the rest of us may benefit. Thank you on behalf of all training and consulting professionals everywhere.

Elaine Biech
Editor
June 2001

About Jossey-Bass/Pfeiffer

Jossey-Bass/Pfeiffer is actively engaged in publishing insightful human resource development (HRD) materials. The organization has earned an international reputation as the leading source of practical resources that are immediately useful to today's consultants, trainers, facilitators, and managers in a variety of industries. All materials are designed by practicing professionals who are continually experimenting with new techniques. Thus, readers and users benefit from the fresh and thoughtful approach that underlies Jossey-Bass/Pfeiffer's experientially based materials, books, workbooks, instruments, and other learning resources and programs. This broad range of products is designed to help human resource practitioners increase individual, group, and organizational effectiveness and provide a variety of training and intervention technologies, as well as background in the field.

Contents

---

*See Experiential Learning Activities Categories, p. 6, for an explanation of the numbering system.

**Topic is "cutting edge."

GENERAL INTRODUCTION
TO THE 2002 ANNUAL

The 2002 Annual: Volume 1, Training is the thirty-eighth volume in the *Annual* series, a collection of practical and useful materials for professionals in the broad area described as human resource development (HRD). The materials are written by and for professionals, including trainers, organization-development and organization-effectiveness consultants, performance-improvement technologists, educators, instructional designers, and others.

Each *Annual* has three main sections: experiential learning activities; inventories, questionnaires, and surveys; and presentation and discussion resources. Each published submission is classified in one of the following categories: Individual Development, Communication, Problem Solving, Groups, Teams, Consulting and Facilitating, Leadership, and Organizations. Within each category, pieces are further classified into logical subcategories, which are identified in the introductions to the three sections.

This year we have added a new subcategory to the Organizations category, which first appeared in the *1999 Annual*. "Change Management" joins "Communication" and "Vision, Mission, Values, Strategy" as the third subcategory within Organizations. Although these topics have been addressed in the past, it may have been difficult to locate them in the former structure. Appropriate past submissions will be cross-referenced in the next update to the *Reference Guide to Handbooks and Annuals*, which indexes all the materials by key words.

A new subcategory, "Technology," was added in the *1999 Annual*. Much has changed for the HRD professional in recent years, and technology has led much of that change. Given the important role technology plays, we will continue to publish material that relates technology to the HRD field and how the HRD professional can use technology as a tool.

We continue to identify "cutting edge" topics in this *Annual*. This designation highlights topics that present information, concepts, tools, or perspectives that may be recent additions to the profession or that have not previously appeared in the *Annual*.

The series continues to provide an opportunity for HRD professionals who wish to share their experiences, their viewpoints, and their processes with their colleagues. To that end, Jossey-Bass/Pfeiffer publishes guidelines for potential authors. These guidelines are available from the Pfeiffer Editorial Department at Jossey-Bass, Inc., in San Francisco, California.

Materials are selected for the *Annuals* based on the quality of the ideas, applicability to real-world concerns, relevance to current HRD issues, clarity of presentation, and ability to enhance our readers' professional development. In addition, we choose experiential learning activities that will create a high degree of enthusiasm among the participants and add enjoyment to the learning process. As in the past several years, the contents of each *Annual* span a wide range of subject matter, reflecting the range of interests of our readers.

Our contributor list includes a wide selection of experts in the field: in-house practitioners, consultants, and academically based professionals. A list of contributors to the *Annual* can be found at the end of the volume, including their names, affiliations, addresses, telephone numbers, facsimile numbers, and email addresses. Readers will find this list useful if they wish to locate the authors of specific pieces for feedback, comments, or questions. Further information is presented in a brief biographical sketch of each contributor that appears at the conclusion of each article. We publish this information to encourage networking, which continues to be a valuable mainstay in the field of human resource development.

We are pleased with the high quality of material that is submitted for publication each year and often regret that we have page limitations. In addition, just as we cannot publish every manuscript we receive, you may find that not all published works are equally useful to you. Therefore, we encourage and invite ideas, materials, and suggestions that will help us to make subsequent *Annuals* as useful as possible to all of our readers.

Introduction
to the Experiential Learning Activities Section

Experiential learning activities ensure that lasting learning occurs. They should be selected with a specific learning objective in mind. These objectives are based on the participants' needs and the facilitator's skills. Although the experiential learning activities presented here all vary in goals, group size, time required, and process,[1] they all incorporate one important element: questions that ensure learning has occurred. This discussion, lead by the facilitator, assists participants to process the activity, to internalize the learning, and to relate it to their day-to-day situations. It is this element that creates the unique experience and learning opportunity that only an experiential learning activity can bring to the group process.

Readers have used the *Annuals'* experiential learning activities for years to enhance their training and consulting events. Each learning experience is complete and includes all lecturettes, handout content, and other written material necessary to facilitate the activity. In addition, many include variations of the design that the facilitator might find useful. If the activity does not fit perfectly with your objective, within your time frame, or to your group size, we encourage you to adapt the activity by adding your own variations. You will find additional experiential learning activities listed in the "Experiential Learning Activities Categories" chart that immediately follows this introduction.

The 2002 Annual: Volume 1, Training includes fourteen activities, in the following categories:

Individual Development: Self-Disclosure

696. The Imposter Syndrome: Getting in Touch with Success, by Adrian F. Furnham

---

[1]It would be redundant to print here a caveat for the use of experiential learning activities, but HRD professionals who are not experienced in the use of this training technology are strongly urged to read the "Introduction" to the Reference Guide to Handbooks and Annuals (1999 Edition). This article presents the theory behind the experiential-learning cycle and explains the necessity of adequately completing each phase of the cycle to allow effective learning to occur.

Individual Development: Diversity

697. Cultural Triangle: Determining the Effect of Values on Customer/Client Perceptions, by Homer Warren, Ann M. McMahon, C. Louise Sellaro, and Carol Mikanowicz

Communication: Awareness

698. Speed Up! Increasing Communication Skills, by Marlene Caroselli

Communication: Styles

699. Memories: Influencing Others, by Saundra Stroope

Problem Solving: Consensus/Synergy

700. Electric Company: Deciding by Consensus, by John E. Fernandes

Groups: Competition/Collaboration

701. Power Poker: What's in It for Me? by Linda Raudenbush and Steve Sugar

Teams: How Groups Work

702. Sweet Tooth: Bonding Strangers into a Team, by Robert Alan Black

Teams: Problem Solving/Decision Making

703. Puzzles: Practicing Team Process, by Kristin J. Arnold

Consulting and Facilitating: Consulting: Diagnosing/Skills

704. Interrogatories: Identifying Issues and Needs, by Cher Holton

Consulting and Facilitating: Facilitating: Blocks to Learning

705. Crochet Hook: Learning How We Learn, by Lynne Andia

Consulting and Facilitating: Facilitating: Closing

706. Certificates: Appreciating Oneself, by Lois B. Hart

Leadership: Interviewing/Appraisal

707. Selection Interview: Practicing Both Roles, by John E. Oliver

Leadership: Styles

708. Second to None: Electronically Mediated Personal Leadership Planning, by Robert C. Preziosi

Organizations: Change Management

709. The Alphabet Game: Developing Confidence and Spontaneity Through Improv, by Izzy Gesell

Locate other activities in these and other categories in the "Experiential Learning Activities Categories" chart that follows or in the comprehensive *Reference Guide to Handbooks and Annuals*. This book, which is updated regularly, indexes all of the *Annuals* and all of the *Handbooks of Structured Experiences* that we have published to date. With each revision, the *Reference Guide* becomes a complete, up-to-date, and easy-to-use resource for selecting appropriate materials from all of the *Annuals* and *Handbooks*.

Experiential Learning Activities Categories

696. THE IMPOSTER SYNDROME: GETTING IN TOUCH WITH SUCCESS

Goals

- To help participants identify their level of comfort with the successes they've achieved.
- To identify ways participants can increase their willingness to succeed.

Group Size

Twenty to twenty-five.

Time Required

One hour and twenty minutes.

Materials

- One copy of The Impostor Syndrome Questionnaire for each participant.
- One copy of The Impostor Syndrome Lecturette for the facilitator.
- One copy of The Impostor Syndrome Score Sheet for each participant.
- Pens or pencils.

Physical Setting

A place for each person to sit and write.

Process

1. Briefly, without bias, describe the goals of the activity. Provide each participant with a copy of The Impostor Syndrome Questionnaire and a pen or pencil. Allow about ten minutes for them to answer the questions. (Ten minutes.)

2. Deliver The Impostor Syndrome Lecturette, encouraging comments and questions throughout. (Twenty minutes.)

3. Provide each participant with The Impostor Syndrome Score Sheet and allow about ten minutes for them to compile their scores. (Ten minutes.)

4. Ask the group for a show of hands: How many scores were higher, lower, and about the same as they might expect?

5. Ask participants to form subgroups of three and to discuss the following questions:

   ■ Why do you believe you scored the way that you did?

   ■ What does the score tell you about yourself?

   ■ How satisfied are you with your scores?

   ■ What could you do to change your attitudes toward your own success?

   ■ How can you monitor yourself in the future to have a more positive attitude toward success?

   ■ Who could support you? In what way? How will you contact this person and make plans to change your behavior?

   (Twenty minutes.)

6. Bring the group back together and bring closure to the activity with these questions:

   ■ What did you learn about yourself from this activity?

   ■ How might this insight affect you in your professional role? Your personal role?

   ■ What do you want to do differently in the future?

   ■ How will you apply what you've learned about yourself to your life?

   (Twenty minutes.)

Variation

■ Instead of arbitrary trios, have participants form subgroups according to their scores.

Submitted by Adrian F. Furnham.

Adrian F. Furnham is *professor of psychology at the University of London. He holds three doctorates and is a self-confessed workaholic. His primary interests are in applied psychology, particularly I/O psychology. He is well-traveled and enjoys lecturing abroad. This article reflects his interest in both personality theory and applied psychology.*

THE IMPOSTOR SYNDROME QUESTIONNAIRE

Instructions: Each statement below indicates your possible feelings and attitudes about yourself and your abilities. Please indicate how true you feel each of the statements is *as it applies to you,* using the scale below:

1 = not true at all	2 = rarely true	3 = sometimes true	4 = always true

1. I feel that other people tend to believe I am more competent than I am.   1   2   3   4

2. I am certain my present level of achievement reflects my abilities.   1   2   3   4

3. Sometimes I am afraid I will be discovered for who or what I really am.   1   2   3   4

4. I find it easy to accept compliments about my intelligence because they are mainly true.   1   2   3   4

5. I feel I deserve the awards, recognition, and praise I regularly receive.   1   2   3   4

6. At times, I have felt I am in my present job and salary level through some kind of mistake.   1   2   3   4

7. I feel pretty confident that I will succeed in the future.   1   2   3   4

8. I often tend to feel like an upstart.   1   2   3   4

9. Fortunately, my personality often makes a strong impression on people in authority.   1   2   3   4

10. So far, my accomplishments for my stage in life are perfectly adequate.   1   2   3   4

11. I am not sure why I have achieved the success I have.   1   2   3   4

12. I often achieve success on a project when I think I may have failed.   1   2   3   4

13. I often feel I am concealing secrets about myself from others.   1   2   3   4

14. My public and private self are precisely the same.   1   2   3   4

15. Very few people really know how average I am.   1   2   3   4

16. Most of my success is due to "lucky breaks" I have exploited.   1   2   3   4

THE IMPOSTER SYNDROME LECTURETTE

"Success," said American poet Emily Dickinson, "is counted sweetest by those who ne'er succeeded." Paradoxically, real success, just like failure, may be difficult to deal with.

It is said that behind every successful man there stands an astounded woman. What is often true is that many talented, conspicuously hard-working and able people who have achieved success somehow believe that they do not deserve it. In fact, they believe that they are impostors. Those who feel they are impostors seem to have difficulty accepting and enjoying the success that they have rightfully earned. Many handicap themselves by stumbling through life, setting unrealistic goals that they (or anyone else) can never achieve. Feeling like an undeserving person can be dangerously self-fulfilling.

The feelings of inadequacy and undeservedness may develop because of particularly lofty early parental expectations, or because one's teachers and peers never expected one to succeed. In this case, when a person does succeed, he or she often assumes it is simply because of chance and that, equally by chance, that success may (and in all likelihood will) go away. Or, just as frequently, the person may have been led to expect moderate success in another field instead. Thus, if an athletic, sporty type became a successful businessman, he or she may believe he or she is an impostor, thinking that success may not be due to business acumen and knowledge at all, but to the fact that people like and admire sporting fitness and prowess.

As Oscar Wilde shrewdly noted: "In this world, there are only two tragedies. One is not getting what we want, and the other is getting it." Sometimes, depression follows success because people with the impostor syndrome worry that they have "peaked" and wonder: "Where do I go from here?" Some believe that, because they are impostors, they cannot continue to be successful— and they somehow make sure that they fail!

One of the greatest dangers of the impostor syndrome is such self-handicapping thinking. Self-handicapping refers to the many self-defeating actions that people use to impede their own success or justify their own failure. People become their own worse enemies. Drink, drugs, and damsels may be used to achieve the unconscious strategic goal: When used in excess, each interferes with a person's ability to perform as well as he or she could. This particular self-defeating tactic enables many a self-defined impostor to obscure the meaning of subsequent evaluations by him or herself or others. The prototype of a career self-handicapper is the alcoholic who began drinking after his or her career was marked by early success, a lucky break, or an important act so spectacular that it seems impossible to equal, let alone surpass. Of course, chronic procrastination, depression, and panic attacks can also be used to justify failure in anticipation of having one's performance evaluated negatively.

In an empirical demonstration of self-handicapping strategies in action, two psychologists asked two groups of students to work on a problem-solving task (Berglas & Jones, 1978). One group received problems that were soluble, but the other group was given problems that actually had no solutions. Before proceeding to a second problem-solving session, each group was given a choice of two drugs that were ostensibly of interest to the experimenter. One of these drugs was supposed to *enhance* performance in problem solving; the other was described as *impairing* performance. The students who had previously worked on solvable problems generally chose the drug that would improve their performance. The other group, whose experience probably led them to believe that they would not do well on the next task either, showed a strong preference for the interfering drug. By handicapping themselves with a drug, they provided themselves with a convenient excuse in case they did poorly on the second task. What they had done was to prepare a "good explanation" for their possible failure.

But don't panic! One can be taught, quite easily, to avoid the success impostor syndrome and the nagging feeling that one is an impostor. A few specific issues must be addressed. First, one can challenge one's own and others' expectations of one's ability to succeed. Next, one can redirect the negative attention to the *process* of succeeding, rather than on the *products* of success. It is also important for people to learn to accept affection and admiration from others, without believing all are sycophants after the spoils of success. Successful people also must avoid the tendency to withdraw from, or be passive in, developing or maintaining personal relationships. The scorn (or paranoia) that successful people develop for those who pursue them is a naturally occurring psychological response to being in a position in which they never have to initiate social contacts.

Reference

Berglas, S., & Jones, E. (1978). Drug choice as an externalisation strategy in response to noncontingent success. *Journal of Personality and Social Psychology, 36*, 405–417.

THE IMPOSTER SYNDROME SCORE SHEET

Instructions: Add together the scores on items 1, 3, 6, 8, 11, 12, 13, 15, and 16. Then reverse score (1 = 4, 2 = 3, 3 = 2, 4 = 1) items 2, 4, 5, 7, 9, 10, and 14 and add them to the first list.

Interpretation:

 0 to 20: You're fine, don't panic!

21 to 40: Perhaps you deserve the success you have.

   41+: A possible, or potential, victim of the success syndrome: watch your self-handicapping strategies.

697. Cultural Triangle: Determining the Effect of Values on Customer/Client Perceptions

Goals

- To give participants a tool for reflecting on the effects of their own values on perceptions of others.

- To identify a broad range of diverse participant identities that are sources of values that impact perceptions of others.

- To give participants an opportunity to articulate how their own perceptions of others might affect organizational life.

Group Size

Maximum one hundred (twenty groups of five people).

Time Required

One hour and forty minutes to two hours and five minutes.

Materials

- One copy of the Cultural Triangle Lecturette for the facilitator.
- A transparency of the Cultural Triangle Model as well as copies for each participant.
- A copy of the Cultural Triangle Values Selection Sheet for each participant.
- A copy of the Cultural Triangle Sample Listing for each participant.
- Note paper and pencils for all participants.
- Overhead projector and transparency markers.
- Flip chart and felt-tipped markers.

Physical Setting

A room with round tables and chairs, each accommodating a group of five people.

Process

1. Introduce the topic of diversity and explain the importance of being aware that individuals' values contribute to their emotional reactions toward other people they do not know and unfamiliar ideas. Give the Cultural Triangle Lecturette. (Ten minutes.)

2. Display the Cultural Triangle Model transparency and give copies to the participants. Make it clear that the Cultural Triangle Model illustrates that we are all composites of the demographic variables that shape our values, which, in turn, affect our emotional reactions to other people we meet and to new ideas. Answer any questions participants may have. (Five minutes.)

3. Ask participants to list their own individual demographic characteristics (age, personal income, education, occupation, gender, ethnicity, race, and religion) at the top of the triangle on their handouts. (Five minutes.)

4. Give participants copies of the Cultural Triangle Values Selection Sheet and have them place an X on each continuum to indicate the degree to which each value listed applies to them. For example, individuals who feel that they are highly ambitious would place an X to the extreme right side of the ambitious continuum (NA _____ X HA). On the other hand, individuals who feel they moderately value change would place an X in the center of the change continuum (NA __ X __ HA). Tell participants to complete the entire sheet to create a values profile for themselves.

5. When everyone has finished, have participants list their checked values down the right side of their Cultural Triangle Model under the heading "Your Values." If participants are concerned about the exact meaning of a value, assure them that they may define it in their own individual terms. (Ten to fifteen minutes.)

6. Optional: Under the heading "Your Values" on the Cultural Triangle Model, have the participants list other values not listed that are highly applicable to themselves, such as candor, hard work, and so forth. (Ten minutes.)

7. Give participants copies of the Cultural Triangle Sample Listing and have them add as many people and ideas to the list as they can in the next five minutes. (Five minutes.)

8. Stop participants and ask them to fill the box on the Cultural Triangle Model with relevant people, places, things, ideas, and events in their lives. When they have finished, discuss the idea that individuals encounter a large number of people and ideas for which highly applicable values consciously and unconsciously produce an emotional reaction. Say that they can record their likely emotional reactions to each of the people or ideas they have listed on a continuum somewhere between the extremes of highly unfavorable and highly favorable. Have them draw such a continuum beside each of the people or ideas they have listed. (Fifteen minutes.)

9. As an illustration, ask the participants to imagine that they are in their place of employment at their usual work stations. Imagine further that a stranger approaches, dressed in a business suit. That stranger would figuratively be put into their box on the Cultural Triangle Model. Ask the participants the following questions:

   - What values are evoked immediately? (Have them write this down.)

   - What is the nature of your internal response? Is it unfavorable (UGH)? Favorable (WOW)? Somewhere in between?

   - Did you presume that the stranger was a customer/client?

   - What other identities did you assign to the stranger in your imagination? (Male/female? Same race as perceiver? Old? Young?)

   - Are any of your values and their related internal responses affected by these additional presumptions?

   - What identity did you play in the imaginary scenario as you perceived the other person (e.g., work role, gender role, social class)?

   (Ten to fifteen minutes.)

10. Now have participants form small groups and discuss some of the people or items they placed inside their boxes earlier. Explain that group members can (and likely will) have different emotional reactions to the same items (i.e., they will be located at different points on the unfavorable/favorable continuum). Also, clearly state there is no *one* way that a highly applicable value contributes to the reaction. The Cultural Triangle Model is simply an introspective tool to explore one's feelings toward an object or another person or situation (the items in the box, whatever they happen to be). Allow time for group members to share their feelings and reactions to the items they listed with one another. (Ten to fifteen minutes.)

11. Bring everyone together to discuss the following questions:

- What were some of the emotional reactions you felt toward the items on your lists?

- Which of your highly applicable values contributed the most to your emotional reactions toward the item?

- What was discussed in your group relative to how the highly applicable values contributed to the emotional reactions?

- Did the exercise allow you to see how an individual's values contribute to his or her emotional reactions toward other people and new ideas? In what way?

(Fifteen minutes.)

12. Remind the participants that, in real life, interactions involve perceptions of everyone present, each reacting to his or her own values and each with identities tied to his or her own demographics and life course. Give the following brief lecturette.

> The interactions occur in specific settings. The box in the model, then, contains "other," others' actions, and features of a setting. Each person is likely to perceive any new person or idea from a different perspective, brought about by his or her different identity and values. An individual's values evoke reactions to multiple dimensions of complex situations. Diversity competence requires that all parties be aware of their own responses to each new interaction, distinguishing those emotional responses from objective descriptions of reality. Further, we must all realize that others have similar reactions (although based on different values and prior experiences) and may (or may not) be aware of their effects. Thus, understanding others (for example, customers, co-workers, friends) requires you to have the ability to listen to others in order to understand their values and how those values are being applied in the current situation.

(Five minutes.)

Variations

- Have participants discuss items they place in their boxes that deal with various diversity situations by:

  - Using key values associated with the participants' organization.

  - Using key values associated with the participants' professions.

- Working with a brainstormed list of key personal values associated with one's religion and family life.
- Suggesting other scenarios from the participants' work settings or target market groups.
- Specifying other scenarios for roles in the participants' work settings.

■ Have participants use the values they list or choose to discuss how the values of "others" contributed to their own emotional reactions.

Submitted by Homer Warren, Anne M. McMahon, C. Louise Sellaro, and Carol Mikanowicz.

Homer Warren, D.B.A., *is an associate professor of marketing at Youngstown State University, Youngstown, Ohio. He publishes in the area of consumer behavior and has given workshops on the effects of cultural values on workplace diversity.*

Anne M. McMahon, Ph.D., *is a professor of management at Youngstown State University, organizer for the Partners for Workplace Diversity initiative with Youngstown area employers, and a member of the National Workplace Diversity Committee of the Society for Human Resource Management. She has published in several interdisciplinary journals.*

C. Louise Sellaro, D.B.A., *is a professor of management at Youngstown State University, Youngstown, Ohio. She teaches and has published teaching cases in the area of strategic leadership. She works with Partners for Workplace Diversity and is an active member of the nationwide organization, Initiative for Competitive Inner Cities (ICIC). She also does consulting related to program development focused on education of the disadvantaged.*

Carol Mikanowicz, Ph.D., *is a professor of health professions and program director of the master's program in health and human services in the College of Health and Human Services at Youngstown State University. She has presented seminars on diversity for national organizations and is a college member of Partners for Workplace Diversity. Her other accomplishments include numerous publications and national presentations in the health field.*

Cultural Triangle Lecturette

As individuals interact with one another, they develop a set of identities, each of which carries social meaning and value. The meaning and value are found in the perceptions of others. Associated with each identity (including, among others, gender, race, ethnicity, sexual orientation, religion, profession/occupation, parents, citizenship) is an associated set of values that contributes to the perspective that the individual will have on all new people and events encountered. Because each individual has multiple identities, each has a diverse set of perspectives on events. Each individual, then, is diverse. As individuals encounter objects, people, and events, the applicable values give rise to immediate internal emotional responses. Such responses are inevitable. Effective work performance in a diverse environment requires that individuals recognize how their own values operate in encounters with others, including how those values shape their initial internal responses. Self-awareness permits individuals to exercise judgment and to control the effects of those responses on their performance decisions. Reactions are always in the hands of the perceiver, as they stem from cognitive and emotional states of the person holding the perception; they are not objective descriptions of the event or the object being perceived.

Some values are associated with multiple identities, and others are activated by specific events associated with particular identities. Some are deeply rooted in a set of integrated values (such as firm religious values), and others are more isolated. The exercise we are about to do is a tool for reflecting on one's own values and the internal responses one feels because of them. Self-reflection about this internal process allows each person a greater measure of choice in how he or she reacts as each situation progresses and in how he or she interprets what is happening.

The effectiveness of any organization depends on its members appreciating the entire mosaic of which they are a part and learning to deal with one another without emotional triggers. Healthy interaction means that members are able to retain their distinctive individual identities and values while contributing to a collective purpose.

Cultural Triangle Model

Your Values

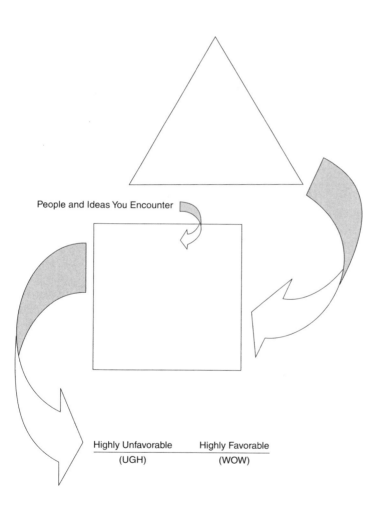

People and Ideas You Encounter

Highly Unfavorable (UGH)   Highly Favorable (WOW)

CULTURAL TRIANGLE VALUES SELECTION SHEET

NA* _____ HA* Polite	NA _____ HA Individual	NA _____ HA Feminine	NA _____ HA Comfortable Life
NA _____ HA Youth	NA _____ HA Performance	NA _____ HA Active	NA _____ HA Inner Harmony
NA _____ HA Technology	NA _____ HA Immediate Gratification	NA _____ HA Exciting Life	NA _____ HA Family Security
NA _____ HA Mature Love	NA _____ HA True Friendship	NA _____ HA Broadmindedness	NA _____ HA Social Recognition
NA _____ HA Clean	NA _____ HA Helpful	NA _____ HA Independent	NA _____ HA Ambitious
NA _____ HA Responsible	NA _____ HA Collective	NA _____ HA Hero Worship	NA _____ HA Forgiving
NA _____ HA Status	NA _____ HA Fatalism	NA _____ HA Passive	NA _____ HA Logical
NA _____ HA Hard Work	NA _____ HA Information	NA _____ HA Peace	NA _____ HA Romance
NA _____ HA National Security	NA _____ HA Equality	NA _____ HA Happiness	NA _____ HA Change
NA _____ HA Self-Respect	NA _____ HA Wisdom	NA _____ HA Capabilities	NA _____ HA Problem Solving
NA _____ HA Courage	NA _____ HA Honesty	NA _____ HA Intellect	NA _____ HA Freedom
NA _____ HA Obedience	NA _____ HA Self-Control	NA _____ HA Masculine	NA _____ HA Helpful
NA _____ HA Cooperation	NA _____ HA Tradition	NA _____ HA Nature	NA _____ HA Risk Taking
NA _____ HA Materialism	NA _____ HA Leisure	NA _____ HA Abstinence	

*NA = This value is not applicable in determining the individual's emotional reactions.
*HA = This value is highly applicable in determining the individual's emotional reactions.

Cultural Triangle Sample Listing

The following is a sample listing of people and ideas that may be placed into the box on the Cultural Triangle Model. You may assume that any of these people or ideas has been introduced to your organization or group or make your own list:

- A teenager
- A senior citizen
- A person with a cane
- A person who speaks a language you do not understand
- A man wearing a turban
- A woman wearing a scarf that fully covers her hair, ears, and neck
- A telecommuting policy covering certain departments
- A new matrix structure for the organization
- Job sharing in some areas

698. Speed Up!
Increasing Communication Skills

Goals

- To learn methods to respond more quickly in business situations.
- To develop the ability to read more quickly and to isolate key details.
- To increase the ability to write more succinctly.
- To develop concentration skills.

Group Size

Any number.

Time Required

Approximately ninety minutes.

Materials

- Overhead transparencies for Speed Up! Reading Speed A through E and Aa through Ee.
- Overhead transparencies for Speed Up! Writing Speed 1 through 3.
- A set of handouts for Speed Up! Concentration Speed 1 through 3 for each participant.
- Paper and pencils for all participants.
- A flip chart and felt-tipped markers.
- A timing device that indicates seconds.

Physical Setting

Any standard room, ideally with tables for groups of five or six.

Process

1. Discuss with participants the need for thinking, reacting, reading, writing, and analyzing information faster than ever in today's business environment. Elicit examples from the fast-paced world in which we live. Remind participants of the demands for maintaining or exceeding production levels, even though there are fewer people to do the work. Point out that roles fluctuate, as do the structures within which their roles were once firmly placed. Review the fact that knowledge increases exponentially, causing a demand for new skills on what seems like a monthly basis. (Five minutes.)

2. Explain that you'll give participants the tools for increasing their speed in three different areas:

    a. Reading

    b. Writing

    c. Concentrating

3a. (Reading.) Begin by advising participants that you will show five separate transparencies to help them to increase their reading and comprehension speed. Give everyone paper and pencils and ask them to identify the key words on each transparency as you show it, to jot them down, and then to formulate one or two sentences making sense of the key words. Show Transparency A for five seconds. Take it off the overhead and ask participants to write down the key words they remember. After a moment or two, ask them to formulate a full sentence or two, using the key words, that reflects the meaning of the passage they saw. Allow one minute for this.

    Next, show Transparency Aa. Ask them to compare their key words with those circled on the transparency. (Answers may differ slightly.) Then call on several participants to read their sentences and briefly discuss how close they were to the original meaning of the passage on the transparency. Repeat the process with Transparencies B through E, calling on different participants each time to share their summaries. With each transparency, encourage reading for key words, skipping over small or insignificant words, and then making better transitions among the important words.

    Remind them that some documents—policy statements or legal matters, for example—should always be read carefully. Advise participants to continue practicing on their own time to further their ability to read quickly and thoroughly. (Twenty minutes.)

4b. (Writing). Share the essence of the following mini-lecture:

> Business writers can reduce their verbiage by 50 percent or more without sacrificing meaning simply by learning to get rid of weak or "helping" verbs, in most cases the "passive" voice rather than "active." Forms of the verb "to be": being, might be, could be, should be, would be, has been, had been, should have been, et cetera can often be eliminated. (You can see the word "be" right in the verb.) In addition, because the verb is an irregular one, its present-tense conjugation includes "is," "am," and "are," while its past-tense form includes "was" and "were." Whenever you see "be" or "am," "is," "are," "was," or "were" standing alone, you know you have something to eliminate. (The only time you absolutely must use a weak verb is when you are giving an example or definition. The preceding sentence is an example and so used the word "is" quite correctly.)

5b. Show the examples (one by one) on transparency Speed Up! Writing Speed 1." Ask for volunteers to revise the sentences by eliminating the weak verbs and substituting strong ones. Point out the verbal economy that resulted—from seven words to three words in this example. (Ten minutes.)

Answer Key

Original: A decision was made by the committee. (seven words)

Revision: The committee voted. (three words)

Original: A report was prepared by the team that was made up of environmentalists. (thirteen words)

Revision: The environmentalist team prepared a report. (six words)

Original: The reliability of a system is determined by its design. (ten words)

Revision: Design determines system reliability. (four words)

6b. Next, show transparency Speed Up! Writing Speed 2. Allow about five minutes for a "translation" of the meaning of the passage. Encourage participants to work in pairs if they wish to do so. (Five minutes.)

7b. Share the revision that appears on Speed Up! Writing Speed 3. Ask participants how their work compares to this revision and note that several good variations are possible. (Listen carefully as they read theirs to ensure they have not used weak verbs or passive voice.) Point out that the revisions are shorter, clearer, and more economical. (Ten minutes.)

8c. (Concentrating) Discuss with participants the answers to these questions:

- What aspects of your work require deep concentration?

- What prevents you from concentrating?

- What are some potential costs of having poor concentration skills?

- Describe how you feel when you have high-intensity moments of intense concentration and understanding.

- What specific actions can people take to concentrate better?

- Medical and law students often engage in mindbenders moments before their exams. What do you do to focus less on your nerves and more on your mental readiness?

(Ten minutes.)

9c. Explain that the ability to concentrate has little to do with intelligence—rather with the ability to focus so intently on the task at hand that all external and internal stimuli recede into the background and the challenge assumes a prominent position in the foreground. So the challenge you're about to present to the group is not a matter of IQ, but rather a question of their talent for marshaling mental energies and concentrating on a single item.

10c. Read the instructions for Speed Up! Concentration Speed Handout 1 aloud. Explain that they will be required to find words whose letters have been separated. Draw the following illustration on the flip chart. Say, "If I write the word 'cat' this way—[c [a [t—you'd have no trouble recognizing it. And if I wrote the word 'dog' like this—d] o] g]—you would decode the word immediately. However, if I write the two words like this—[c d] [a o] [t g]—the two words are much harder to read. The worksheet I'm handing out contains six business-related words, two on each of three lines. Work as quickly as possible to figure out what they are."

11c. Distribute, face down, Speed Up! Concentration Speed Handout 1. Ask participants not to turn it over until you give the signal. Also ask the first person to finish to raise his or her hand. Then ask them to begin.

12c. When the first hand goes up, ask everyone to stop and call on the "winner" to share his or her answers with the group at large. (Approximately five minutes.)

13c. Repeat the process twice more with Speed Up! Concentration Speed Handouts 2 and 3. Ideally, different individuals will finish first. If this happens, discuss the fact that it's possible to become faster with mental processes and also to develop one's powers of concentration. If the same person continues to win each time (unlikely), ask him or her to share the secrets of his or her ability to focus. (Ten minutes.)

Variations

- (Reading) Rather than show transparencies to encourage speed in reading and comprehension, prepare up to ten handout packages—one for each leader of a group of five or six. The handouts should be written in 24-point font size. Begin by having the leaders read the first selection to themselves, without letting others see it. Once they understand the first passage, they will hold it up so everyone in their small group can see it. Five seconds later, the leader will cover the sheet and ask participants to record the key words they recalled and then to string the key words together into a meaningful equivalent of what they saw. The leader calls on each person in the group to read what he or she has formulated and then shares the original, asking participants to assess their own results.

- (Writing) Have participants speculate about the money that could be saved if everyone in their organization were using strong verbs instead of weak ones on all documents produced.

- (Concentration) Discuss when concentration skills are most critical—e.g., during interviews, crises, or conflict situations. Ask participants to prepare comparable exercises. Collect them and then ask for a volunteer to type them and then send them to participants for their future use.

- (Concentration) Lead a discussion on the words contained within split brackets. For example, with the first two words on the first two lines (Peters and Powell), ask participants what they know about these two giants in the field of management. What have they read by these men? Have they heard either speak? What are quotations each has made that have penetrated the world of management?

Submitted by Marlene Caroselli.

Dr. Marlene Caroselli conducts corporate training on a variety of subjects. She also presents motivational keynote addresses and writes—forty-five books to date. View them at her website: http://hometown.aol.com/mccpd or at Amazon.com.

SPEED UP! READING SPEED TRANSPARENCY A

You're comfortable living in your own

skin, aren't you? It may be a thick skin,

it may be a thin one, but it's yours,

all yours. The skin that covers you is

the result of experiences you've had,

people you've met, places you've been,

books you've read, and so on.

The 2002 Annual: Volume 1, Training/© 2002 John Wiley & Sons, Inc.

Speed Up! Reading Speed Transparency B

This all-encompassing membrane is actually a metaphor for the person you are. Your "skin" guides the actions you take, the thoughts you think, the ego, id, and superego that make you who you are. Over the years, a finely polished patina has developed over your basic being. A psychological shellac has hardened over your view of the world.

Speed Up! Reading Speed Transparency C

True, this veneer protects you from hard knocks, but—if you're not careful—it can also block new possibilities from reaching the deepest parts of your personality.

There's nothing wrong with a certain constancy of thought and action. However, if you're clinging to old patterns simply because they're comfortable, then you're stunting your creative growth.

Speed Up! Reading Speed Transparency D

You may be allowing your flexibility muscles to atrophy. And, as natural scientists will tell you, those members of the animal kingdom with the widest range of behaviors are the ones who survive. There are ways to cleave your cover, to expose it to the refreshing air of change. Pump some fresh blood to your cerebral synapses on occasion.

Speed Up! Reading Speed Transparency E

Develop new habits. Most mean only small changes to your current patterns and practices. Others endorse flexibility and change. All of them, though, can make you more receptive to life.

Make a list of the philosophical viewpoints most important to you. Decide which are unalterable and which, perhaps, need a tune-up. And read extensively in and outside your field.

Speed Up! Reading Speed Transparency Aa

You're (comfortable) living in your own skin, aren't you? It may be a thick skin, it may be a thin one, but it's yours, all yours. The skin that covers you is the result of experiences you've had, people you've met, places you've been, books you've read, and so on.

Speed Up! Reading Speed Transparency Bb

This all-encompassing membrane is actually a metaphor for the person you are. Your "skin" guides the actions you take, the thoughts you think, the ego, id, and superego that make you who you are. Over the years, a finely polished patina has developed over your basic being. A psychological shellac has hardened over your view of the world.

The 2002 Annual: Volume 1, Training/© 2002 John Wiley & Sons, Inc.

SPEED UP! READING SPEED TRANSPARENCY Cc

True, this veneer protects you from hard knocks, but—if you're not careful—it can also block new possibilities from reaching the deepest parts of your personality.

There's nothing wrong with a certain constancy of thought and action. However, if you're clinging to old patterns simply because they're comfortable, then you're stunting your creative growth.

SPEED UP! READING SPEED TRANSPARENCY DD

You (may be allowing) your flexibility (muscles) to atrophy. And, as natural (scientists) will tell you, (those members) of the animal (kingdom) with the widest range of behaviors (are the (ones) who survive. There are ways to cleave your cover, to expose it to the refreshing air of change. Pump some fresh blood to your cerebral synapses on occasion.

Speed Up! Reading Speed Transparency Ee

Develop new habits. Most mean

only small changes to your

current patterns and practices.

Others endorse flexibility and change.

All of them, though, can make you

more receptive to life.

Make a list of the philosophical

viewpoints most important to you.

Decide which are unalterable and

which, perhaps, need a tune-up.

Speed Up! Writing Speed Transparency 1

A decision was made by the committee.

A report was prepared by the team that was made up of environmentalists.

The reliability of a system is determined by its design.

Speed Up! Writing Speed Transparency 2

If the proposal is rejected by your office, clear and logical reasons must be submitted in sufficient detail to permit transmittal to the proposer with editing or revision being needed.

Speed Up! Writing Speed Transparency 3

If your office rejects the

proposal, you must submit

clear, logical, and detailed

reasons for transmittal to

the proposal.

The 2002 Annual: Volume 1, Training/© 2002 John Wiley & Sons, Inc.

Speed Up! Concentration Speed Handout 1

[P P] [e o] [t w] [e e] [r l] [s l]

[C D] [r e] [o m] [s i] [b n] [y g]

[m c] [a r] [n e] [a a] [g t] [e e]

Speed Up! Concentration Speed Handout 2

[c f] [h u] [a t] [n u] [g r] [e e]

[i e] [n v] [v e] [e n] [n t] [t s]

[f m] [o e] [r n] [c t] [e a] [s l]

SPEED UP! CONCENTRATION SPEED HANDOUT 3

[m a] [o s] [t s] [i u] [v m] [e e]

[p r] [o e] [w p] [e o] [r r] [s t]

[r d] [e a] [s m] [i a] [s g] [t e]

699. MEMORIES: INFLUENCING OTHERS

Goals

- To increase participants' awareness of behaviors or factors that make influencing others challenging.

- To identify various approaches to or styles for influencing others.

- To learn which behaviors are most effective for influencing others.

Group Size

Ten to twenty participants.

Time Required

Forty to forty-five minutes.

Materials Required

- Flip chart and markers.

Physical Setting

A room with enough space for participants to sit comfortably in pairs for discussion and to hold a large group discussion.

Process

1. Explain the goals of the activity and instruct participants to find partners they do not know very well and to sit together.

2. Say to the group: "For the first part of this activity, think of something that you have with you—in your pocket, purse, or wallet—that is valuable to you. It may have either monetary or sentimental value." Demonstrate by

showing an item of your own and telling participants a brief story about its unique qualities and importance to you. For example, "My purse has value to me, not just because of what's in it, but because it reminds me of my trip to Italy. I bought it in a leather shop in Florence. When I carry it, I remember the trip and the friends I made while I was there." (Five minutes.)

3. Ask participants to share with their partners the unique characteristics of the items they have selected. After the pairs have finished, ask a few pairs to share with the large group. (Five to ten minutes.)

4. Announce to the group, "Now, for the second part of this activity, get back together with your partners and use all of your influence to take that item from your partner. You will only have about two minutes each; your goal is to do whatever it takes to influence your partner to give you the item." (Five minutes.)

5. Bring the group together and provide closure to the activity with the following questions:

   ■ How many of you were successful in obtaining an item from your partner?

   ■ What were some of the approaches you used to influence your partners?

   ■ What specific behaviors seemed to work best to influence them?

   ■ Which of these behaviors and approaches might be useful to influence others on the job?

   ■ What special challenges did you face in trying to influence your partner during this activity?

   ■ How are these challenges similar to ones you face on the job when trying to influence others?

   (Fifteen minutes.)

6. List the key behaviors and challenges brought up by participants during this discussion on the flip chart. You might also wish to link the approaches and comments you observe to conflict management styles and steps in the influencing process. Typical behaviors participants identify as helpful might include: listening, acknowledging the other person's feelings about the importance of the item, compromising or making a deal, and pointing out the benefits to the other person. Typical challenges might include: it's difficult to ask for something important to the other person; it's hard when the person has very strong personal feel-

ings about the item; it's hard to influence when you aren't prepared or don't know why you need the item. (Ten minutes.)

Variation

■ Form trios and assign one person as an observer to identify behaviors that were effective and challenges that were overcome.

Submitted by Saundra Stroope.

Saundra Stroope *is a senior training and development consultant at WorldCom who specializes in leadership, communication skills, coaching, and team development.*

700. ELECTRIC COMPANY: DECIDING BY CONSENSUS

Goals

- To practice using the consensus decision making process.
- To become proficient in and see the advantages of the consensus decision making process.
- To develop participants' awareness of poor decisions that can be made in a crisis situation.

Group Size

Ten to twenty participants.

Time Required

Approximately one hour.

Materials

- A copy of the Electric Company Task Sheet for each participant.
- A set of Electric Company Option Sheets (I through V), enough for each participant, but handed out according to what has happened previously.
- One copy of the Electric Company Trainer's Guide for the facilitator.
- Pencils or pens for participants.

Physical Setting

A room in which several subgroups can work without interfering with or overhearing one another.

Process

1. Present this activity following a session on consensus decision making to reinforce the learning or as an introduction to the process.

2. Announce to the group that they will now have an opportunity to practice consensus decision making.

3. Hand out the Electric Company Task Sheet and pens or pencils to all participants.

4. Have the participants read through the introductory material at the beginning of the Task Sheet and then review the exercise and answer questions for the entire group. (Ten minutes.)

5. Divide the group into teams of four to six members each and have them seat themselves far enough from other groups that they cannot be overheard.

6. Instruct the participants to individually choose an option from the list of possible steps. (Five minutes.)

7. Once each individual has filled in his or her choice, ask the subgroups to come together and use the consensus decision making process (in case you are just introducing the process here, explain it at this point), then record the team's choice. (Ten minutes.)

8. Once the teams have made their choices, give each subgroup the handout associated with the option chosen (I, II, III, IV, or V). Remind participants that individual choices should always be made first, and then the subgroup should use the consensus decision making process to choose an option. Also remind them NOT to look ahead. (Twenty minutes.)

9. When all the teams have completed the exercise, reconvene the entire group. In the group setting, discuss each team's results, problems, insights, etc. Make sure the group does not get hung up on the *right* answer. The groups were simply to decide on the *best* course of action for the team using the consensus decision making process. Of course, taking an elevator is always a wrong answer, but nearly everyone will know that.

Much of the learning while finding the *right* answer comes from the discussions that are held during the exercise. Each person will have knowledge of some sort to contribute. At the close of discussion, share the Electric Company Trainer's Guide with the entire group.

10. When each group has had a chance to discuss the activity and interacted with the other groups, sum up by reminding everyone of the power of consensus decision making. (Five minutes.)

Variation

- If group size increases beyond twenty participants, an additional facilitator may be required to keep the subgroups on task.

Submitted by John E. Fernandes.

John E. Fernandes holds a B.S. degree in mechanical engineering from the University of Connecticut. He served as a project engineer for United Aircraft Products in Forest, Ohio, and since 1976 has worked for Potomac Electric Power Company, now a part of Southern Energy Incorporated, as a results engineer. He has held several positions at the Morgantown Generating Station, where he is currently general superintendent of fuel and ash.

ELECTRIC COMPANY TASK SHEET

The Situation

You work for Consensus Electric Company (CEC) at the coal-fired Station at Frightful End (SAFE). The station has a good record of performance and electrical production. You are part of a maintenance crew assigned to work on a start-up steam valve on the tenth floor of the twelve-story plant. Your crew is made up of individuals of equal grade; there is no specified leader(s).

While performing your maintenance tasks, the members of the team suddenly realize that the building is filling with coal dust. Your reaction is to look over the hand rail and to observe that the area below is filled with coal dust also. There is no other discernable activity that exists.

There are no working telephones or a paging system on the ninth, tenth, or eleventh floors, and none of your crew has any form of communication (no cell phones or emergency beepers). One of your crew has a complete toolbox with the normal assortment of screwdrivers, wrenches, sockets, hammers, and so forth. The plant lighting has remained illuminated. The paging system is amazingly quiet.

Instructions

1. Each member of your group should decide *independently* on an appropriate reaction to the situation.

2. After each individual has decided, the team should use the consensus decision making process to decide an appropriate reaction to the situation.

3. *After your team has made its decision, ask the facilitator for the remainder of the exercise.*

4. Once again, each individual should *independently* decide on an appropriate reaction to each of the additional situations.

5. After all individuals have finished, the team should get together and use the consensus decision making process to decide on an appropriate reaction to each of the additional situations.

NOTE: Do not look ahead at the upcoming situations. Make your decisions based on the information you have as of that point.

Decide the first step to take from the list below:

I. Stay put, do not move, remain calm, and wait to see what happens next.

II. Climb the stairs to the roof and try to signal someone from the roof.

III. Cautiously descend the stairs along an outside wall looking for a phone to communicate with the control room.

IV. Get in the elevator and descend as quickly as possible to the mezzanine level, escape to the front of the plant, and try to understand the situation at that point.

V. Take a different action.

Check the box below that corresponds with the choice you made individually. When your team has made a choice, mark that box also before asking for the next page of the exercise.

	I	II	III	IV	V
Self					
Team					

ELECTRIC COMPANY OPTION SHEET I

Instructions: Based on what you decided during the first step, here are some additional situations. Make consensus decisions for them, first individually, and then as a group.

You have decided to stay put, not move, remain calm, and wait to see what happens next. Now decide the next step to take based on the following information: There is smoke in the plant coming from below.

    a. Find a corner and set up some kind of protection to huddle behind.

    b. Elect one individual to go to the twelfth floor and find a phone, page, or communicate with someone and then report back to the group.

    c. Spread out to find individual areas of protection for each member of the crew.

    d. Take a different action.

As before, fill out your individual choice below and make your team decision before proceeding.

	a	b	c	d
Self				
Team				

    Below you a fireball expands and extinguishes quickly near the fuel-firing levels of the boiler. Decide which of the following you should do:

    a. Reconsider the decision to stay put and suggest moving down toward the control room.

    b. Reconsider the decision to stay put and suggest moving to the roof for fresh air.

    c. Using some of the tools, create an opening in the side of the building to allow for fresh air.

    d. Take a different action.

As before, fill out your individual choice below and make your team decision before proceeding.

	a	b	c	d
Self				
Team				

All alarm units trip and the trouble alarm sounds that by established procedure means you must evacuate the building.

- a. No choice but to plan the safest route to get outside the building and to the ground.
- b. Send a scout out to find the best way to get to the outside ground floor while the remainder of the team finds a secure place to stay.
- c. Because of the dust and fire, stay together, fortify a position, and stay put until the emergency passes.
- d. Take a different action.

As before, fill out your individual choice below and make your team decision before proceeding.

	a	b	c	d
Self				
Team				

Electric Company Option Sheet II

Instructions: Based on what you decided during the first step, here are some additional situations. Make consensus decisions for them, first individually, and then as a group.

You have climbed the stairs to the roof and tried to signal someone from the roof. Now decide the next step to take based on the following information: There is smoke from the fire coming out of the roof access doors.

    a. Have members of the crew look over the side to see what is going on below.

    b. Find a corner and set up some kind of protection to huddle behind.

    c. Elect one individual to go to the twelfth floor, find a method to page or communicate with someone, and then report back to the group.

    d. Take a different action.

Do NOT read ahead. As before, fill out your individual choice below and make your team decision before proceeding.

	a	b	c	d
Self				
Team				

    Below you, a fireball expands and puffs out the various openings to the roof. Decide individually which of the following options to take and then decide as a group.

    a. Devise some way to communicate with someone in order to let people know that your group is on the roof.

    b. Reconsider the decision to be on the roof and proceed to head down to the control room.

    c. Continue to fortify your position on the roof.

    d. Take a different action.

As before, fill out your individual choice below and make your team decision before proceeding.

	a	b	c	d
Self				
Team				

All units trip and the trouble alarm sounds that by standard procedure means that you are to evacuate the building.

a. No choice but to plan the safest route to get outside to the ground level.

b. Send a scout out to find the best way to get to the ground while the remainder of the team finds a secure place to stay.

c. Because of the dust and fire, stay together, fortify a spot on the roof, and stay put until the emergency passes.

d. Take a different action.

As before, fill out your individual choice below and make your team decision before proceeding.

	a	b	c	d
Self				
Team				

Electric Company Option Sheet III

Instructions: Based on what you decided during the first step, here are some additional situations. Make consensus decisions for them, first individually, and then as a group.

You have just cautiously descended the stairs along an outside wall looking for a phone to communicate with the control room.

Now there is smoke in the plant coming from below. Decide individually and then as a group what to do.

a. Continue to descend but consider a way to ensure the ability to breathe.

b. Stop your descent, find a place that is protected from the coal dust, and find clean air to breathe.

c. Reconsider the team's decision and take refuge on the roof.

d. Take a different action.

As before, fill out your individual choice below and make your team decision before proceeding.

	a	b	c	d
Self				
Team				

Below you, a fireball expands and extinguishes quickly near the fuel-firing levels of the boiler. Decide individually which of the following options to take and then decide as a group.

a. After the fireball passes, hastily escape below to the outside and make contact with the control room at that time.

b. Pay no attention to the fireball. Continue with the action decided on previously.

c. Reconsider the team's previous decision.

d. Take a different action.

As before, fill out your individual choice below and make your team decision before proceeding.

	a	b	c	d
Self				
Team				

All units trip and the trouble alarm sounds that by standard procedure means you must evacuate the building. Decide individually which of the following options to take and then decide as a group.

a. No choice but to plan the safest route to get downstairs and outside.

b. Send a scout to find the best way to get to the ground floor and outside while the remainder of the team finds a secure place to stay.

c. Because of the dust and fire, stay together, fortify a spot in the plant, and stay put until the emergency passes.

d. Take a different action.

As before, fill out your individual choice below and make your team decision before proceeding.

	a	b	c	d
Self				
Team				

ELECTRIC COMPANY OPTION SHEET IV

Instructions: Based on what you decided during the first step, here are some additional situations. Make consensus decisions for them, first individually, and then as a group.

You have just entered the elevator to descend as quickly as possible to the mezzanine level, escape to the front of the plant, and try to understand the situation at that point.

There is the smell of number 2 start-up oil in the plant. Decide individually and then as a group which is the best of the following options:

a. Say good-bye to each other because you realize this was the wrong decision.

b. You need to rethink your solution.

c. Go back to the first step and pick a different choice.

d. That was your final answer!!!!!!!

	a	b	c	d
Self				
Team				

Electric Company Option Sheet V

Instructions: Based on what you decided during the first step, here are some additional situations. Make consensus decisions for them, first individually, and then as a group.

You have just taken the action you agreed to in the previous situation. Now some other problems have arisen. What should you do?

There is smoke in the plant coming from below. What should you do?

Your Response	Team Response

Below, a fireball expands and extinguishes quickly near the fuel firing levels of the boiler. What should you do?

Your Response	Team Response

All units trip and the trouble alarm sounds that by standard procedure means you must evacuate the building. What should you do?

Your Response	Team Response

ELECTRIC COMPANY TRAINER'S GUIDE

Responses to Option I

- It's not a good idea to go separate ways. Staying together is always the best course of action.

- A hole in the wall will most likely cause the fire to explode toward a new source of oxygen.

- As stated, procedure calls for everyone to evacuate the building. The trouble alarm only sounds in an emergency.

Responses to Option II

- People should never be sent out alone.

- As stated, procedure calls for everyone to evacuate the building. The trouble alarm only sounds in an emergency.

Response to Option III

- As stated, procedure calls for everyone to evacuate the building. The trouble alarm only sounds in an emergency.

Response to Option IV

- Whenever there is an emergency situation or the possibility of an emergency situation, never get into an elevator. If there is an emergency, you could become caught with no escape.

Response to Open-Ended Questions and Option V

- Generally speaking, the team should not send team members out alone, should plot a path out of the building when the trouble alarm sounds, and should use common sense in terms of not putting team members in harm's way.

701. POWER POKER: WHAT'S IN IT FOR ME?

Goals

- To demonstrate the dynamics of negotiating, competition, and power.
- To explore issues involved in comparing individual values to group values.
- To discuss issues of hidden and open agendas.
- To explore issues of group member status.
- To demonstrate issues of trust.

Group Size

Up to thirty-six, preferably a number divisible by six.

Time Required

Forty-five to ninety minutes to play a minimum of two rounds and discuss all the issues. If time is limited, select only the most pertinent discussion questions.

Materials

- One copy of the Power Poker Facilitator Notes for the facilitator.
- One Power Poker Sample Play Sheet for the facilitator
- One Poker Power Swap Sheet per player per round.
- One Power Poker Ranking/Scoring Chart handout per participant.
- One deck of fifty-two playing cards per subgroup.
- Three index cards per player.
- Pens or pencils for participants.
- A flip chart and felt-tipped markers.
- (Optional) Colorful markers or crayons.

Physical Setting

Tables, preferably round, with five or six seats per table.

Process

1. Prior to the workshop, read through the Power Poker Facilitator Notes and Power Poker Sample Play Sheet so that you understand the process thoroughly.

2. First, discuss the goals of the activity in general terms. Then divide the participants into subgroups of five or six players each. Have additional participants act as observers. Seat each subgroup at its own table.

3. Distribute one deck of playing cards to each group. Distribute one Power Poker Swap Sheet, one Power Poker Ranking/Scoring Chart, three index cards, and a pen or pencil to each player. Go over the Power Poker Ranking/Scoring Chart to demonstrate the points awarded for each type of poker hand. (Ten minutes.)

4. Have each subgroup select one player to act as dealer. The dealer also plays the game after dealing the cards. Explain that the deal will rotate clockwise on each new round of play and that the game play and ranking of hands is based on the standard rules for poker.

5. Go over the following rules for Round 1 with the group:

Round 1: Distributing the Cards: The dealer distributes five cards to each player. Each player records his or her original five cards on the Power Poker Swap Sheet. Each player places one card face down (hole card) and the other four cards face up. (*Note:* Experience has shown that players prefer to place the cards they wish to trade in the face-up position.)

Round 1: Preparing the Index Card: Each player represents the value and suit of the hole card on the index card, using the colored markers and crayons if desired, and then places the index card in a place that can be seen by all other players. The dealer then selects one card from the deck—the "power" card—and places it face up on the table. All players may use this card to help form their hand.

Round 1: Trading Period: Players have five minutes to trade cards with any other player in their subgroup. Rules of the trade:

- Players may trade only the cards that are face up.

- Players may trade only one card at a time.

- All trades are voluntary; no one is required to trade any of their cards during the trading period.

- All players must record each of their trades on their Power Poker Swap Sheets.

When the trading is complete, give the players two minutes to verify their Power Poker Swap Sheets.

After all trades are completed and recorded, tell players they may trade in one to three cards for new cards from the deck. Say that before receiving the replacement card(s), the player must turn over his or her hole card and place it next to the index card. Players receive all replacement cards face down. (Fifteen minutes for the first round, less time for subsequent rounds.)

6. Now tell players that they may wager pennies or chips on their final hand if they wish to do so. When everyone is ready, have all players reveal all of their cards to the rest of their subgroup. Tell them to score points for their hands based on the Power Poker Ranking/Scoring Chart. Remind them that the winning hand receives a twenty-point bonus. (Five minutes.)

7. Post the points for each player in the subgroup and then tally the total of each subgroup as one score. Record each subgroup's score on the flip chart. (Five minutes.)

8. Allow each subgroup to meet for five minutes and then continue with the next round. All rounds are played in the same way. (At least two rounds should be played, but you may allow five or six rounds if desired.) Declare the team with the most points the winner. (Ten minutes.)

9. Help people reflect on their experiences and find meaningful learning around any or all of the following ten issues.

Group Dynamics: Individual and Group Efforts

- How did you begin playing the game? Did you see it as an individual or group effort?

- Did you want to improve your hand at the cost of all others? Some others? One other?

- When (if you did) did you begin to see that it was a group effort? Why?

- What did you do to help others?

- How are issues of individual and group efforts played out in your workplace?

Group Dynamics: Hidden and Open Agendas

■ What did you write on the index card? Were you open or closed with how much you revealed?

■ What did the index card represent for you?

■ Did the index card represent how you wanted to be seen?

■ How are issues of hidden and open agendas relevant to your workplace?

Group Dynamics: Honest and Open Communication

■ What did you write on the index card? Were you honest about the card you held?

■ What did the index card represent for you?

■ Did the index card represent how you wanted to be seen?

■ What would you think/do if a player's index card did not match his or her hole card? How would that affect your future dealings with that player? If this happened, could you leave it in the training room?

■ How are issues of hidden and open agendas relevant to your workplace?

Group Dynamics: Cooperation and Competition

■ How did you see yourself and others as you played the game? As collaborators? As competitors? Explain.

■ Were you never/sometimes/always actively participating?

■ Did you experience conflicting self-talk?

■ Were you able to listen carefully to others? Stay focused? Stay on track?

■ How are issues of cooperation, collaboration, and competition relevant to your workplace?

Group Dynamics: Loyalty and Factionalism

■ Was your subgroup marked by individualism? Factionalism? Loyalty to the whole? Loyalty to the individual?

■ How are issues of individuality, group loyalty, and factionalism relevant to your workplace?

Group Dynamics: Individual and Group Goals

■ What was your individual goal during Round 1? Round 2? Round 3? Etc.

- What were the goals of others in your group for each round?
- Did individual and group goals coalesce? How did this happen?
- In your workplace, how important is it for individual goals to coincide with group goals to accomplish your organization's mission?
- What can be done to merge individual and group goals?

Group Dynamics: Incentive and the Role of Money in Motivation

- How did you recognize and then celebrate success? Describe individual/group success recognition and celebration.
- How did you/others reinforce success?
- During the poker game, what were your incentives?
- At work, what are some effective incentives for you?
- Many play poker for money. How did you/others react when you found out you were playing for points instead of cash?
- If you used the "penny option," how did the use of real money affect the play of the game? Did it carry over into the next round(s)?
- At work, is money a low/medium/high motivator for you/for others?
- How are issues of recognition/celebration of success relevant to your workplace?

Group Dynamics: Group Member Status

- Was there a hierarchy in your poker group? If so, how was the ranking established?
- How would an observer recognize high/low status individuals in your group?
- At work, what are the individual/group/organizational effects of status? Are the effects mostly positive or negative?
- At work, how can the positive effects of status be promoted and the negative effects be reduced?
- What can/should be done to close the status gap in your workplace?

Group Dynamics: Urgency/Faster Work Completion

- Was your subgroup eager to complete each round quickly?
- Did the timed segments help/not help/hinder play?
- Were some individuals faster paced than others?

- How did the subgroup, as a whole, feel in terms of urgency?
- Was urgency achieved by strategic thinking/planning? Effective communications?
- How can a sense of urgency in the workplace contribute to better customer service? More effective competition?
- What roles do leaders/workers play in creating a sense of urgency for faster product/service delivery?

Group Dynamics: Trusting the Group Process to Succeed

- When confronted by a challenge or problem in playing poker, how did you proceed as an individual? As a subgroup?
- How did you solve the problem? Individually, or as a subgroup?
- Once successful at a problem solution, did you/your subgroup use the same process for the next play/round?
- How is this problem-solving process similar/different from work? Do you solve problems individually or as a group?
- Do you individually or with others develop successful processes to meet challenges/solve problems?
- To what extent do you trust this individual/group problem-solving process? (*Note:* Research shows that, with additional time, most group/participative problem-solving processes result in solutions of higher quality than those achieved by individuals working alone.)
- How can you and others trust the group process to succeed when confronted with challenges and problems in the workplace?

(Twenty minutes.)

Submitted by Linda Raudenbush and Steve Sugar.

Linda Raudenbush, Ed.D., has more than twenty-five years of marketing, managing, training, and consulting experience in both the private and public sectors. She has been an adjunct professor at the National-Louis University and Strayer University and is currently teaching at the University of Maryland, Baltimore County (UMBC). Dr. Raudenbush contributed a chapter for the 1996 Sage publication, The Adjunct Faculty Handbook, *and has been published in the* HRD Quarterly. *She has been a regular session presenter at the annual University System of*

Maryland Women's Conference. Dr. Raudenbush is currently employed by the U.S. Department of Agriculture in the National Agricultural Statistics Service (NASS).

Steve Sugar *is a writer and teacher of learning games. He is the author of* Games That Teach *and co-author of* Games That Teach Teams *(Jossey-Bass/Pfeiffer). Mr. Sugar contributed chapters on instructional design to* The ASTD Handbook of Instructional Technology *(McGraw-Hill) and* The ASTD Handbook of Training Design and Delivery *(McGraw-Hill).* Personnel Journal, Training & Development, *and* TRAINING *have interviewed Mr. Sugar about game design. He has presented at all major conferences and has been on the faculties of the University of Maryland University College, the New York Institute of Technology, and The Johns Hopkins University.*

POWER POKER FACILITATOR NOTES

Here are some thoughts you may wish to consider before conducting your first session of the game:

Poker Deficient? If you wish to be more familiar with the rules of poker, refer to the rules in a reference, such as the *Encyclopedia of Card Games*. You may also want to play a few rounds to learn the basics of the game.

Observers. You might consider using one player-observer for each subgroup. The observer should be briefed or given a "behavior checklist." The observer could also track the cards traded between players.

Swap Sheet Option. The Swap Sheets act as the group memory, documenting the trades between the players. If you feel that the Swap Sheet may slow down or impede game play, then eliminate its use during play. This duty could be assigned to the observer.

Hole Card. Placing one card face down—the hole card—represents the personal agenda we all bring to the game. An entire discussion could be based on sharing and openness—what we know about ourselves and what we are willing to share with others. As the players create the index:

- Do they hesitate or write down the value immediately?

- Do they look around to "size up" the rest of the group?

- Do they write down the true value?

Reality Check. If you feel that the "reality check" (when the hole card is turned face up and does not match the index card) presents too much of a risk of a player losing face with the rest of the group, then remove this element of the game. For example, in the Power Poker Sample Play Sheet, when Player 2 shows his hole card, surprise is expressed by the other players because the hole card does not match the index card. This disclosure can be a very powerful discussion item, with special relevance to the workplace.

Secret Role. You can assign the task of misrepresenting the hole card to one of the players. This would protect the "role player," while allowing the dynamic of deceit and disclosure to be part of the game play.

Confidentiality. The issues of trust and openness explored in this game may require reminders to the players that the behaviors shown in each subgroup are part of the game play and must remain confidential to this game session.

Continuing Behavior. The first round involves negotiation, collaboration, strategizing, and communicating as players try to improve their own hand—hence: "What's in It for Me?" Some players and groups might continue this behavior into the second round. By the third round, all players and groups should realize that working together to maximize the group score is to everyone's advantage. After Round 1 and/or Round 2, watch for the players to experience this "aha!" awareness.

The Penny Option. Add an economic challenge to the first round of play by distributing pennies to all of the players and then allowing them to wager on their final poker hands. Determine whether this first round dynamic imprints the competition-cooperation issue in the following rounds.

POWER POKER SAMPLE PLAY SHEET

The participants form a subgroup of four players (for simplicity of the example, only four players). The subgroup is seated at a table equipped with one deck of playing cards. Each player receives a Power Poker Swap Sheet and three index cards. The subgroup selects a dealer.

Round 1

Card Distribution and Set-Up*

- The dealer distributes five cards, face down, to each of the players, including herself. Player 1 is dealt 2c, 2h, 4d, 8d, and 9s. Player 2 is dealt Ad, Ac, Ah, 3h, and Qs. Player 3 is dealt 3c, 5d, 7d, 8s, and Js. The dealer, or Player 4, is dealt 3d, 4h, 6d, Kc, and Kd. Each player records his or her original hand on the Swap Sheet. Each player reviews his or her hand and then shows the following cards face up: Player 1 shows 2h, 4d, 8d, and 9s—the 2c is the hole card. (Rationale: Player 1 wants to build on his pair of twos.)

- Player 2 shows Ad, Ah, 3h, and Qs. The Ac is the hole card. (*Rationale:* Player 2 wants to collect four aces or a full house.)

- Player 3 shows 3c, 7d, 8s, and Js. The 5d is the hole card. (*Rationale:* Player 3 is hoping to collect a straight.)

- Player 4 shows 3d, 4h, 6d, and Kd. The Kc is the hole card. (*Rationale:* Player 4 wants to build on her pair of kings.)

- Each player then depicts his or her hole card on an index card and places it face up in front of his or her hand.

  - Player 1's index card represents the 2c as the hole card.

  - Player 2's index card represents the 5c** as the hole card.

  - Player 3's index card represents the 5d as the hole card.

  - Player 4's index card represents the Kc as the hole card.

- The dealer draws the "power" card*** from the deck and places it in the middle of the table. The power card = 4s.

---

*Note: c = clubs; h = hearts; d = diamonds; s = spades; A = ace; K = king; Q = queen; J = jack.
**Note: The facilitator asked Player 2 to misrepresent his hole card.
***Note: Any player can use this card to help form a hand.

The Trading Period

- Player 2 needs a pair to create a full house. Player 2 offers to trade the Qs to Player 3 for the 3c. Player 3 agrees and the trade is made. Both players record the trade on their Swap Sheets.

- Player 2 holds a full house: Ad, Ah, 3h, 3c, and Ac (hole card). Player 3 now holds 7d, 8s, Js, Qs, and 5d (hole card).

- Player 3 needs another spade card to create a flush. Player 3 offers to trade the 7d to Player 4 for the Ks. Player 4 refuses, wanting to keep the pair of kings.

- Player 3 offers to trade the 7d to Player 1 for the 9s. Player 1 agrees and the trade is made. Both players record the trade on their Swap Sheets.

- Player 3 now holds a flush: 8s, 9s, Js, Qs, and 4s (power card**). Player 1 now holds 2h, 4d, 7d, 9d, and 2c (hole card). This ends the trading period.

Replacement Cards

- Player 1 holds 2h, 4d, 7d, 8d, and the 2c (hole card). Player 1 decides to keep the two pairs (2h, 2c, and 4d, 4s—power card). Player 1 turns over the hole card and turns in the 7d and 8d for replacement cards. Player 1 receives the 2d and 10s. Player 1 holds a full house: 2c, 2d, 2h, and 4d, 4s (power card***).

- Player 2 holds a full house: Ad, Ah, 3h, 3c, and Ac (hole card). Player 2 does not want to replace any cards.

- Player 3 holds a flush: 8s, 9s, Js, Qs, and 4s (power card***). Player 3 does not want any replacement cards.

- Player 4 holds 3d, 4h, 6d, Ks, and Kc (hole card). Player 4 turns over the hole card and turns in the 3d, 4h, and 6d for replacement cards. Player 4 receives the 3s, Qh, and Kh. Player 4 holds three of a kind: Kc, Kh, and Ks.

Show and Score

- Player 1 has a full house: 3 twos and 2 fours. Player 1 receives 25 points from the Ranking and Scoring Chart.

- Player 2 has a full house: 3 aces and 2 threes. Player 2 receives 25 points from the Ranking and Scoring Chart. Player 2 has the winning hand and receives a 20-point bonus. (When comparing two full houses, the three-of-a-kind cards are compared to each other. In this case, the aces are ranked higher than the twos.)

- Player 3 has a flush: 4, 8, 9, J, Q of spades. Player 3 receives 20 points from the Ranking and Scoring Chart.

- Player 4 has three of a kind: three kings. Player 4 receives 10 points from the Ranking and Scoring Chart.

Final Tally

- The facilitator tallies the final scores.

    Player 1 = 25 points

    Player 2 = 25 + 20 = 45 points

    Player 3 = 20 points

    Player 4 = 10 points

    Subgroup Total = 100 points

POWER POKER SWAP SHEET

Original Hand

Hole Card _____

Trade 1

Hole Card _____

Trade 2

Hole Card _____

Trade 3

Hole Card _____

POWER POKER RANKING/SCORING CHART

Scores

Straight Flush = 45 points

Four of a Kind = 30 points

Full House = 25 points

Flush = 20 points

Straight = 5 points

Three of a Kind = 10 points

Two pairs = 7 points

Two of a Kind = 5 points

Winning Hand = 20-point bonus

Definitions

Straight Flush. Any five cards of the same suit in numerical sequence, such as the ten, nine, eight, seven, and six of any one suit.

Four of a Kind. Any four cards of the same denomination, such as 4 tens.

Full House. Three cards of one denomination and two of another, such as 3 jacks and 2 tens.

The 2002 Annual: Volume 1, Training/© 2002 John Wiley & Sons, Inc.

Flush. Any five cards of the same suit, but not in sequence, such as the jack, nine, eight, six, and two of any one suit.

Straight. Any five cards in numerical sequence, such as the ten, nine, eight, seven, and six of any suit.

Three of a Kind. Any three cards of the same denomination, such as 3 tens.

Two Pairs. Two different pairs of cards, such as 2 tens and 2 jacks.

Two of a Kind. Any two cards of the same denomination, such as 2 kings.

702. SWEET TOOTH:
BONDING STRANGERS INTO A TEAM

Goals

- To provide a fun icebreaking experience at the start of a workshop or with a fun challenge for people who do know one another.

- To introduce the concept of teamwork.

- To provide participants an opportunity to experience key points and learning related to teamwork.

- To help establish a comfortable and supportive environment.

Group Size

Any size in subgroups of five.

Time Required

Fifteen minutes.

Materials

- Sweet Tooth Sample Exercise for each participant.

- A stop watch.

- Paper (optional) and a pencil or pen for each participant.

- Sweet Tooth Sample Exercise Answer Sheet for the facilitator.

Physical Setting

Room arranged with tables that accommodate subgroups of five.

Process

1. Explain that the general idea is just to relax, have fun, and get to know one another while completing a task.

2. Have participants form groups of five each and arrange them at tables. Either ask for one person from each group to "volunteer" to be the leader and to come forward, or use a light-hearted approach for selecting the volunteer: most blue on, traveled the farthest to get to workshop, has the most buttons on.

3. Hand out copies of the Sweet Tooth Sample Exercise to the volunteers to distribute to their table mates.

4. Briefly explain that all the groups in the room will be competing to see which table can give the correct answers to the listed items first, using candy/sweet names. Tell them they will have five minutes to complete the list. (Five minutes.)

5. Tell everyone to begin and start the stop watch. When the time is up or a group claims to be finished, review their answers. (Five minutes.)

6. Ask for a volunteer scribe to record the group's answers on a flip chart at the front of the room. Reward prizes, perhaps candy, if the group answered all the questions correctly. If not, give the prize to the group that had the most correct answers.

7. Bring closure with the following questions:

   ■ What lessens about effective teamwork can be learned from this activity?

   ■ What caused each subgroup to be successful?

   ■ What might be learned about effective teamwork from what happened during this activity.

   ■ What might be done next time to increase the chances of success?

Variation

■ Have the individual subgroups create their own lists of clues for the names of candies/candy bars/sweets. Collect the lists and make a grand list using one or two from each group's contribution. Then hold a competition among the total group.

Submitted by Robert Alan Black

Robert Alan Black, Ph.D., CSP, founder and president of Cre8ng People, Places & Possibilities, is a creative thinking consultant and award-winning professional speaker who specializes in the S.P.R.E.A.D.ng™ of Cre8ng™ and Creative Thinking throughout workplaces around the world. Each year he speaks at many executive development institutes, conferences, and conventions in the United States, Canada, Turkey, and South Africa. He has written eleven books and over two hundred articles that have been published throughout the United States, Canada, Malaysia, Turkey, and South Africa.

SWEET TOOTH SAMPLE EXERCISE

Instructions: Complete the items below with the name of a candy bar or sweet treat. The team that completes the most items correctly first will win a prize.

1. Pee Wee . . ., baseball player.
2. Dried up cows.
3. Kids' game minus toes.
4. Not bad and more than some.
5. Explosion in the sky.
6. Polka . . . .
7. Rhymes with Bert's, dirts, hurts.
8. Happy place to drink.
9. Drowning prevention device.
10. Belongs to a mechanic from Mayberry's cousin.
11. They're not "lesses"; they're . . . .
12. Two names for a purring pet.
13. Takes 114 licks to get to the center of these.
14. Sounds like asteroids.
15. A military weapon.
16. A young flavoring.
17. Top of mountains in winter.
18. To catch fish you need to . . . .
19. Sounds like riddles and fiddles.

The 2002 Annual: Volume 1, Training/© 2002 John Wiley & Sons, Inc.

SWEET TOOTH SAMPLE EXERCISE ANSWER SHEET

1. Reese's® Peanut Butter Cups
2. Milk Duds®
3. Tic®Tacs
4. Good & Plenty®
5. Starburst®
6. DOTS®
7. Certs®
8. Mr. Goodbar®
9. LifeSavers®
10. Goobers
11. S'mores
12. Kit-Kat®
13. Tootsie Roll® Pops
14. Altoids®
15. Bazooka® gum
16. Junior® Mints or Sugar Babies®
17. Sno-Caps®
18. Raisinets®
19. Skittles®

703. Puzzles: Practicing Team Process

Goal

- To demonstrate the team process of generating ideas, organizing them, building a consensus to selection, and taking action.

Group Size

Any number in subgroups of three.

Time Required

Fifty minutes.

Materials

- A small, easy-to-assemble thirty-piece jigsaw puzzle for each subgroup.
- Paper and pencil or pen for each observer.
- Large Post-it® Note pads.
- Black felt-tipped markers.
- Flip chart.

Physical Setting

A room with table(s) so that each subgroup can work separately.

Process

1. Tell the group they will be modeling a typical team process of generating information, then organizing that information so that the team can select one or more options to act on. (Two minutes.)

2. Ask people to form groups of three; two people will be putting each puzzle together while the third person will observe the process.

3. Hand out one puzzle and paper and pens or pencils to each subgroup. Tell them to choose an observer and that the other two people will assemble the puzzle while the observer records just "how" the pairs put the puzzle together. For example, the first step will be to "open the box." Encourage the observers to take careful notes and assure the participants that this is NOT a competition. (Five minutes.)

4. Allow the subgroups to complete their puzzles and cheer when each completes its puzzle. (Five minutes.)

5. When all subgroups have completed their puzzles, debrief the activity by asking process observers "How did your team put the puzzle together from the starting point of opening up the box to the puzzle being complete?" (While you are asking this question, write "open box" at the top of the flip chart and "puzzle complete" at the bottom of the flip chart. (Five minutes.)

6. Ask for one idea from each observer in turn, and with a large felt-tipped marker, legibly write each idea on a large Post-it Note. Place the Post-it Notes on the flip chart, with all the "generation" ideas toward the top, "organization" ideas toward the middle, "decisions" in the lower half and "take action" on the bottom. Place communication issues along the side of the flip chart. Depending on the level of detail and number of teams, the group will identify ten to fifteen steps in the process. (Five minutes.)

(*Note:* Step 6 models the "generation" of information—specifically the steps to assemble a jigsaw puzzle. By placing the Post-it Notes in predetermined categories, you are "organizing" the information into categories, as well as into a flow chart).

7. Congratulate the subgroups on "generating" the many steps used to assemble a jigsaw puzzle, which you have posted on the flip chart. Point out the similarities to "brainstorming," one of the primary tools used to generate information.

8. Reinforce the analogy that teams generate ideas, organize them, select what needs to be done, and then take action—just like they put puzzles together. (Five minutes.)

9. Using the Post-it Notes, compare the notes to the process that teams use, with the following translation:

Generate

Look at/open the box. Define what you are brainstorming.

Dump the pieces out. Brainstorm/generate ideas.

Turn the pieces over. Make sure everyone understands what was said or meant.

Organize

Find the corners. Organize or sort the ideas by categories.

Group same colors/animals/puzzle subjects together. Organize or sort the ideas by categories.

Decide

Agree to focus on the frame. Decide what to do/how to proceed.

Agree that one person will assemble one part of the puzzle, and the other person will assemble another part. Decide roles.

Act

Put puzzle together. Take action.

Clap hands. Celebrate success!

(Five minutes.)

10. Point out the different ways the pairs organized their pieces (by color, by picture objects, corners, or sides). Draw the parallel that many teams organize the information differently, depending on the subject. They might flow chart it from one point to another, prioritize it by importance, sort it into categories, place it on a timeline, etc. (Five minutes.)

11. Point out the subtle ways that teams are always making small decisions—often without verifying that they have made a decision! Ask the group how they made decisions while putting the puzzle together—relying on the "puzzle expert," the loudest voice, a majority vote, or a consensus. Discuss the different ways teams make decisions and quickly move into action. (Five minutes.)

12. Finally, debrief the communication flow—checking with each other, referring to the goal (the picture of the completed puzzle on the box), as well as roadblocks to effective team communication. (Five minutes.)

13. From your specific observations as well as the discussion, summarize the key learnings from this activity. (Two minutes.)

Submitted by Kristin J. Arnold.

Kristin J. Arnold, M.B.A., specializes in coaching executives and their leadership, management, and employee teams, particularly in the areas of strategic and business planning, process improvement, decision making, and collaborative problem solving. An accomplished author and editor of several professional articles and books, as well as a featured columnist in The Daily Press, *a Tribune Publishing newspaper, Ms. Arnold is regarded as an expert in team development and process improvement techniques. With building extraordinary teams as her signature service, she has provided process facilitation, training, and coaching support to both public- and private-sector initiatives.*

704. INTERROGATORIES: IDENTIFYING ISSUES AND NEEDS

Goals

- To build immediate rapport among team members or group participants.
- To identify questions related to the topic or issue.
- To create a comfort zone and open climate for questioning and sharing.

Group Size

Any size up to fifty.

Time Required

Twenty to thirty minutes. Time varies depending on number of interrogatories used and input from the participants.

Materials

- An Interrogatories Topic List for the facilitator.
- A flip chart and felt-tipped markers.
- Masking tape.

Physical Setting

Any.

Process

1. Introduce this activity as an opportunity to discover what issues and questions people have brought to the session. Share with the group how important questions are and the fact that you want to be sure everyone has his or her questions answered as a result of the session. (Two minutes.)

2. Explain that for the next ten or fifteen minutes, they will simply be asking questions. You will introduce a topic. Once you have shared the topic area, the participants are to ask any questions they have related to that topic. You will be jotting down their questions on the flip chart, but no one is to *answer* a question at this time. Say: "The goal is to come up with as many questions as possible in the time allowed. Feel free to build on a question already asked, or share a completely different question. You may initially feel a bit uncomfortable with this activity, but try to flow with it." (Two minutes.)

3. Using the Interrogatories Topic List (or a list you have customized for the session), write the first topic on the flip chart as you share it verbally with the group. Remain quiet and wait for someone to ask a question. Write the key components of the question on the chart. As individuals ask questions, continue recording the essence of their statements. Do not make any comments about any questions. Once all the questions appear to have been asked about a particular topic, or at your own discretion, introduce another topic, and continue the process. As you finish a flip-chart page, have someone tape it to the wall as you continue recording questions. Continue the process for approximately ten to fifteen minutes, then stop. (Ten to fifteen minutes.)

4. To debrief, ask the group the following questions:

   ■ How did you feel about this process?

   ■ What common themes did we hear?

   ■ What are the benefits of this questioning process?

   (Five minutes.)

5. Emphasize the following points:

   ■ Everyone has questions related to every issue. No one should feel "on the spot" for asking a question.

   ■ There are often questions that individuals are afraid to bring up, for fear of looking stupid or uninformed (out of the loop). This method puts the questions out on the table in a nonthreatening way.

- Everyone can begin to spot trends as the questions come out. This will help a group to focus its energy as they tackle the issues during a session.

(Five minutes.)

6. Conclude by identifying the questions that will be answered in the current session and which ones will be put on a "parking lot" to deal with later. (Five minutes.)

Variation

- In a team-building session, have the team members review the questions they have generated under each topic. Facilitate the process of consolidating the questions, then prioritizing them in terms of importance to the team.

Submitted by Cher Holton.

Cher Holton, Ph.D., *president of The Holton Consulting Group, Inc., is an impact consultant focusing on the topic of Bringing Harmony to Life: with customers, among team members, and in life. She is one of fewer than two dozen professionals worldwide who have earned both the Certified Speaking Professional and Certified Management Consultant designations. She has authored* The Manager's Short Course to a Long Career, Living at the Speed of Life: Staying in Control in a World Gone Bonkers!, *and* Suppose . . . Questions to Turbo-Charge Your Business and Your Life.

INTERROGATORIES TOPIC LIST

Instructions: Choose from the following topics those that relate to your session topic, or develop your own to customize the activity.

- Coaching
- Communication
- Customers
- Email
- Leadership
- Management
- Meetings
- Mission
- Performance Appraisal
- Priorities
- Quality
- Rules
- Service
- Success
- Teamwork
- Training
- Values

705. Crochet Hook: Learning How We Learn

Goals

- To understand ways in which one learns.

- To see that trainer attitude plays a role in learning.

- To learn how one's own attitude toward the task can influence learning.

- To appreciate the role of proper instructions and supplies in learning a task.

- To understand various aspects of the learning process.

- To delve into the Experiential Learning Cycle.

Group Size

Eight to twenty participants.

Time Required

Ten minutes for the activity. Up to two hours to process the results.

Materials

- Crochet hooks, one per person. Provide crochet hooks in various sizes, but not matching the sizes specified in the instructions.

- A set of instructions for making a crocheted chain, one per person. Either write them from experience, or obtain them from the Internet. If you use instructions from a published work, be sure to obtain permission from the publisher. (*Note:* It is best to provide more instructions than are needed and to photocopy from photocopies, which will decrease the copy quality. Provide the poorest quality materials possible. Instructions that are hard to read—light in color, too small, or photocopied at an angle or with words at the end of sentences cut off, instructions that are too small or too light to read, and so on.)

- Pieces of yarn or string or shoelaces in varying sizes from 6 inches to 24 inches long. (These materials also should not match the instructions and should make it more difficult to complete the task, perhaps by being too thick or too thin or made from a stiff material.)
- A transparency of the Experiential Learning Cycle.
- A Crochet Hook Discussion Guide for the facilitator and one copy for each participant.
- A flip chart and felt-tipped markers.
- Masking tape.
- An overhead projector and screen.

Physical Setting

A room large enough for the participants to work separately and to record the debriefing results on flip chart paper on the walls.

Process

1. Explain that for the time being the goals of the activity will not be discussed, but that later they will be covered in detail.

2. Give each person (or assign partners) a page of crochet directions, a single crochet hook, and yarn or other material.

3. In a firm and not friendly tone of voice, say to the group, "You are to produce an eight-inch crochet chain in the next ten minutes using the instructions you have been provided. Everything you need to complete the task has been given to you. Work quickly. Do not talk to one another because you must concentrate." Do not use a tone of voice or body language that conveys receptivity to questions, special kindness, or supportiveness. (Two minutes.)

4. After they begin, circulate throughout the room, making a crochet chain yourself if you are able to do so. As you make the chain, in a firm voice say, "See how easy this is." (If you are unable to complete this task, just walk and watch the participants.) Listen to comments and make observation notes. Tell them to "hurry, the clock is ticking." After five minutes, announce, "There are five minutes remaining." Then call out the

remaining time every minute thereafter. After ten minutes announce, "Time is up. Stop working."

5. As people complete their chains, praise them loudly and excessively: "That's wonderful!" "How fast you are!" "You are a quick learner!" "Nice job!" Allow those who finish early to take a break. Do not encourage those who are having difficulty. Instead, say such things as, "Hurry, you are taking an awfully long time." "Focus on the directions and concentrate." "What seems to be the problem?" If anyone complains that the directions are difficult, ensure him or her that the directions are complete and accurate and to follow them. If any completed products appear to be inconsistent in their appearance (that is, some loops are large and some are small), do not praise the person for completing the task, but judge the work by saying something like: "This isn't right; look how lopsided it is. All the loops should be the same. This isn't good." To get the kinds of responses you want during the debriefing, it's best to appear distant, disinterested in helping the learners, nonsupportive, and unapproachable through both your demeanor and tone of voice. Model the kinds of behaviors trainers should avoid. (Ten minutes.)

6. Process the exercise by displaying the Experiential Learning Cycle transparency as you lead participants through it. First, post the model, uncovering one section at a time as you discuss it: "You've just finished the 'experience' portion of the Experiential Learning Cycle. Let's discuss what we learned from this activity in terms of the model. The activity gave everyone the same experience, so we can talk about it together. This is 'publishing' or sharing our reactions to the experience we had in common and how we felt about what happened."

Pause now and have participants share their reactions by asking the following questions.

- What was your reaction to the experience?

- Was it easy or hard to do as you were asked. Why was that?

- How did you feel about your accomplishment? Did you feel good about yourself or not? Why was that?

- Who else had a similar experience? Tell us about it.

(Ten to fifteen minutes.)

7. Encourage responses from as many participants as possible. The comments will be negative in most cases.

8. After learners have shared their feelings of displeasure, discomfort, and lack of success, explain that you will now move to the "processing" part of the model. Uncover it on the transparency. Say, "Let's make sense of this. How many of you were able to complete the task and how many were not? Please separate into two groups: Those who did complete the task should form one group and those who did not should form another group." Once the participants are in one of the two groups, give them flip charts and markers and say, "Talk within your groups and record on flip chart paper what helped you complete the task or what interfered with your being able to finish." Tell them to mark one flip chart "What Helped Us Learn" and the other "What Interfered with Our Learning." Allow 10 minutes for both groups to capture their ideas. (Ten minutes.)

9. When both groups have finished, ask each group to present its list to the plenary group. Some of the ideas that should appear on the lists are these:

What Helped the Learning

- Received instructional materials (directions).

- Received materials to complete the task (yarn and crochet hook).

- Persons who are intrinsically motivated were challenged by the exercise.

What Interfered with the Learning

- Learning environment was unpleasant: trainer was unwilling to help, trainer pressured the group (announced time remaining), trainer didn't allow enough time to complete the task, trainer did not seem willing to answer questions.

- Individuals were unable to learn by the method presented (reading directions).

- There was no demonstration, and no product was shown from which learners might copy.

- There was no need to learn to do the task, and no benefits for completing the task were presented.

It is possible that each group will record the flip sides of the same thing on their lists. For example, the "successful" group may have listed that the instructional materials were good; the other group may record that the instructional materials were bad. Listen to any discrepancies and probe. In the example above, ask: "Why would one group be pleased with the instructional method and the other group be unhappy with it?"

Supplement their comments by explaining that people learn differently and that successful learning in a group depends on the inclusion of several instructional methods in the design. To increase the chances for 100 percent learner success, the trainer could have used additional instructional methods, such as modeling or demonstrating the task. Also, learners may have been able to partner and teach one another how to complete the task, which would have increased the number of successful learners, or "experts" in the room could have been used to help the others. (Fifteen minutes.)

10. When the groups finish presenting their lists, suggest other learning principles they may have missed, using the Crochet Hook Discussion Guide. Ask:

- How did the trainer's style help or hurt the learning process?

  Learning can occur when external threats are at a minimum (Knowles, Holton, & Swanson, 1990). The more supportive, accepting, and caring the environment, the freer a person is to experiment with new behaviors and attitudes. If learners are in a setting in which others may see them performing a new task, the lack of privacy may affect their ability to learn. Were, for example, any of the learners embarrassed that they may have been seen crocheting?

- If you were having difficulty, did you ask questions? If not, why not?

  The most likely reason, they will say, is that the trainer's demeanor did not invite questions, and so the value of feedback and engaging the learners in dialogue was not gained.

- What value was there in having the trainer complete the chain?

  There was no value because the trainer did not show the completed product nor demonstrate the process of making the chain. If the trainer did complete the task, he or she may have demeaned the learners who were not able to complete what appeared to be a very simple task.

- Were you motivated to complete the project? What could the trainer have done to motivate you?

  Adults are motivated to learn when they have a need to do so. They want to know how the training will help them. Part of preparing to learn is to understand the benefits of the learning, as well as the disadvantages of not learning. If learners appear to be resistant to a task, a trainer should ask questions to find out the source of the resistance. In this case, the trainer did not make the learning activity relevant to the students' learning objectives nor did the trainer explain the objectives prior to beginning the task. To stay motivated, learners must see the benefits of the task and feel that they can accomplish the task. In this case, there was no trainer encouragement; and slow learners were even belittled.

- Were any of you who completed the task in the military or Boy or Girl Scouts? How might that experience have affected your ability to complete the task?

  Adults possess a large bank of previous learning and can tap into their experiences. Because crocheting is all about making knots, those who knew how to make knots may have been able to use that knowledge in this new task. The trainer could have helped the learners link new knowledge and skills to knowledge and skills they already possessed. This would have encouraged the group and made the task less difficult. However, although existing knowledge and skills can help, they can also hinder learning because learners may dismiss or reject the new knowledge and skills and stick with what they know and can do. Or learners may experience interference from their existing knowledge and skills as they try to learn something new. In this case, they may have had to unlearn previous learning. To illustrate this concept, ask the group whether anyone already knew how to knit. People who can knit may have found it difficult to change their hand position to use the new tool.

11. Complete the discussion of the Experiential Learning Cycle model. "We have discussed the experiencing, publishing, and processing parts of the model. Next is 'generalizing' (show the model), which is about helping learners to turn specific knowledge and ideas into larger, abstract ideas. This is known as the 'So what?' part of the cycle." Ask:

- What might we infer/conclude from our experience?

- What did you learn that you can apply in the rest of your life from this experience?

- What does that suggest to you about learning in general?

- What does that help to explain about the ways in which you learn best?

(Ten minutes.)

12. Next, ask the group to sum up (generalize) what the experience taught them about being an effective trainer. List the learning principles they have discovered during the activity and debriefing on the flip chart.

13. Say, "Finally, we must be able to *apply* the learning. The final stage in the Experiential Learning Cycle is 'applying.'" Ask the group members how

they can apply what they learned through the experience to the real world.

- How can you use what you have learned the next time that you are instructing someone else?
- What will you do with what you just learned?

Record their ideas on the flip chart. (Ten minutes.)

14. Conclude by explaining that the model is depicted as a cycle and that, although you started with the experience, it's possible to begin the cycle at any point. However, to maximize learning, be certain to follow the model completely from beginning to end.

15. Give out copies of the Crochet Hook Discussion Guide to all participants. Check that all points have been covered and encourage questions about anything participants have not understood about the Experiential Learning Cycle or the points on the discussion guide. (Ten minutes.)

Variations

- Substitute another learning task for the crocheting activity, such as origami. Be sure to choose something that would be difficult for the group to learn simply by reading instructions and that most would not already know how to do.

- If there are a lot of participants and you have additional breakout space, split the group: one group of participants working individually and the second group working together, sharing their ideas and teaching one another.

- The Crochet Hook Discussion Guide could be used as the basis for a lecturette before the activity, thus giving participants something to look for as they proceed. They could be given paper and pencils and asked to take notes about the learning process as they make their crochet chains.

Reference

Knowles, M., Holton, E.F., & Swanson, R.A. (1990). *The adult learner: The definitive classic in adult education and human resource development.* Houston, TX: Gulf.

Submitted by Lynne Andia.

Lynne Andia is director of organization development for a gas supplier and teaches in the master's program at West Chester University, West Chester, Pennsylvania. She is a partner in Pathways to Performance Improvement, a consulting firm specializing in meeting facilitation, strategic planning, training, and management development. She has an M.Ed. and M.S. in organization development.

THE EXPERIENTIAL LEARNING CYCLE

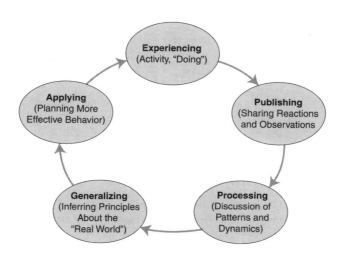

From Introduction to Experiential Learning Activities in *The 1999 Reference Guide to Handbooks and Annuals*. San Francisco: Jossey-Bass/Pfeiffer.

CROCHET HOOK DISCUSSION GUIDE

Learning Principles

1. We learn best when external threats are at a minimum (Knowles, Holton, & Swanson, 1990). "The more supportive, accepting, and caring the social environment, the freer a person is to experiment with new behaviors and attitudes" (Johnson & Johnson, 1991, p. 43).

2. The starting point of change is discontent. If learners see no reason to change their behavior, they probably won't (Yelon, 1995).

3. "People will believe more in knowledge they have discovered themselves than in knowledge presented by others" (Johnson & Johnson, 1991, p. 43). This approach to learning is based on inquiry and discovery, which increases learners' motivation to learn and commit to implement their conclusions in the future. The Experiential Learning Model builds on that self-discovery method (Segal, 1997).

4. "Learning is more effective when it is an active rather than a passive process" (Johnson & Johnson, 1991, p. 42).

5. Learners must believe that they are capable of doing the needed behaviors and must see the behaviors as being appropriate to the situation before they will engage in them (Johnson & Johnson, 1991).

6. It is easier to change a person's attitudes and behavioral patterns in a group context than in an individual context. A person accepts a new system of action theories, attitudes, and behavioral patterns when he or she accepts membership in a new group (Johnson & Johnson, 1991).

7. Skills should be learned one at a time, and each new skill should build on previously acquired skills (Gagne & Medsker, 1996).

8. Learning and knowledge are hierarchical in nature (Gagne & Medsker, 1996).

9. Learning will be made easier to the extent that:

   - The learner is motivated to learn. (How many teenagers fail Driver's Ed class?) "Adults are motivated to learn as they experience needs and interests that learning will satisfy" (Knowles, Holton, & Swanson, 1990, p. 31).

   - The responses to what is being learned are meaningfully related to each other and to the motives that the learner brings with him (Yelon, 1995).

- From B.F. Skinner we know that something in the environment preceding a behavior—the antecedent—and something in the environment following the behavior—the consequences or result—influences the likelihood of a behavior's reoccurrence (Hellriegel, Slocum, & Woodman, 1989). Therefore, the new, correct responses should be reinforced or followed by some reward or information that the response has been made correctly; in organizations, these rewards range from the material, such as salary and bonus, to the intangible, such as approval.

- The learning situation provides opportunities to practice the new responses. Whether learning verbal or motor skills, practice—"repeated attempts by the learner to achieve the desired performance"—can facilitate learning (Gagne & Driscoll, 1988, p. 100). Both arranging repeated practice opportunities and furnishing immediate feedback aid in achieving learning outcomes (Gagne & Driscoll, 1988).

- The new responses to be learned are broken up into learnable units and presented in an appropriately paced sequence. Sequencing instruction is about ordering content. The teaching of crochet, for example, could be aided by "known-to-unknown" sequencing, where learners become aware of what they already know to help them learn the new material. Both Herbart and Knowles advocate this approach to bringing the learners' experiences to the learning situation (Rothwell & Kazanas, 1998).

- Coaching or guidance helps the learner develop new responses. Gagne and Driscoll (1988) suggest that verbal explanation, as well as visual demonstrations, can help individuals learn motor skills. Break a procedure into parts that can be demonstrated separately and guided with verbal cues.

- Learner characteristics provide direction for developing training, such as choosing the instructional methods, recognizing factors that affect motivation, etc. The individual differences of the learners, such as how much they already bring to the situation (prerequisite knowledge, skills, and attitudes), their preferred learning styles, their physical and mental aptitudes, and their experiences, should be identified during a needs assessment so that the trainer can design appropriate and effective instruction (Rothwell & Kazanas, 1998).

References

Gagne, R., & Driscoll, M.P. (1988). *Essentials of learning for instruction.* Englewood Cliffs, NJ: Prentice Hall.

Gagne, R., & Medsker, K. (1996). *The conditions of learning: Training applications.* Stamford, CT: Wadsworth.

Hellriegel, D., Slocum, J.W., Jr., & Woodman, R.W. (1989). *Organizational behavior.* Cincinnati, OH: South-Western College Publishing.

Knowles, M., Holton, E.F., & Swanson, R.A. (1990). *The adult learner: The definitive classic in adult education and human resource development.* Houston, TX: Gulf.

Johnson, D.W., & Johnson, F.P. (1991). *Joining together: Group theory and group skills.* Needham Heights, MA: Allyn & Bacon.

Rothwell, W.J., & Kazanas, H.C. (1998). *Mastering the instructional design process.* San Francisco, CA: Jossey-Bass.

Segal, M. (1997). *Points of influence: A guide to using personality theory at work.* San Francisco, CA: Jossey-Bass.

Yelon, S.L. (1995). *Powerful principles of instruction.* Reading, MA: Addison-Wesley.

706. CERTIFICATES: APPRECIATING ONESELF

Goals

- To allow participants to identify an area in which they would like to be appreciated.
- To experience public appreciation.
- To provide an innovative activity to celebrate the end of a workshop.

Group Size

A minimum of five; no maximum, but use small groups of four to six people if there are more than twenty.

Time Required

Approximately thirty minutes.

Materials

- Printed certificates*.
- Fine-point colored markers.
- Ribbons.
- Stickers.
- Large stars.
- Graphic tapes in many widths and colors.
- Stapler.
- Tape.
- Scissors.

---

*For unique certificates and supplies for recognition ceremonies, contact Baudville Inc. at 800–728–0888 or www.baudville.com and ask for a catalogue.

Physical Setting

Tables and chairs facing the front of the room.

Process

1. Prior to the workshop, purchase pre-printed or prepare computer generated certificates for each participant. Enhance the certificate's appearance by keeping the content simple. Center the words "Certificate of Self-Appreciation for" and leave the area blank below this. Add a graphic image, emblem, or logo that represents your organization or geographic location (for example, a half-tone outline of your area's skyline, a photograph of your building, or a graphic image from clip art.) Select a special paper such as parchment or glossy finish. Be sure to include the following information on each certificate:

   - Name and date(s) of the workshop
   - Name of the trainer
   - Name of the sponsor or company

   Place ribbons, stickers, stars, and other supplies on a table at the front of the room for easy accessibility.

2. At least thirty minutes prior to closing a workshop session, explain to the participants that everyone likes to be appreciated and to receive certificates to display or show others; however, this activity will give them the chance to give a certificate of appreciation to themselves. (Two minutes.)

3. Distribute the certificates and fine-point markers. Have participants write their own names in the appropriate space.

4. Next, tell the participants to think of what they deserve recognition for while attending this workshop. Examples might be:

   - Someone who is usually quiet might write, "I freely contributed ideas."
   - Someone who is usually talkative might write, "I listened attentively before speaking up!"
   - Someone who is usually an avoider of conflict might write "I was willing to deal with conflict."
   - Someone who is usually anxious about returning phone messages might write, "I resisted returning phone calls during the session."

Tell participants to fill in the space below "Certificate of Self-Appreciation for" using the fine-point colored markers. (Five minutes.)

5. Ask the participants to add special touches to their certificates, using the supplies you have placed at the front of the room. (Ten minutes.)

6. Collect the completed certificates. Conduct a ceremony for giving out the certificates. Everyone faces to the front. Call the person who is listed on the top certificate. Verbally embellish the reason the certificate is being given such as:

> "Sue, we are so proud to present this certificate to you because we know how much you love to talk and that it is hard to not speak up with every one of your ideas and opinions. Therefore, we are giving you a certificate for listening attentively before you spoke up! Congratulations!"

Lead the group in applause as you shake hands and give out the certificates. (Approximately one minute per certificate.)

7. Continue this type of presentation for each participant. Then ask for comments from participants on how they felt about the activity. (Five minutes.)

Variations

- Form small groups of four to six participants who have worked together during the workshop. Have them give the certificates to one another in their small groups after they are finished.

- The participants decide from whom they would like to receive a certificate and that individual is asked to present the award to the recipient.

- Make a pile of completed certificates placed upside down. Each person draws a certificate and presents it to the person named on it.

- Give yourself a certificate as the trainer.

Resource

Hart, L.B. (1995) *Connections.* Lafayette, CO: Leadership Dynamics.

Submitted by Lois B. Hart.

Lois B. Hart, Ed.D., is director of the Women's Leadership Institute and president of Leadership Dynamics. She has twenty-nine years of experience as a trainer, facilitator, and consultant, presenting programs on leadership, teams, conflict, and facilitation. She is co-author with Ken Blanchard and Mario Tamayo of Celebrate! *(2001). She has written twenty-one other books, including* Connection: Saying Hello and Saying Good-bye, 50 Activities for Developing Leaders, Learning from Conflict, Training Methods That Work, *and* Faultless Facilitation.

707. Selection Interview: Practicing Both Roles*

Goals

- To give participants an opportunity to prepare for a personnel selection interview from the perspectives of both the interviewer and the applicant.

- To allow each participant to experience the roles of interviewer, applicant, and observer.

- To provide participants with an opportunity to give and receive feedback on their interview techniques.

Group Size

Any number of triads.

Time Required

Approximately two hours.

Materials

- One copy of the Selection Interview Interviewer's Role Sheet for every participant.

- One copy of the Selection Interview Applicant's Role Sheet for every participant.

- One copy of the Selection Interview Observer's Role Sheet for every participant.

---

*The author asked thirty-nine personnel management students to evaluate this exercise by secret ballot on the following scale: 1 = excellent experience; 2 = good experience; 3 = okay/average learning experience; 4 = not a good experience; 5 = terrible experience (a waste of time). All responses were 1, 2, or 3. There were no 4's or 5's. Mean rating was 1.79.

- Blank paper and a pencil for each participant.
- A writing surface for each participant.
- A newsprint flip chart and felt-tipped markers.
- Masking tape.

Physical Setting

A room large enough for triads to work without disturbing one another.

Process

1. Explain the goals of the activity. (Five minutes.)

2. Ask the participants to assemble into triads and give one member of each triad a copy of the Selection Interview Interviewer's Role Sheet; another member of each triad a copy of the Selection Interview Applicant's Role Sheet; and the third member a copy of the Selection Interview Observer's Role Sheet. Give blank paper, a pencil, and a writing surface to every participant.

3. Instruct participants to read their sheets and to ask for clarification on any point they do not understand. Answer all questions and then tell participants that they have ten minutes to prepare for their interviews. (Ten minutes.)

4. After ten minutes, stop the preparation and ask interviewers to begin their interviews. Tell observers to take notes as the interview progresses. After ten minutes, announce that the interviews should come to a close. (Ten minutes.)

5. When all triads have finished, announce that each member of the triad should make notes silently for three minutes before the observers give their feedback. Feedback should take about five minutes. (Eight minutes.)

6. Announce that, in the next round, each participant will play a different role. Give participants sheets for roles they did not play during the last round.

7. Repeat Steps 3 through 6. Then repeat Steps 3 through 5 with participants receiving new instruction sheets. (Sixty minutes.)

8. Reassemble the total group and lead a discussion that includes the following questions:

- How did you feel when you played the interviewer role? Answers in the past have included the following:

  - Confident, in control, empowered

  - Preparation is important

  - Practice is needed

  - Important to be flexible

  - Developing a natural flow is important

  - Felt applicant could/could not be trusted

  - Questions control the interview

  - Silence is powerful

  - Receive information only when applicant talks

  - Listening is important

- How did you feel when you played the applicant role? Answers in the past have included the following:

  - Anxious or intimidated at first

  - Later, relaxed or cautious, depending on how interviewer acted

  - Felt better after opening up

  - Preparation helped

  - Practice needed

  - Role sheet helped me realize that interviews are not win/lose competitions

  - Friendly smile, eye contact, gestures relaxed me

  - Positive information being given made me comfortable

  - Negative information being given made me uncomfortable

  - Turned a negative to a positive by admitting a weakness and telling how I overcame the weakness

  - Applicants can use questions and silence too!

- When you were playing the observer role, what seemed to work well for interviewers? Past answers include:
  - Make applicant comfortable
  - Allow applicant to talk (listen)
  - Establish flow by linking questions to applicant's answers
  - Pose hypothetical problems to the applicant
  - Ask job-related questions
  - Allow applicant to ask questions
  - Wait for more after briefing responses
- What didn't work well for interviewers? Past answers have included the following:
  - Making applicants uncomfortable
  - Doing all the talking
  - Not listening
  - Not probing for more detail
  - Asking questions unrelated to the job
  - Not inviting the applicant to ask questions
  - Rushing; being impatient
- What worked well for applicants? Past answers have included the following:
  - Eye contact
  - Thinking before answering
  - Preparation
  - Relaxing
  - Being friendly but not overly familiar
  - Giving positive, upbeat answers
  - Being open and honest
- What has not worked well? Answers in the past have included the following:
  - Pretending to be perfect
  - No preparation or practice

The 2002 Annual: Volume 1, Training/© 2002 John Wiley & Sons, Inc.

- Answering before thinking
- Being overly humorous or sarcastic
- Giving negative answers
- Being guarded or overly serious
- What did you learn from this experience? Answers should include:
  - Practice at three roles
  - A list of questions that could be used in the future
  - Overcame anxiety about interviewing
  - Desire to prepare and practice

Variations

- Have all participants bring a résumé for use during the interviews.
- Have job descriptions available for interviewers.
- Allow triads to decide the job for which the applicant is being interviewed.
- If the group is small, have all or some of the triads role play while the others observe.
- Interviews may be videotaped for later analysis and discussion.

Submitted by John E. Oliver.

John E. Oliver received his Ph.D. degree from Georgia State University. He is a professor and head of the Department of Management at Valdosta State University. He has published several instruments and experiential learning exercises in the Annuals, *as well as made over eighty other contributions to journals, books, and magazines. His research and consulting interests are in the areas of human resource development, organization development, and team development. He serves on the editorial review boards of several journals.*

Selection Interview Interviewer's Role Sheet

Instructions: In this round, you will play a manager interviewing an applicant for the position of management trainee, an entry-level management position in a large bank. You are seeking to fill the position with a person who is intelligent, educated, and motivated and who can make decisions, communicate with people at all levels (managers, employees, and customers), and protect and use the bank's assets efficiently.

A good interviewer uses three tools effectively:

1. *Questions* to probe for information (what, how, why),

2. *Silence* to be receptive to information and to prompt further comment by the interviewee, and

3. *Observation* to see things that are not verbally transmitted.

In addition, a good interviewer recognizes that an effective interview process has three stages: *before* the interview, *during* the interview, and *after* the interview. Several important activities are accomplished during each stage.

Before the interview, the effective interviewer reviews key job requirements, reviews the applicant's resume or application if available, plans questions to ask based on the applicant's apparent strengths and weaknesses compared to job requirements, and ensures compliance with equal employment opportunity guidelines.

During the interview, the interviewer uses an opener (statement or question) to relax the applicant. For example, "Let me tell you a little about the company" or "I see you're from Albany. I used to live there, too." When the applicant is relaxed, he or she uses *lead-in statements* to begin the interview. Something like, "What college did you attend?" works well. The interviewer should make statements and ask planned questions about *relevant* issues using lead-in questions followed by more in-depth probes such as, "Tell me more about that," "When did that happen?" "Why?" "Who else was involved?" and "What did you learn from that?"

Relevant issues might include the following:

- Education and training
- Work experience and skills
- Job performance evaluations
- Career interests and work goals

- Interest in job and company
- Salary and benefits
- Self-assessment (*if job related*)
- What has led to your success to date?
- What motivates you?
- What are the important traits of a manager?
- What would be a good reason to fire an employee?
- What strengths do you have that would help you be successful in this job? Weaknesses?

As the interview progresses, the interviewer gives the applicant a chance to ask questions. He or she closes the interview with a "thank you" and a definite date, time, place, and method of next contact, for example, "We'll call you at this number next Friday to let you know what comes next. We still have three people to interview."

Ordinarily, a good interviewer waits until after all candidates have been interviewed, then reviews his or her notes on all applicants again before making a decision. The decision is then communicated as promised.

Remember, *your goal is to determine whether the applicant has the necessary skills, knowledge, abilities, and motivation to perform the job well.* The interview should last ten minutes. Afterward, you will be given time to take notes on what occurred during the interview and to hear feedback from the observer.

Selection Interview Applicant's Role Sheet

Instructions: In this round, you will play the role of a recent college graduate interviewing for the position of management trainee, an entry-level management position in a large bank. The position requires a person who is intelligent, educated, and motivated and who can make decisions, communicate with people at all levels (managers, employees, and customers), and protect and use the bank's assets efficiently.

As an applicant, you can prepare for the interview in three ways:

1. Learn all you can about the job and the organization before the interview;

2. Prepare a list of questions you would like to ask about the job, the organization, promotional opportunities, pay, and benefits; and

3. Prepare yourself mentally by relaxing.

Remember that the interview is *not* a competition. It is an activity that allows you to see whether there is a match between the job requirements and your qualifications. If the match does not exist, you don't want the job. If the match does exist, the more relaxed you are, the more qualified you will appear. If you do not get the job, you are still a "good person." There is nothing you can do in the short run to better qualify yourself for a job, and you do not want to get a job for which you are unqualified. This leads to dishonesty, failure, or both. Therefore, relax, be confident, and approach the interview as a fact-finding mission. Find out whether you can do the job, and also whether you *want* the job. You may want to ask questions such as the following:

- What would my duties and responsibilities be?

- Who would I be working with?

- If I do a good job, how will I be rewarded?

- What other jobs could I expect to do in the future?

- What do you like about being a manager in this organization? Dislike?

- What is the pay range for people in this job?

- What fringe benefits does the company offer?

As the interview progresses, you may be asked questions to determine your qualifications. Opening questions such as, "What college did you attend?" may be followed by probes such as, "In what subjects did you do well?" and "Why?" Try to be relaxed and honest.

As the interview comes to a close, try to find out when, where, and how you will be contacted again.

Remember, *your goal is to determine whether this job is one for which you are qualified and one in which you will be satisfied and successful.* The interview should last ten minutes. Afterward, you will have an opportunity to take notes on what occurred and then hear feedback from the observer.

Selection Interview Observer's Role Sheet

Instructions: In this round, you will observe while a manager interviews an applicant for the position of management trainee, an entry-level management position in a large bank. The position requires a person who is intelligent, educated, and motivated and who can make decisions, communicate with people at all levels (managers, employees, and customers), and protect and use the bank's assets efficiently.

As an observer, you should take notes on three things:

1. *What worked well for the interviewer?* This includes questions that elicited good information and actions, such as smiling, making eye contact, or using silence that led the applicant to share more information.

2. *What worked well for the applicant?* This could include questions, answers, or behavioral responses that resulted in positive responses by the interviewer.

3. *What questions or behaviors did not work well for either party?* How do you think that these less effective efforts could be redesigned to make them more effective?

The interviewer is trying to learn as much as possible about whether the applicant is qualified for the job based on what he or she knows about job requirements. The following is a list of some types of information that can be gained from the interview:

Ability to work in a group

Adaptability

Appearance

Attitudes toward achievement

Basic values and goals

Breadth and depth of knowledge

Cultural breadth

Diversity of interests

Emotional and social adjustment

Intellectual abilities

Interpersonal relations

Leadership

Level of accomplishment

Management of time, energy, and money

Maturity and judgment

Motivation

Reaction

Relevance of schooling

Relevance of work experience

Responsiveness

Self-expression

Self-image

Skill and competence

Social interests

Sufficiency of schooling

Sufficiency of work experience

Versatility

Vitality and energy

The interview should last ten minutes. After the interview is over, all three of you (you the observer, the interviewer, and the applicant) are to take three minutes to reflect, silently and in writing, any feelings, ideas, or comments you may wish to share during later discussion of the interview.

Only after the three minutes of silent note taking will you begin giving feedback to both the interviewer and applicant on the things that worked well or that could be improved. Be sure to let them discuss your comments and suggestions, their own notes, and anything else they want to discuss.

Remember, *your goal as observer is to give positive feedback to both the interviewer and applicant and to make sure they have shared their feelings and knowledge in order to ensure that maximum learning occurs during the experience.* Your feedback should take only about five minutes.

708. Second to None: Electronically Mediated Personal Leadership Planning

Goals

- To identify key tasks and people for ongoing personal leadership development.
- To review personal action plans and receive feedback from fellow leadership development planners.
- To appreciate the value and insight that others' opinions have in determining personal leadership goals.
- To develop a community of leaders by establishing a framework for sharing perspectives and experiences.

Group Size

Twelve to sixteen participants who have previously attended a leadership seminar.

Time Required

Two hours face-to-face in addition to two or three hours online.

Materials

- Copies of the online summary report for everyone.
- One Second to None Personal Leadership Planning Guide for each participant.
- One Second to None Celebration Sheet for each participant.
- A flip chart and felt-tipped markers for the facilitator.
- Masking tape.
- A pen or pencil and note paper for each participant.

Physical Setting

A room large enough for participants to sit comfortably with plenty of table top room to spread materials out. A U-shaped room arrangement is preferred to enhance interactions between and among participants.

Process

1. The process begins at the closing of a leadership development program. Explain the need for reflective thinking about the almost-completed program. State that the need exists to continue to grow and develop as leaders. Announce that a Personal Leadership Planning Guide will be sent to each participant as an email attachment in five days. Explain that it consists of a series of questions divided into nine areas of personal planning.

2. Five working days after the program has concluded, send a copy of the Second to None Personal Leadership Planning Guide as an email attachment, asking each participant to complete it online and email their responses back to you within ten working days.

3. Review the responses from all of the participants and prepare a summary of participant responses. Be sure to highlight dominant themes. Post the summary on an electronic bulletin board that all participants can access.

4. Ask the participants to respond to the posting by putting their responses directly on the electronic bulletin board within five working days.

5. Ask participants to review the entire bulletin board (summary report and responses) in relation to their own Personal Leadership Planning Guides. Suggest to them that if they want to make any changes on their Planning Guides, they should do so at this juncture.

6. Invite participants to a face-to-face debriefing of the personal leadership planning process as it has been carried out up to this point. The timing for this two-hour face-to-face debriefing should be about thirty working days from the conclusion of the leadership development program.

7. After everyone has gathered, explain the goals of the activity. (Ten minutes.)

8. Hand out copies and review the summary report briefly to create a framework for the debriefing. (Fifteen minutes.)

9. Lead a discussion on the following question: "In general terms, what did you change as a result of the electronic bulletin board activity?" Post the responses on a flip chart. (Fifteen minutes.)

10. Break the participants into small groups of three or four and ask them to discuss the following questions, while recording their responses to present to the total group:

- What would the workplace be like if you were a better leader?
- How well-aligned is what you intend to do with what the organization needs to have done?
- Which actions stand the best chance of being successful?
- How will any roadblocks to success be overcome?
- When and how often will you review the progress of your total plan?

(Thirty minutes.)

11. Reconvene the total group and have them present the information on their flip charts. (Twenty minutes.)

12. Conduct a large group discussion on the following questions:

- What additional learning has resulted from this debriefing?
- How effective has this overall planning process been for you?
- What other observations can you offer about this experience?

(Twenty minutes.)

13. Tell the participants that all the flip charts from the debriefing will be made available in a file online.

14. Conduct a closing toast and hand out Second to None Celebration Sheets to everyone. Give them a few minutes to fill them out and suggest that they keep these sheets handy to review them at least every quarter. (Ten minutes.)

Variations

- The timing of the electronic activity can be changed based on participant availability.
- Each of the electronic elements could be accomplished in a face-to-face setting using flip charts.
- Participants could bring laptops to the debriefing and type notes into an electronic file.
- If participants are geographically dispersed after the leadership program, the debriefing could be accomplished using teleconferencing methods.

Submitted by Robert C. Preziosi.

Robert C. Preziosi, D.P.A., is a professor of management at the Huizenga Graduate School of Business and Entrepreneurship at Nova Southeastern University in Fort Lauderdale, Florida. In 1997 he received the school's first Excellence in Teaching Award, and in 2000 he was named Professor of the Decade. He is also president of Preziosi Partners, Inc., a consulting firm. He has worked as a human resources director, a line manager, and a leadership-training administrator. As a trainer, his areas of interest include leadership, adult learning, and all aspects of management and executive development. In 1984 he was given the Outstanding Contribution to HRD award by ASTD, and in 1996 he received his second ASTD Torch Award. He is a regular contributor to the Annuals.

The 2002 Annual: Volume 1, Training/© 2002 John Wiley & Sons, Inc.

Second to None Personal Leadership Planning Guide

Instructions: Answer the following questions in as much detail as possible so that you will be able to use this guide later and know what you intended.

Building on Successes

1. What are two or three personal successes I've experienced during the last three years?

2. What are two or three professional successes I've experienced over the last three years?

3. What are two or three leadership successes that I envision over the next three years?

4. How will I turn the successes I envision into reality?

5. Who will assist me? How will he or she assist me?

Learning from Peers and Others

1. What specific knowledge and skill do I need for building new leadership successes?

2. Who among my peers can help me attain the knowledge and skills that I need?

3. Who are others from whom I can learn?

4. What is my plan for gaining the new knowledge and skill that I need?

5. How will I evaluate my success in gaining the new learning?

Helping Others Learn

1. Whom that I work with needs new knowledge and skills?

2. How will I help the person acquire the new learning?

3. Who else will provide assistance for new learning?

4. How will we determine that the new learning has taken place?

Championing for the Future

1. What vision of the future do I and my organization share?

2. What actions am I currently taking to create that future?

3. What actions remain to be taken? What's my plan for taking action?

4. How have I created excitement about the future?

5. What must I do to sustain excitement about the future?

Creating Newness

1. What have I done recently to develop my creative abilities?

2. What new ideas have I produced lately?

3. What has helped me be successful in implementing new ideas?

4. How have I been evaluating the results of my creative efforts?

5. How have I been encouraging others to be creative?

Getting It Done with Fun

1. What are the things that I know I must do to increase my leadership impact?

2. How do I know that I am intensely absorbed when getting things done?

3. How perfectly am I practicing when preparing to do things I have not done before?

4. How far am I stretching my own limits and those of others?

5. How well am I using mental rehearsal?

6. What's my plan for reviewing and improving business processes?

Building the Team

1. In what ways do I put others first?

2. In what other ways do I pay value to people?

3. How have I been embracing diversity?

4. What actions have I taken to express my belief in equity?

5. What actions have I taken that exhibit mutual accountability?

Walking My Talk

1. What does the big picture look like to me?

2. What am I doing that I love to do?

3. What am I doing that exhibits high standards of personal conduct?

4. How do I respond to customer needs?

5. How do I ensure doing it right the first time?

Driving for Change

1. What needs to be changed?

2. How can I create excitement about the need for change?

3. What new state of affairs must be developed? Who will help develop it?

4. What resources will be required during the change?

5. What behaviors on my part will help bring about the change?

Second to None Celebration Sheet

This is how I will celebrate when I:

1. Build on Successes

2. Learn from Peers/Others

3. Help Others Learn

4. Champion the Future

5. Create Newness

6. Get It Done with Fun

7. Build the Team

8. Walk My Talk

9. Drive Change

709. The Alphabet Game: Developing Confidence and Spontaneity Through Improv

Goals

- To demonstrate how behavior is determined by beliefs about a situation.
- To experience how a change in thinking can lead to a change in results.
- To understand how spontaneity can be developed through practice.
- To develop participants' confidence in dealing with change and uncertainty.

Group Size

Five to fifty participants.

Time Required

Approximately fifty to sixty minutes.

Materials

- Flip chart.
- Felt-tipped markers.

Physical Setting

A room set up so all participants can see and hear the facilitator and another person in a demonstration area at the front of the room.

Process

1. (*Note:* Play this and other improv games as much as possible before you use them with a group. You can really never know how the game is going to turn out, so you have to be as comfortable with uncertainty as you want your participants to be. Your confidence comes from knowing that you can deal with WHATEVER comes up, not from knowing WHAT will come up.) Begin by asking for a show of hands of people who have seen or are familiar with Improv theater. Ask whether they enjoy Improv theater. Solicit reasons for liking Improv. (Likely replies include, "It's fun," "The players are so quick," and "The spontaneity of it.") Ask whether those who have seen or experienced Improv think they can play the same games as the performers they've seen. Some, if not most, will say "No." Solicit reasons for their answers. (Likely answers include, "They are professionals," "I can't think that fast.") (Five minutes.)

2. Say to the group:

   "I am going to teach you an Improv game that you may have seen previously. This is a game that is easy to learn, a lot of fun to play, you CANNOT fail, and all you need to know to play this game is the letters of the English alphabet." Pause for a moment and say, "You don't even have to know that perfectly. Can I have one volunteer to come up and play the game with me?"

3. People will be looking around. Some will encourage others to get up. Say to the group, "You cannot volunteer anyone else. Just yourself." If no one volunteers immediately, point out to the group that if this were a room full of the same people at the age of eight, most hands would be up and folks would be shouting, "Pick me first!" Yet as adults we think, "Pick someone else first!"

4. Choose the first volunteer you see and ask him or her to stay seated for a moment while you ask the audience a question. Say to the group, "I'd like to take a second and have you share with me the thoughts that went through your mind when I asked for a volunteer. What were the exact words you heard yourself say to yourself? If this were a foreign movie, how would the subtitles read?" Objectively, repeat what is said or transcribe the answers onto flip-chart paper. Do this without comment on the content. (Five minutes.)

5. Now have the volunteer come to the front of the room. Greet the volunteer and encourage the audience to give the volunteer a round of applause for having the courage to step up. Introduce the volunteer to the

audience and yourself and thank this person for stepping forward. Ask the volunteer what thoughts went through his or her mind that encouraged participation. Note or record what is said, as before. (Five minutes.)

6. Say to the group, "How did you feel when you saw that [name of person] had volunteered?" Likely responses include, "relieved," "grateful," "happy that I'm off the hook." Repeat the answers as the group offers them. (Five minutes.)

7. Say (while indicating that you are referring to the volunteer):

> "This person is a leader. This volunteer stepped into the unknown for you! And by doing so managed to relieve the tension, fear, and anxiety that were present in this room. In other words, ONE person, by taking an action, managed to change the emotional climate in this room. This shows the power one person has to affect others in a group, family, organization, or company."

Turn to the volunteer and say:

> "Let's play! This is a simple game. You and I are going to talk to each other as friends do, about a topic, which will be chosen in a minute. The way we play is this. If I begin the conversation, I must begin my part with a word beginning with the letter 'A.' When it's your turn, you start with a word beginning with the letter 'B.' Then I will go with a 'C' word, you with a 'D' word, and so on.
>
> "For example if the topic is 'travel' and I begin, I might say, 'Any time I have to go on a trip, I always watch the Weather Channel to see what the weather is like where I'm going.' And you might reply, 'Barbados is my favorite destination. Have you ever been there?' I could answer, 'Can't say that I have, but I'd like to go. What do you like about it?'
>
> "We'll attempt to get through the whole alphabet. Remember that this is not a word association game. We want to have as real and fluid a conversation as possible. Is that clear?
>
> "Know that you cannot fail. There is no time limit, and nothing you say can be wrong. Don't try to think too much about the subject matter or whether it is making sense. Anything you say will be okay. I will help you succeed, and you will help me succeed. Any questions? If not then let's begin."

(Five minutes.)

8. Turn to the audience and ask them to shout out a topic that two friends might talk about. Likely responses include "weather," "politics," and "sex." *Choose the first one you hear.* The topic doesn't matter to the usefulness of the game. (*Note:* This, in fact, is a good opportunity to model a basic tenet

of Improvisation Theater known as "Accept Any Offer." A topic such as "sex" will likely cause the player to be nervous and a bit embarrassed. It will also create a nervous energy in the audience. Even with a seemingly neutral topic such as "sewing" or "golf," some players may also feel that they don't know anything about the topic and will be visibly nervous.)

9. Assume "politics" was the chosen topic. Say to the player, "Do you want to go first or do you want me to go first?" Assume you are chosen to go first. Begin a conversation with a word that starts with the letter "A."

For example, "Anytime I think of politicians, I get angry" or you might say, "An election can show how fragmented we are in this country." (*Note:* Remember that it does not matter what you say as long as you are abiding by the rule.) Once you've finished your part, stop and let the other player begin, so the conversation may continue and develop in a fashion such as:

Babies are what the politicians sound like when they campaign against each other.

Could you imagine what it would be like if everyone told the truth as they saw it?

Don't believe that's possible!"

Even if we made them take a lie detector test?

And so on through the alphabet. When you are finished, thank the volunteer for doing a great job and have the audience applaud the person. (Five minutes.)

Facilitator Notes: Be prepared for the following situations during the activity:

- When a player pauses for longer than a few seconds or seems obviously to be thinking of a strategy, stop the action and say, "Time out! One of the interesting things about Improv is that it lets us see our minds working in real time. Would you share with us what you were thinking when you hesitated?"

  The opportunity here, as it was earlier when exploring why people did or did not volunteer, is to explore what thinking is going on and to show how thinking drives behavior. Remind the player that any answer is the correct one and that there is no way to make a mistake because you will help your partner succeed and your partner will help you. The only responsibility either player has is to come up with a word beginning with the next letter. And even that rule is flexible because both players can just move on over the missed letter without consequence.

- Often a player inadvertently skips a letter. You, as the facilitator, may or may not notice it. You may even be the one skipping the letter. Chances are that someone in the room—an audience member or one of the players—will notice. Either it will be allowed to pass without comment or someone may bring it to everyone's attention.

  If it is allowed to pass, ask either then or during the debriefing, "Did anyone notice that one of the letters was skipped? Why didn't you bring it up?"

  If it is not allowed to pass, ask, "Why point out this small flaw? What benefit does it bring? Is there a benefit to letting it go?"

You may stop the action at any point in the game to highlight what is going on. You can then pick up the game where you left off or start over. It doesn't matter for your purpose because the learning comes from understanding and experiencing the process. The real gift here is for the participants to understand that whatever happens is useful.

Strive to have everyone who comes up to the front feel successful. You can always remind a player who is struggling with the possibility of failure that there is no time limit to the game, or you can even stop a game that is not working and start over.

10. Once the volunteer is seated again, have each person in the room choose a partner so that everyone is part of a duo. Ask each duo to self-select which partner will be called "A" and which is to be called "B." If there is an uneven number of participants, you may play or allow a triad to be formed, in which case there will be a "C" in that triad.

11. Say the following to the entire group:

    "Each team is going to play the Alphabet Game just as it was demonstrated. We will all use the same topic, which will be chosen in a moment. Remember that when it is your turn to speak you begin your sentence with a word that begins with the next consecutive letter of the alphabet. There is no need to rush, and it doesn't help to be fixed on a particular outcome or story line. Things always change! Someone call out a topic that friends talk about."

    Choose the first topic you hear and have the pairs begin. (Five minutes.)

12. When the majority of the pairs have finished, debrief with the following questions:

    - Did you have a successful experience? Was it a self-fulfilling prophecy?
    - What did you do that made it work? Did you feel relaxed?

- If you were not successful, why not? Where did you get stuck? Was it before the game actually began?

- What would you do differently next time?

- What did you think as you prepared and went through the experience? What was your mental state?

- How did what you were thinking or, in other words, your beliefs about what was happening, affect the process or the outcome of the game?

- Where is the opportunity to change in this game?

- Do you feel any differently about yourself and your ability to play this game than when I first asked you to volunteer?

- What is different? What caused this change?

- How is what you experienced, thought, or did relevant to any other part of your personal or professional life?

- Are there situations you can change back at work simply by the way you think about and approach them?

(Fifteen minutes.)

13. Give everyone a few minutes to write down a situation in which he or she has been unsuccessful on the job, think of it in a new way, and share with his or her partner some actions to take the next time the situation comes up. (Ten minutes.)

Submitted by Izzy Gesell

Izzy Gesell, M.Ed., CSP, head honcho at Wide Angle Humor, helps organizations and individuals worldwide through seriously humorous and humorously serious keynotes, training, coaching, and consulting sessions that are entertaining, informative, and very practical. Topics include managing stress and change through humor, team building, communication, leadership through Improv theater techniques, and overcoming gender differences and other obstacles to effective communication. He has presented at many conferences and is the author of Playing Along: Group Learning Activities Borrowed from Improvisation Theater.

Introduction
to the Inventories, Questionnaires, and Surveys Section

Inventories, questionnaires, and surveys are valuable tools to the HRD professional. These feedback tools help respondents take an objective look at themselves and their organizations. These tools also help to explain how a particular theory applies to them or to their situations.

Inventories, questionnaires, and surveys are useful in a number of training and consulting situations: privately for self-diagnosis; one-on-one to plan individual development; in a small group to open discussion; in a work team to help the team to focus on its highest priorities; or in an organization to gather data to achieve progress.

You will find that the use of inventories, questionnaires, and surveys enriches, personalizes, and deepens training, development, and intervention designs. Many can be combined with other experiential learning activities or articles in this or other *Annuals* to design an exciting, involving, practical, and well-rounded intervention.

Each instrument includes the background necessary for understanding, presenting, and using it. Interpretive information, scales, and scoring sheets are also provided. In addition, we include the reliability and validity data contributed by the authors. If you wish additional information on any of these instruments, contact the authors directly. You will find their addresses and telephone numbers in the "Contributors" listing near the end of this volume.

Other assessment tools that address a wider variety of topics can be found in our comprehensive *Reference Guide to Handbooks and Annuals*. This guide indexes all the instruments that we have published to date in the *Annuals*. You will find this complete, up-to-date, and easy-to-use resource valuable for locating other instruments, as well as for locating experiential learning activities and articles.

The 2002 Annual: Volume 1, Training includes four assessment tools in the following categories:

Individual Development

The Archetype Inventory for Organizations, by Patrick J. Aspell and Dee Dee Aspell

Communication

Organizational Values and Voice Audit, by Diane M. Gayeski

Leadership

Why Don't They Do What I Want? Understanding Employee Motivation, by Janet Winchester-Silbaugh

Organizations

Empowerment Inventory, by K.S. Gupta

THE ARCHETYPE INVENTORY™ FOR ORGANIZATIONS

Patrick J. Aspell and Dee Dee Aspell

Abstract: The Archetype Inventory™ for Organizations identifies four basic archetypes in organizations: King/Queen, Warrior, Magician, and Lover. An Archetype Chart is provided, which explains what each archetype represents and the traits, functions, ineffective side, and limitations for the person who fits that profile. The relationships among people with the types and their likely work styles are briefly described. Personal reflections challenge individuals to apply the archetypes model to their present work lives.

INTRODUCTION

This instrument was designed to be used by trainers or consultants to give co-workers a model to discuss their similarities and differences and through so doing to work more closely together. It is not intended to be used as a substitute for true psychological profiling nor is it to be treated as an absolute categorization system.

Although the topic is closely related to spirituality, it is not the same thing. Archetypes refer to psychological concepts. In fact, they can be considered a higher form of integration for personality types. Archetypes are primordial forms from which types derive. For example, the aggressive or assertive salesperson, in a sense, is like the archetype of warrior.

DESCRIPTION OF THE INVENTORY

The Archetype Inventory is a thirty-six item forced-choice questionnaire intended to be given to people who work together so that they can compare scores and learn more about themselves and others in an effort to improve their relationships on the job and increase organizational performance.

No reliability or validity studies have been done on this inventory, although it does have face validity for previous respondents.

ADMINISTERING THE INVENTORY

Respondents should be members of the same organizational group who work together regularly. Give copies of the Inventory and pens or pencils to everyone and go over the directions. Be sure everyone understands the concept of forced choice and the rating system provided (1 through 3) for amount of agreement with a statement. This particular system gives respondents an "out" when they do not really agree with one answer completely, but it is still their best choice from the two presented. Answer any questions and give respondents ten or fifteen minutes to complete the thirty-six forced-choice items.

Next, give respondents the Scoring Sheet and go over the directions. Then give everyone time to score their own inventories. When they have finished, tell them to look at the Interpretation provided and give everyone copies of the Discussion Sheet, which they are to fill out individually, and the Profile Sheet. After they have read all the material and finished filling out the Discussion Sheet, have them form small groups or pairs to go over their results with others for fifteen or twenty minutes. After that, bring the entire group together to discuss personal insights, what they have learned about one another, and next steps for the organization and for themselves personally.

Resources for Further Study

Aspell, D.D., & Aspell, P.J. (1994). *Archetype inventory.* San Antonio, TX: Lifewings.

Aspell, D.D., & Aspell, P.J. (1995). *Art of building better relationships with people.* San Antonio, TX: Lifewings.

Aspell, D.D., & Aspell, P.J. (1995). *Enneagram communication styles.* San Antonio, TX: Lifewings.

Aspell, D.D., & Aspell, P.J. (1995). *Enneagram Inventory®:72 questions, scoring, descriptions.* San Antonio, TX: Lifewings.

Aspell, D.D., & Aspell, P.J. (1995). Leadership styles and the Enneagram. In J.W. Pfeiffer (Ed.), *The 1995 annual: Volume I, training,* p. 227. San Francisco, CA: Jossey-Bass/Pfeiffer.

Aspell, D.D., & Aspell, P.J. (1996). *Art of relating: Forty-five interpersonal relationships.* San Antonio, TX: Lifewings.

Aspell, D.D., & Aspell, P.J. (1996). *Enneagram Inventory® and the Jungian Personality Type Inventory™.* San Antonio, TX: Lifewings.

Aspell, D.D., & Aspell, P.J. (1996). What drives you crazy? In E. Biech & J.E. Jones (Eds.), *The HR handbook* (Vol. I), p. 97. Amherst, MA: HRD Press.

Aspell, D.D., & Aspell, P.J. (1997). *Enneagram personality portraits: Enhancing professional relationships.* San Francisco, CA: Jossey-Bass/Pfeiffer.

Aspell, D.D. & Aspell, P.J. (1998). Uncover the nine different thinking styles to enhance your problem-solving skills. In N.J. Anderson (Ed.), *Supervisor's guide to quality and excellence,* *IV*(7), 3. Concordville, PA: Clement Communications.

Aspell, D.D., & Aspell, P.J. (1999). *AESOP (Enneagram Spirituality of Personality).* San Antonio, TX: Lifewings.

Aspell, D.D., & Aspell, P.J. (2000). *Aspell Type and Style Indicator.* San Antonio, TX: Lifewings.

Aspell, D.D., & Aspell, P.J. (2000). *Enneagram Inventory® software.* San Antonio, TX: Lifewings.

Patrick J. Aspell, Ph.D., is a licensed professional counselor and an organization consultant with Aspell Empowerment Enterprises, Inc. He presents workshops and seminars to public and private organizations. In addition to numerous articles, Dr. Aspell has co-authored a number of inventories and books for business.

Dee Dee Aspell is the founder and principal of Aspell Empowerment Enterprises, Inc. She presents workshops and seminars specializing in leadership, empowerment, team development, and conflict and emotional management. She is a professional coach and the co-author of numerous inventories and books.

THE ARCHETYPE INVENTORY™ FOR ORGANIZATIONS*

Patrick J. Aspell and Dee Dee Aspell

Instructions: This inventory is intended to help you discover the typical ways you experience yourself in the workplace. There are no right or wrong answers.

Learning how you prefer to behave and knowing how other people like to behave can be beneficial to you. It will help you to know how you respond to others in different situations and to understand how people with different characteristics relate to one another. With this knowledge, you can recognize the ways in which people differ in their styles of working and discover the unique contribution each person makes to the workplace.

You have a choice of two statements for each of the thirty-six items below. First, go through the entire Inventory, circling the letter of your preferred statement in each case. Respond as candidly as possible to each question so you will receive the most benefit. Although there is no time limit, do not think too long about any statement. If you cannot decide which statement to select, skip it and return to that choice later. When in doubt, it is a good idea to go with your first impression. Remember: For each item, choose the *one* statement that comes closer to describing you.

When you have finished your sentence choices, go back through the Inventory and, in the space under each pair of sentences, circle the 1 if the statement you chose *sometimes* describes you, the 2 if the statement you selected *often* describes you, and the 3 if the statement *almost always* describes you.

Once you are sure you understand the directions given above, go to the next page and begin.

---

*The Archetype Inventory™ in its complete form is published by the co-authors.

1. A. I like to be responsible.

   D. I like to enjoy the beauty of nature.

   1   2   3

2. A. It is important for me to have stable emotions.

   C. It is important for me to be detached from my emotions.

   1   2   3

3. A. I am inclined to be concerned about the welfare of people.

   B. I am inclined to challenge people who oppose my views.

   1   2   3

4. C. I like to be with spiritual-minded persons.

   D. I like to be with feeling-minded persons.

   1   2   3

5. D. I am willing to do almost anything for someone I love.

   B. I am willing to bear most hardships to attain my goals.

   1   2   3

6. B. I like to be disciplined in mind and body.

   C. I like to be knowledgeable in situations.

   1   2   3

7. A. It is important for me to be right about what I do.

   C. It is important for me to be clear about what I think.

   1   2   3

8. D. I want to be close to people I care for.

   C. I want to know a lot about people.

   1   2   3

9. B. I tend to take action to get things done.

   C. I tend to observe what is happening in situations.

   1   2   3

10. A. I am likely to behave according to standards.

   D. I am apt to express affection by a hug.

   1   2   3

11. C. I like to reflect on what is going on in my experience.

   D. I like to touch and be touched.

   1   2   3

12. B. I like to control my emotions to achieve my goals.

   D. I like pleasing colors, sounds, tastes, and aromas.

   1   2   3

13. A. I want people to be treated justly.

   D. I want people to love each other.

   1   2   3

14. A. I am inclined to arrange things to happen in an orderly way.

   C. I am inclined to arrange my thoughts in a logical way.

   1   2   3

15. A. It is important for me to be fair.

   B. It is important for me to be loyal.

   1   2   3

16. A. It is important for me to be reasonable.

   B. It is important for me to be strong in will.

   1   2   3

17. C. I can empathize with people in distress.

   B. I can get people to accomplish a task.

   1   2   3

18. C. I reflect carefully in making decisions.

   B. I take action promptly in making decisions.

   1   2   3

19. A. I tend to encourage people to develop their talents.

   C. I tend to calmly observe what is going on among people.

   1   2   3

20. D. I like to share my feelings with people.

   C. I like sharing my ideas with people.

   1   2   3

21. B. I like to respond to challenges.

   C. I like to analyze ideas.

   1   2   3

22. A. I see myself as a confident person.

   D. I see myself as a sensitive person.

   1   2   3

23. C. I value thinking more than feeling.

   D. I value feeling more than thinking.

   1   2   3

24. B. I like to take action to attain my goals.

   D. I like to do things for persons I love.

   1   2   3

25. A. I tend to be concerned about the welfare of most people.

   D. I tend to be concerned about the feelings of most people.

   1   2   3

26. A. It is important for me to order things around me.

   C. It is important for me to clarify my thoughts.

   1   2   3

27. B. It is important for me to be faithful to my commitments.

   A. It is important for me to live by my principles.

   1   2   3

28. A. I am inclined to harmonize differences among those under my care.

B. I am inclined to sacrifice my personal interests for those to whom I am committed.

1   2   3

29. D. I like to be close to persons I love.

B. I like to plan strategies for succeeding.

1   2   3

30. C. I see myself as a knowledgeable person.

B. I see myself as a decisive person.

1   2   3

31. C. It is important for me to use my knowledge to change situations.

A. It is important for me to provide for those in my charge.

1   2   3

32. C. I am likely to observe people in different situations.

D. I am likely to touch people in different situations.

1   2   3

33. C. I like to change my ideas so I can change my behavior.

B. I like to take action to achieve my goals.

1   2   3

34. D. I enjoy the sights and sounds of nature.

A. I enjoy order and peace.

1   2   3

35. C. I like to know the workings of the universe.

D. I like to experience the oneness of the universe.

1   2   3

36. B. I like disciplining my mind to face life's challenges.

D. I like living life to the fullest.

1   2   3

The Archetype Inventory™ for Organizations
Scoring and Interpretation Sheet

Instructions for Scoring the Inventory

1. Add the numbers you have circled for all of your A choices and put the *total* in the appropriate box below.

2. Follow the same procedure for the rest of your choices for letters B, C, and D.

Total Scores

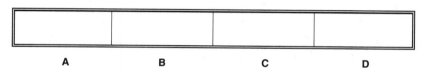

| A | B | C | D |

3. The letters (A, B, C, D) below the boxes represent the four basic archetypes. Transfer your total scores from the four boxes to the scoring grid by counting upward from zero on the matrix for each of your archetypes and marking an A, B, C, or D at the appropriate point on the grid. Next, connect the letters to form a line graph of your personal profile.

Your Profile

	A	B	C	D
45				
44				
43				
42				
41				
40				
39				
38				
37				
36				
35				
34				
33				
32				
31				
30				
29				
28				
27				
26				
25				
24				
23				
22				
21				
20				
19				
18				
17				
16				
15				
14				
13				
12				
11				
10				
9				
8				
7				
6				
5				
4				
3				
2				

Interpretation

Now that you have your profile, consider what it means for you. If you have the same score for two different archetypes, determine which fits you better by reading the descriptions of the four basic types, King or Queen, Warrior, Magician, or Lover, on the Discussion Sheet.

1. The letter with the highest score on the graph shows your major or dominant archetype.

2. If one of your scores is significantly higher than the rest, then your soul tends to have a distinctive presence or charisma.

3. If you have tie scores, then read the descriptions of the archetypes on the Discussion Sheet to discern which archetype comes closer to how you see yourself, although you have strong traits for both categories.

4. A flat profile, three or more scores the same or almost the same, may suggest a flexible person who is able to adapt to a variety of situations with moderate ease. Situations at work may be challenging you to draw on the gifts that characterize other archetypes. It may also suggest that you might experience some difficulty in being able to name some of your preferences.

5. It is worth noting your lowest score(s) on the profile, which indicates features of your soul for which you have a low preference. Low scores indicate your limitations, shadow qualities that you may wish to explore or develop further.

N.B. You are the ultimate determiner of what archetype fits you the best. However, in later discussions, listen intently for insight from others about how they see you.

Archetype Inventory Discussion Sheet

The following is a brief outline of the various types of personality commonly found within an organization, provided as a way for you to interpret your results and to serve as discussion points with others who will help you gain insight into your results. Through discussion, you will also learn more about one another and be able to plan ways to work together in the future.

Personal Manifestations of the Archetypes

King/Queen

- Is attracted to honorable and responsible persons.
- Reminds others of rules and the right thing to do.
- Encourages people to develop their talents.
- Defends the just rights of others.
- Promotes order and peace.

Warrior

- Is attracted to people offering opportunities for accomplishment.
- Likes persons who succeed.
- Experiences relationships as tasks to be achieved.
- Feels close to persons with whom he or she does something.
- Communicates in an assertive and persuasive manner.

Magician

- Does not usually initiate relationships.
- Apt to reflect a lot on ideas about a relationship.
- Is attracted to people who listen to his or her views and theories.
- Likes to observe what is happening in a relationship.
- May come across as aloof and hard to figure out.

Lover

- Is attracted to warm and friendly persons.
- Likes to feel wanted or loved by another.
- Wants to be accepted and approved of by people.

- Enjoys imagining what it is like being together with loved ones.
- Likes to be with people.

Work Style Manifestations of the Archetypes

King/Queen

- Works conscientiously to do a job correctly.
- Can stay at one task for a good period of time.
- Wants to follow administrative or operational procedures.
- Takes one step at a time in coming to a reasonable conclusion.
- Wants to treat people fairly.

Warrior

- Motivates others to do their jobs.
- Enjoys talking with others about tasks.
- Works efficiently to get things done.
- Communicates by talking about results.
- Can work under pressure to get things done quickly.

Magician

- Is good at analyzing problems.
- Reflects on the theory behind a project.
- Is satisfied working by himself or herself.
- Prefers silence in order to concentrate.
- Dislikes being interrupted on the job by phone calls.

Lover

- Supports people at work.
- Helps others do their work.
- Likes to be with people in the workplace.
- Focuses on how people are affected by decisions.
- Tends to be sympathetic to other people's needs.

Reflections

Answer the following questions silently for yourself. When you have finished, you will be asked to share your responses with others as directed by the facilitator.

What was your dominant archetype, according to the Inventory?

What do you think about that archetype?

Do you feel comfortable or uncomfortable with what your profile reflects?

If you are comfortable, what rings true for you about your archetype? Describe a specific situation that illustrates how your archetype is expressed in your life and/or work.

How could you use the knowledge of your archetype(s) to benefit you at home or at the office?

THE ARCHETYPE INVENTORY PROFILE SHEET

Archetype	King/Queen	Warrior	Magician	Lover
Represents	Order, stability, right	Power, strength, action	Knowledge, wisdom	Giving, joy, body awareness
Traits	Confidence, integrity, foresight, responsibility, organization, competence	Alertness, assertiveness, achievement, decision, enterprise, doer, discipline	Observation, information, understanding, insight, consciousness	Caring, empathy, relater, intimacy, feeling, sensitivity, responsive
Functions	Takes charge, arranges activities, treats others fairly, focuses on common good	Sets goals, aims to succeed, motivates others, confronts challenges, faces opposition	Monitors situations, formulates ideas or theories, wants to discern, discovers meanings of things	Motivated by love, synchronizes with the sensory world, relates to all creatures
Ineffective Side	Tyrant who is domineering, weakling who is fearful, bungler who lacks insight and decision	Aggressor who is oppositional, angry, and heartless; coward who is fearful, powerless, and helpless	Superior-minded ego, obsessed with knowledge, inferior-minded ego with deflated self-image	Over-responsive to sensory impressions, under-responsive to sensations, lacks feeling
Limitations	May try to do too much, may not express feelings, may have difficulty with disorder or disorganization	May be aggressive and ruthless, may pick on weak individuals, may be domineering, may become oppositional	May become self-inflated with knowledge, may control information for profit or prestige	May not limit sensual experience, may be overwhelmed by sensory impressions, may be drawn by every pleasurable stimulus

The 2002 Annual: Volume 1, Training/© 2002 John Wiley & Sons, Inc.

ORGANIZATIONAL VALUES AND VOICE AUDIT

Diane M. Gayeski

Abstract: Many organizations suffer from poor employee performance and attitudes because policies do not support the firm's stated goals and initiatives. Nowhere is this more significant than in employee communication and training practices, as these are the primary "voices" of the company to its constituencies. The Organizational Values and Voice Audit is an instrument through which organizational members can pinpoint areas that, in their perception, may be out of alignment with their organization's values and goals. A table of common disconnects is used to guide a discussion in which participants share their own responses to the questionnaire and can then recommend changes in communication and training practices.

INTRODUCTION

The phrase "walking the talk" is a common reference to managers' ability and willingness to behave in ways that encourage their subordinates to act in accordance with the organization's espoused values and culture. Unfortunately, employees in all types of organizations often perceive that management does not, in fact, walk the talk. This leads to a lack of executive credibility, employee cynicism, mixed messages, and lack of focus, all of which contribute to impaired individual and organizational performance.

Although the actions of individual members in an organization carry strong messages, so do its internal and external communications and training policies and practices. Training courses, manuals, newsletters, and employee meetings all represent the "voice" of the company. When the messages contained in these channels are mixed or when policies and practices around communication and training do not reinforce the organization's stated values and goals, the organization's culture and success are impaired. Often, employees are unaware of the source of their discontent and confusion; the Organizational Values and Voice Audit helps to uncover misaligned policies and practices so that discrepancies can be resolved.

The audit is an aid to discussion and helps to suggest possible changes in organizational communication and training management; those who administer it should therefore have a thorough grounding in these areas. It is used most fruitfully with small groups of employees (six to thirty people at one time) who have some exposure to management values and goals, as well as to the organization's communication and training practices. Therefore, the participants should be training or communication practitioners or managers who frequently request and use training and communication interventions.

DESCRIPTION OF THE INSTRUMENT

The instrument consists of two sets of lists. The first asks participants to identify the initiatives that their organization is pursuing or espousing. The second asks participants to identify common communication and training practices in their organization. Participants fill out the instrument individually, but then discuss their responses in a facilitated session. An Interpretation Sheet is provided that helps participants to see which initiatives actually are misaligned with typical training and communication policies and approaches.

Administration of the Instrument

The process takes twenty to forty minutes, depending on the size of the group, and should take place in a room where there is a convenient writing surface for each person and where group discussion can take place. The ideal size of the group is about fifteen people, although the audit can be done with fewer or with more. The facilitator will need an overhead projector and screen, along with at least one felt-tipped marker; it is often useful to have flip charts or blank acetate to jot down remarks as they are made during the discussion. Make a copy of the Organizational Values and Voice Audit for each respondent and make a separate copy of the Interpretation Sheet for each person.

It is important that the people selected to participate have a clear idea of the organization's espoused values and goals, as well as of the typical ways that training and communication programs (including employee communication and customer communication) are generated and accessed. Before the meeting, make an overhead transparency of each question set and of the Interpretation Sheet.

Begin the assessment by introducing its purpose: to identify common disconnects between organizational values and goals and the way that organizational communication and learning actually take place. It is important to point out that every organization has at least a few misalignments in this regard, even the best-performing ones. Instruct the respondents to think over their own experiences in the organization and to use their own perceptions and opinions, rather than to try to represent the views of others.

Hand out the instrument and give the respondents about five minutes to fill it out. Ask them not to discuss their responses with one another during the process.

The Scoring Process

If the group is small, read each item and ask people to raise their hands if they checked it off. If the group is larger, collect the instruments and let the participants take a break or begin discussion while you (and/or an assistant) tally up the total number of check marks for each item. In either case, write the number of total check marks next to each item on the overhead transparency copy of the question sets.

Once you have the totals, ask the participants what this activity made them think about their organization's values and policies. Prompt them to recognize that many of the practices in the second list are actually at odds with the statements in the first list. Explain that many training and communication activities the organization engages in are sending the wrong messages to their employees about what's really important in the organization. Either the value statements (such as empowerment, diversity, and participatory management) are not really supported or are unattainable, or the communication about these issues is at odds with the activities.

Hand out a copy of the Interpretation Sheet to each person, and display the sections one at a time on the overhead projector. Highlight and discuss the ones that were most frequently mentioned by participants. Ask them what effect they believe the "disconnects" are having or will have on their organization's productivity, image, and morale. Then ask them what other values or initiatives the organization is pursuing and to think about which communication and training practices strengthen those values or initiatives and which appear to be at odds with them. Take notes on the overhead transparency or on a flip chart.

OTHER SUGGESTED USES FOR THE AUDIT

This instrument can be used as part of a formal employee communications or training audit, along with other typical measures of employee satisfaction with those functions. Additionally, it can be used as a part of a professional development program for public relations, employee communication, and training/development staffs to help them think about how their policies and projects impact organizational goals.

Diane M. Gayeski, Ph.D., is principal of Gayeski Analytics, LLC, through which she helps clients assess and improve their communications and learning systems. She is also professor of organizational communication, learning, and design at Ithaca College. Dr. Gayeski is the author of eleven books and frequently conducts executive briefings and workshops on employee communications, training, performance consulting, and new technologies.

ORGANIZATIONAL VALUES AND VOICE AUDIT

Diane M. Gayeski

Instructions: Check each of the initiatives or approaches from the list below that your organization currently is pursuing.

☐ Continuous improvement/total quality management

☐ Cost-containment/downsizing

☐ Diversity awareness/diversity appreciation

☐ Employee empowerment

☐ Globalization

☐ High-performance workplace/performance-based compensation

☐ Just-in-time manufacturing

☐ Learning organization/continual learning

☐ Participatory decision making

☐ Relationship marketing/customer orientation

☐ Self-managed teams/teamwork

☐ Work-life balance/family-friendly workplace

On the list that follows, check the items that characterize your organization's *typical* communication and training practices.

☐ Communication interventions such as training and newsletters are evaluated (if at all) by "smile sheets" measuring how much the audience liked them.

☐ Communication/training/marketing staff are rewarded for the amount of materials or programs they produce, rather than on their return on investment.

☐ Company materials do not include or acknowledge input of employees or customers.

☐ Employees are typically sent to training courses or conferences either because of an organization-wide or department-wide mandate or as a "reward" for good performance.

- [ ] Employees are typically sent to training courses or conferences by managers, rather than making the decision to attend themselves.
- [ ] Most learning activities consist of courses led by a professional instructor.
- [ ] Most meetings with management consist of announcements and/or formal presentations.
- [ ] People are often expected to attend training courses and meetings before or after work or on weekends.
- [ ] People are not rewarded for doing what they've been taught in training.
- [ ] People often throw out memos and newsletters or delete email and voice mail messages before even reading/listening to them.
- [ ] Policies and procedures documentation is often not kept up-to-date.
- [ ] There is no established way to solicit and organize good ideas from customers and employees.
- [ ] Training and documentation generally present one "best" way to approach a task, based on the input of one or two subject-matter experts.
- [ ] Training and employee communication programs are based on requests from managers who think that the person has a training or communication problem.
- [ ] We don't really know how much the company spends on communication and training each year (including the time employees are away from their "real" work).

ORGANIZATIONAL VALUES AND VOICE AUDIT INTERPRETATION SHEET

Instructions: Look at each of the initiatives you checked off on the audit form and determine whether you also checked any of the negative characteristics that provide a "disconnect" between that espoused value and its practice in your organization. Consider how each affects your own work life and be ready to discuss your thoughts with others.

Initiative(s)	Possible Disconnects
Continuous improvement/ total quality management	Communication interventions such as training and newsletters are evaluated (if at all) by "smile sheets" measuring how much the audience liked them. (Is this any way to measure improvement or focus on quality?)
	Communication/training/marketing staff are rewarded for the amount of materials or programs they produce, rather than on their return on investment. (Is this a good metric of quality?)
	Policies and procedures documentation is often not kept up-to-date. (If we improve processes, why is this information often not accessible?)
	There is no established way to solicit and organize good ideas from customers and employees. (Do process improvement ideas only happen in meetings or quality circles?)
	We don't really know how much the company spends on communication and training each year (including the time employees are away from their "real" work). (Is this any way to manage resources?)
Cost containment/downsizing	Communication/training/marketing staff are rewarded for the amount of

Initiative(s)	Possible Disconnects
	materials or programs they produce, rather than their return on investment. (Do we reward waste?)
	We don't really know how much the company spends on communication and training each year, including the time employees are away from their "real" work. (We cut costs by laying off hourly workers, yet spend untold resources disseminating information to those who are left.)
Diversity awareness/diversity appreciation/globalization	Employees are typically sent to training courses or conferences either because of an organization-wide or department-wide mandate or as a "reward" for good performance. (Forget about what you need or want as an individual; you are just a part of a group.)
	Training and documentation generally present one "best" way to approach a task, based on the input of one or two subject-matter experts. (Forget about acknowledging or encouraging diversity.)
Employee empowerment/ participatory decision making/ self-managed teams/teamwork	Company materials do not include or acknowledge input of employees or customers. (So much for partnerships; it's just top-down communication as usual.)
	Employees are typically sent to training courses or conferences by managers rather than making the decision to attend themselves. (So this is empowerment?)
	There is no established way to solicit and organize good ideas from customers and employees. (Do process improvement ideas only happen in meetings or quality circles?)

The 2002 Annual: Volume 1, Training/© 2002 John Wiley & Sons, Inc.

Initiative(s)	Possible Disconnects
	Training and documentation generally present one "best" way to approach a task, based on the input of one or two subject-matter experts. (Is there any way to encourage and capture new approaches?)
	Training and employee communication programs are based on requests from managers who think that the employee has a training or communication problem. (Does the employee or team get to decide? Could there be other problems that are not training or communication related, such as the way people or projects are managed?)
High-performance workplace/ performance-based compensation	Employees are sent to courses or conferences by managers either because of an organization-wide or department-wide mandate or as a "reward" for good performance. (Ignore individual performance gaps; just put everybody through a course or train people when they don't really need it.)
	People are not rewarded for doing what they've been taught in training. (Let's just ignore that investment and teach people to be cynical.)
Relationship marketing/ customer orientation	Company materials do not include or acknowledge input of employees or customers. (Where can people see evidence of their own input in the partnership?)
	There's no established way to solicit and organize good ideas from customers and employees. (How can we forge relationships with people we don't really pay attention to?)

Initiative(s)	Possible Disconnects
Just-in-time manufacturing	Policies and procedures documentation is often not kept up-to-date. (We can eliminate millions of dollars of inventory, but we can't replace our old pages in manuals.)
Learning organization/ continual learning	Company materials do not include or acknowledge input of employees or customers. (Who's in the best position to decide what is examined and discussed?)
	Most learning activities consist of courses led by a professional instructor. (Forget about sharing knowledge informally; learning consists of taking courses.)
	Most meetings with management consist of announcements and/or formal presentations. (Is this any way to gather new information or challenge assumptions?)
	There is no established way to solicit and organize good ideas from customers and employees. (Where do good ideas come from anyway?)
Work-life balance/ family friendly workplace	People are often expected to attend training courses and meetings before or after work or on weekends. (Does this provide a hardship for people with family or community obligations?)

WHY DON'T THEY DO WHAT I WANT? UNDERSTANDING EMPLOYEE MOTIVATION

Janet Winchester-Silbaugh

Abstract: Managers are often puzzled and frustrated when employees and others are not motivated to support their projects or new ways of doing things. Why won't employees use the new software correctly? Why can't they be more helpful to customers? Why won't suppliers deliver on time? Why doesn't the boss support me in this project? Regretfully, organizations often unwittingly reward people for doing the wrong things. This survey is designed to diagnose when reward structures are causing problems.

Organizations usually think of rewards in terms of money: salary, incentives, and bonuses. But research shows that people are rewarded by many other things: pride in their work, challenging projects, the support of their peers, future opportunities, family needs, and personal goals. Understanding these complex and often conflicting rewards can help managers change their reward systems so that the system supports their goals.

INTRODUCTION

People are motivated by many things, among them pay, job satisfaction, opportunity, pride in their work, family needs, and status. We often think of
rewards in terms of money: how much salary people earn or whether they
receive a bonus or not. It's easy to forget that people are motivated by a complex set of needs that varies by the person. Of course, needs such as pay and
job security are essential for people to come to work. Motivation, however,
which encourages people to contribute their reputations, their creativity, and
their special talents, comes from intrinsic personal values. Top-performing
employees reported in a recent survey (Avery, undated) that they were motivated by a good reputation, important work, appreciation by others, and the
opportunity to prove their capability to others much more than they were
motivated by money.

Employee motivation is complex, and employers can give conflicting
messages. For example, a manager who emphasizes "personal accountability" may send employees powerful messages about the benefit of taking no
risks, avoiding blame, or even covering up mistakes. Workplaces that focus
on "productivity" may find that employees don't take time to serve customers.
Employees who enjoy face-to-face interactions with customers may resist
communicating with customers by email and form letters, even when those
forms of communication would be very effective. Employees who are proud
of their work may not want to use a new procedure because they have not
mastered it and see it as reducing their quality of work.

The Why Don't They Do What I Want? Understanding Employee Motivation Survey can be used to help managers analyze the rewards and the
costs that each employee associates with a situation. Managers who understand what employees are responding to can find ways to send the right message and reward what they intend to reward.

THEORY BEHIND THE SURVEY

People do things based on their own perceptions of what is important. This
survey was based on a combination of many people's ideas on the topic.
Goldratt's (1997) work on system constraints showed that there are often

conflicting and overlapping constraints on a system. People react to those constraints in equally conflicting and confusing ways. Maslow, through his Hierarchy of Needs (Maslow, 1943), illustrated that not all needs are equal and that needs change over time. Vroom and Yetton (1976) pointed out that a decision will be successful only if it is accepted by the people who must implement it. Kohn (1993) combined many studies to caution that rewards can actually serve as punishment and carry subtle negative messages for people. Ryan and Oestrich's (1998) research into the causes of fear in the workplace showed that people are afraid of the loss of credibility and the damage to their relationships with their bosses if they speak out about common management practices. Vroom, in his Expectancy Theory (Vroom, 1964), said that people are motivated to action if they expect that their actions will be successful and that those actions will lead to a useful result. The Harvard Center for Risk Analysis (Slovic, 2001) found that the perception of a risk, such as for an airplane crash, can be even more important than the statistical chance of an event happening in motivating people to action. I have found the survey presented here to be a useful tool in understanding why people act in seemingly irrational ways.

ADMINISTERING AND SCORING THE SURVEY

This survey can be used as a personal or group tool to diagnose how the reward structure of an organization influences resistance to change. Some suggestions for administration with a group follow.

1. Adjust the survey to fit your particular situation. Add or delete reward categories.

2. Give a copy to each group member to fill out and go over the directions with them for clarity.

3. Write the decision, project, or issue you want the respondents to analyze on the "Issue" line.

4. Tell them to determine who the key stakeholders are for this project or issue. (A stakeholder is any person, organization, or group that has a vested interest in the project or its outcome.) Stakeholders include employees, other departments, government regulators, the public, customers, and suppliers, to name a few. They should write the names of the four or five key stakeholders on the lines titled "Stakeholder."

5. For each stakeholder, they are to write several comments about how this stakeholder may think about this issue. The key is for a respondent to look at the issue from the stakeholder's point of view, to see it through his or her eyes. For instance, if your town is putting in a new intersection with an interstate highway, the local gathering place café may lose business, but may also receive a payment for some of its land (financial and resource impacts). It may lose its status as a neighborhood meeting place (social cost), but the town's payment for part of the property may also give the owner the resources to become an upscale restaurant (professional opportunities). The owner may be both sad to lose the daily conversation with neighbors and excited about the possibilities for a new restaurant (psychological costs and rewards). As you can see, rewards and costs are often contradictory. Include what is most important in your particular situation.

6. Now they should rate each element from the point of view of each stakeholder, using the scale of 1 to 5 shown on the survey. Explain that it is realistic for the same stakeholder to have both positive and negative impacts from the same project. If they don't know what the impacts will be, tell them to put a question mark in the blank.

7. When they have finished, they are to add the scores for each stakeholder. The lower the score, the less support the project has and the greater the risks.

A careful review of the risks that respondents point out will give you practical ideas for reducing problems. Look for important costs for a particular key stakeholder that are not critical for the success of a project.

INTERPRETING THE RESULTS

The following ranges of scores can be used to interpret stakeholders' support for the issue in question.

18–20 Active Supporters/True Believers

- This stakeholder will probably go out of his or her way to support the project, put his or her reputation on the line for the project, convince others that the project is a good one, and come up with creative ways to solve problems. This person may even be willing to make significant sacrifices to make this project work.

- The project is good for these stakeholders. Try to make sure they aren't disillusioned. Don't forget this group, but active supporters alone will not be able to carry the whole project. Support other groups as well.

- These stakeholders are important because they can be the true believers who carry the project through tough times. On the other hand, they can flip to being active resisters if they lose faith in the project's value. The wrath of a spurned supporter can be strong.

14–17 Passive Supporters

- These stakeholders think the project is okay, but may not go out of their way to make it happen. Expect them to work faithfully as long as it doesn't involve a heavy cost of some kind, such as putting their reputation on the line, working overtime during holidays, moving, or taking a different job.

- This group will contribute creative energy, if you can hold these people's support. Make sure they have intrinsic rewards, such as working on an excellent team, training in new areas, pride in doing a good job, or the possibility of job growth.

- These stakeholders are important because they can seed support in other groups. They have more credibility with resistant groups than the true believers do.

8–13 Neutral Stakeholders, Waiting for Results

- These stakeholders start out neutral, but will swing to the negative or positive side, depending on how the project goes and on how other people respond.

- Think about what is rewarding to these stakeholders and build up those aspects of the job. Many stakeholders are in this category, so you must pay a lot of attention to them. Their wait-and-see attitude makes them easy to overlook.

- Neutral stakeholders are important because there are so many of them. Most successful projects require that you gain the support of a significant number of neutral stakeholders.

4–7 Quiet Nonsupporters

- These stakeholders may do a good job at their work, but will notice all the problems with the project and will probably talk about these problems with other people.

- These people have something important to lose. If their reactions are emotional, see what social or psychological costs there may be. Often, employees who are good at their current jobs, but who don't think they will get enough training or time to learn a new system, will be in this category. They will lose a lot of professional pride if they cannot become proficient at the new system. They may become supporters if you can show them a safe path to do well with the project.

- These stakeholders, along with the neutral stakeholders, are the most important swing votes. If you can win their honest support, your chances of success rise dramatically.

0–3 Active Nonsupporters

- There are two kinds of active nonsupporters, vocal and quiet. Both can be just as damaging to a project.

- Develop a clear strategy for dealing with active nonsupporters and then follow it to the end. Listen to their arguments because they may tell you about weaknesses in the project that no one else will. It is important to understand what drives their vehemence against the project. Sometimes you can turn the tide by persuading active nonsupporters; other times, the best you can do is to limit their impact.

- These stakeholders are important because they can polarize opinion and poison the well for many other stakeholders. They will work hard to make their points known, so do not take their actions personally.

To get an overall sense of the resistance you'll face, add the stakeholders' scores together. The lower the score, the less support the project has and the greater the risks. A careful review of the risks will give you practical ideas for reducing problems. Look for important costs for a particular key stakeholder that are not critical for the success of a project.

WAYS TO INCREASE SUPPORT FOR A PROJECT

You can decrease the resistance to a project by changing the reward system, especially the subtle costs and rewards. Here are some helpful methods:

1. Make sure managers and employees both have roughly equal benefits and costs. For instance, if employees must work mandatory overtime to

complete a project, so must managers. If managers receive rewards for meeting goals, build in commensurate rewards for employees. This balance makes the decision makers more aware of the full cost of their decisions and increases the employees' perceptions of fairness.

2. Ensure that the people who make decisions feel the effects if things go wrong. If they don't feel the pain, they may not notice the changes that need to be made.

3. Rely on many different types of rewards, including a mix of financial rewards (such as an incentive check), social rewards (a celebration to say thanks for a job well done), psychological rewards (noticing employees who are making special contributions), and opportunities for growth (such as training and assigning interesting work). Simply receiving additional money to change a system or do things in a different way is almost never enough.

4. Choose rewards that are important for each stakeholder based on his or her life goals. Treating all people identically will not be treating them fairly, because their goals are different. For some people, overtime to earn extra money for a down payment on a house is important. For others, well-timed time off so they can attend their child's basketball game is critical. For still others, learning that new computer tool is really interesting. The most effective rewards are things that people want, and this will be different for each person.

5. Practice what you preach. Nothing kills support for a project faster than telling your employees to take risks, then criticizing them when things go wrong. If you say you'll get back to someone by Tuesday, make sure you do it. If you say training will be available, make it happen. If you ask for honest feedback, be prepared to hear the bad as well as the good.

References

Avery, D. (undated). *Recruiting for retention* [On-line]. Available: www.shrm.org/whitepapers/documents/default.asp?page=61264.asp [last accessed May 17, 2001]

Goldratt, E. (1997). *Critical chain.* Great Barrington, MA: North River Press.

Kohn, A. (1993). *Punished by rewards.* Boston, MA: Houghton Mifflin.

Maslow, A. (1943, July). A theory of human motivation. *Psychological Review, 50,* 370–396.

Ryan, K., & Oestrich, D. (1998). *Driving fear out of the workplace*. San Francisco, CA: Jossey-Bass.

Slovic, P. (2001). *The perception of risk*. London, England: Earthscan.

Vroom, V. (1964). *Work and motivation*. New York: John Wiley & Sons.

Vroom, V., & Yetton, P. (1976). *Leadership and decision making*. Pittsburgh, PA: University of Pittsburgh Press.

Janet Winchester-Silbaugh, MBA, CEBS, CCP, and SPHR, *is an organization development consultant with Change Management Resources in Albuquerque, New Mexico. She works with organizations to remove barriers to change, develop compensation plans that support strategic growth, and find the leverage points that trigger organizational change.*

Understanding Employee Motivation Survey

Janet Winchester-Silbaugh

Instructions: Use this survey each time you wish to assess the likelihood of encountering employee or other stakeholder resistance to a new process or project or a change in a present process. Write in the name of the issue to be analyzed and then each key stakeholder on the lines provided. Attempt to describe the person's motivation for supporting (rewards) or resisting (costs) the issue. Then rate the impact that the issue would have on each, using the scale from 1 to 5 shown below.

| 1 = strong negative impact; this project is big and bad | 2 = mild but noticeable negative impact; this project is annoying, but not worth putting a lot of energy into blocking | 3 = no noticeable impact; "who cares" OR has an equal negative and positive impact | 4 = mild, noticeable, positive impact; a pretty good idea, but not worth too much effort | 5 = strong positive impact; worth going out on a limb for |

Issue to Be Analyzed: _____

Stakeholder Rewards or Costs from the Stakeholder's Point of View

Stakeholder 1: _____

Rewards or Costs in Finances or Resources

Social Rewards or Costs

Impact on Professional Growth or Opportunities

| 1 = strong negative impact; this project is big and bad | 2 = mild but noticeable negative impact; this project is annoying, but not worth putting a lot of energy into blocking | 3 = no noticeable impact; "who cares" OR has an equal negative and positive impact | 4 = mild, noticeable, positive impact; a pretty good idea, but not worth too much effort | 5 = strong positive impact; worth going out on a limb for |

Personal Psychological Rewards and Costs

Total Points for Stakeholder 1: _____

Stakeholder 2: _____

Rewards or Costs in Finances and Resources

Social Rewards or Costs

Impact on Professional Growth or Opportunities

Personal Psychological Rewards and Costs

Total Points for Stakeholder 2: _____

1 = strong negative impact; this project is big and bad	2 = mild but noticeable negative impact; this project is annoying, but not worth putting a lot of energy into blocking	3 = no noticeable impact; "who cares" OR has an equal negative and positive impact	4 = mild, noticeable, positive impact; a pretty good idea, but not worth too much effort	5 = strong positive impact; worth going out on a limb for

Stakeholder 3: _____

Rewards or Costs in Finances and Resources

Social Rewards or Costs

Impact on Professional Growth or Opportunities

Personal Psychological Rewards and Costs

Total Points for Stakeholder 3: _____

Stakeholder 4: _____

Rewards or Costs in Finances and Resources

Social Rewards or Costs

Impact on Professional Growth or Opportunities

Personal Psychological Rewards and Costs

Total Points for Stakeholder 4: _____

1 = strong negative impact; this project is big and bad	2 = mild but noticeable negative impact; this project is annoying, but not worth putting a lot of energy into blocking	3 = no noticeable impact; "who cares" OR has an equal negative and positive impact	4 = mild, noticeable, positive impact; a pretty good idea, but not worth too much effort	5 = strong positive impact; worth going out on a limb for

Stakeholder 5: _____

Rewards or Costs in Finances and Resources

Social Rewards or Costs

Impact on Professional Growth or Opportunities

Personal Psychological Rewards and Costs

Total Points for Stakeholder 5: _____

Sample Completed Understanding Employee Motivation Survey

Issue to Be Analyzed: *My customer service representatives don't work very hard to make customers happy. They won't make the extra effort; they just follow the book and no more.*

Stakeholder 1: *My department director*

Rewards or Costs in Resources
My year-end bonus looks good. I'm under budget so far. (5 points)

Social Rewards or Costs
I hate to look stupid in front of the other directors.
My family gets mad when I bring work home at night. (2 points)

Impact on Professional Growth or Opportunities
I've heard the vice president is thinking of leaving. I'll be in good position if my statistics look good. (4 points)

Personal Psychological Rewards and Costs
We do good work in my department. (3 points)

Total Points: *14*

Stakeholder 2: *The customer service representatives*

Rewards or Costs in Resources
There's never enough help. I'm too tired to care about overtime.
Why work too hard? The pay is the same either way.
You'd think they'd get a computer system that worked right. (2 points)

Social Rewards or Costs
My kids hate it when I have to work overtime.
The last time I went out on a limb for a customer, the boss told me I was wrong.
I had to call the customer back and explain why we couldn't do what I said we could do. I felt pretty stupid. (1 point)

Impact on Professional Growth or Opportunities
Mary was promoted last year. I wonder why she was instead of me?
The education budget is all used up—again. (2 points)

Personal Psychological Rewards and Costs
I hate to tell customers it will be next week before I can get something done.
I was proud of my work before this new director came. (1 point)

Total Points: *6*

EMPOWERMENT INVENTORY

K.S. Gupta

Abstract: Empowerment became a buzzword in the late 1990s, when industry professionals started looking at employee empowerment as a competitive edge for the new millennium. The Empowerment Inventory measures employee empowerment based on a conceptual framework from the research. The key variables that affect empowerment have been shown to be respect among team members, top-management attitudes toward employees, amount of open communication in the organization, opportunities for learning, organizational support for employees, responsive supervisors, opportunities for self-development, level of formality, performance-linked feedback, and level of autonomy. Reliability and validity, as well as the utility of the instrument, are also discussed.

INTRODUCTION

Empowerment has been described as an act of building, developing, and increasing employee power through cooperation, sharing, and working together. For our purposes here, empowerment can be defined as "the process of sharing power and providing an enabling environment in order to encourage employees to take initiative and make decisions to achieve organizational and individual goals."

The conceptual framework of empowerment, like any other construct, is perceptual. Figure 1 shows the perceptual framework for empowerment used in this instrument, including the empowering variables and the consequences. The degree to which any empowering variable is present is associated with an increase in the level of employee empowerment, which increases

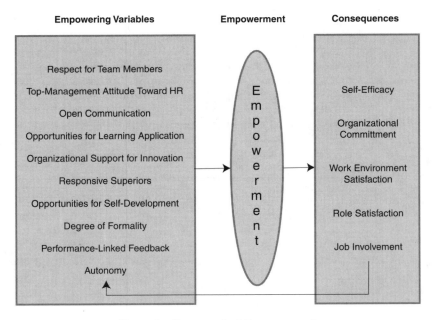

Figure 1. Framework of Empowerment

the positive consequences. This creates a spiral effect in which the more employee empowerment, the more positive organizational consequences.

Empowering variables and consequences measured by the inventory, as shown in the figure, are

- Respect for team members (RTM);
- Top-management attitude toward human resources (TMA);
- Open communication (OC);
- Opportunities for learning application (OLA);
- Organizational support for innovation (OSI);
- Responsive superiors (RSR);
- Opportunities for self-development (OSD);
- Degree of formality (DF);
- Performance-linked feedback (PLF); and
- Autonomy (AMY).

CONSEQUENCES

The consequences for the organization of empowering employees are seen as increased:

- Self-efficacy (SE);
- Organizational commitment (OCT);
- Work environment satisfaction (WES);
- Role satisfaction (RS); and
- Job involvement (JI).

MEASUREMENT OF VARIABLES AND CONSEQUENCES

The instrument measures the ten variables of an empowered environment and their consequences in the following ways:

Respect for Team Member. This dimension is captured by number of times an individual's views are asked, as ranked by the following three items:

- My boss asks for my views before making decisions about my work.
- Superiors invite their subordinates for informal discussions about their work.
- My colleagues share their views before any decisions are made about their work.

Top-Management Attitude Toward Human Resources. This variable is shown by the ways that top management treats people, measured by the following two items:

- Top management treats people as a vital resource for gaining competitive advantage.
- The top management of this organization believes that human resources are extremely important and that everyone should be treated humanely.

Open Communication. The feeling that employees feel free to express their ideas and ask for clarification was measured by the following five items:

- Problems between departments are generally resolved through mutual effort and understanding.
- Everyone has a chance to express opinions on how to do the work.
- Communication within this organization is very open.
- It is easy to ask for advice from anyone in my organization.
- People in my organization solve their work-related problems through mutual discussions.

Opportunities for Learning Application. This variable is measured by the following item:

- Employees returning from training programs are given opportunities to try out what they learned.

Organizational Support for Innovation. The amount of encouragement shown for new ideas and how easily they are accepted, as well as the degree of risk taking and flexibility that are encouraged, were measured by the following five items:

- My organization is flexible enough to adopt any change quickly.
- My organization encourages innovation.
- Top management encourages new ideas and risk taking.
- This organization is receptive to new ideas.
- This organization facilitates and provides opportunities for individual creative work.

Responsive Superiors. The way that employees feel about their managers' decision-making process is measured by the item:

- When important decisions must be made regarding any work process, the tendency of managers here is to pass the files on to somebody else for making decisions.

Opportunities for Self-Development. The feeling about opportunities for continuous self-development is measured by the following two items:

- People here have an opportunity to develop their skills further.
- My organization facilitates employee self-improvement.

Degree of Formality. The formality of procedures is measured by the item:

- Operating procedures are used as guidelines only and may not be followed strictly at all times.

Performance-Linked Feedback.   The amount of performance feedback received and the manner in which it is given are measured by the following five items:

- I am satisfied with my career progress in this organization.
- I receive the necessary information in time to carry out my work efficiently.
- I receive regular feedback on my work performance.
- Any weaknesses are communicated to employees in a nonthreatening way.
- Employees are sponsored for training on the basis of genuine training needs.

Autonomy.   The level of freedom given to employees for making decisions regarding their own areas of work is measured by the following two items:

- I make most of the decisions regarding my own work and area of responsibility.
- I allow my subordinates to make their own decisions while carrying out their work.

Self-Efficacy.   The way employees feel about their own capability and the confidence shown by their supervisors is measured by the following item:

- Here people are able to do their jobs without much help from their supervisors.

Organizational Commitment.   The amount of responsibility employees feel for the progress of the organization is measured by the following two items:

- I feel that I am responsible for whatever happens to my organization, whether good or bad.
- I care about the growth of this organization.

Work Environment Satisfaction.   Satisfaction about the work itself and the work environment is measured by the following four items:

- I am satisfied with the people in my work group.
- I am satisfied with my supervisor.

- I am satisfied with my job.
- I am satisfied with my organization, compared to most other organizations I have heard about or worked for.

Role Satisfaction. Individual role satisfaction is measured by the following item:

- I am not always satisfied with my role in the organization.

Job Involvement. Employees feeling that their work suffers in their absence shows their level of job involvement and is measured by the following two items:

- While away from the job, I often worry that my work is suffering.
- I am willing to devote my free time to work.

VALIDITY AND RELIABILITY

The reliability of the instrument was found by computing Cronbach's alpha on the items. The value of Cronbach Alpha was 0.9584 for the thirty-seven-item scale. Internal consistency (homogeneity of the items) was tested by isolating the items. A value greater than 0.80 indicates very high consistency or internal agreement between a particular item and the entire set of all the remaining items in the questionnaire. The discriminatory capability of the instrument has also been tested.

ADMINISTERING THE INVENTORY

Respondents must be members of the same organization for best results. First, discuss the concept of empowerment and the empowering variables and consequences as they pertain to one's work life. Show Figure 1 as a transparency. Be sure that participants understand the purpose of taking the inventory, then hand out copies and pencils and give them about ten minutes to complete the thirty-seven items. When they have finished, hand out the Scoring Sheet and allow everyone enough time to add the scores they have given to their organization. Lead a discussion of the results, leading to what they, in the spirit of empowerment, can do themselves to improve low scores. Discussions that lead to actions that can actually be taken by the participant himself or herself are best and most likely to lead to participant satisfaction. Remember that respondents must not come away feeling that someone else must act on their needs, as the other person may not be willing or able to do so.

UTILITY

This instrument measures the perceived level of employee empowerment within an organization. It also could be used to measure the change in perceived level of empowerment after efforts are made to improve.

Reference

Gupta, K.S. (1999). *Empowerment: A conceptual and exploratory study.* Unpublished doctoral dissertation, IIT Mumbai, Bangalore, India

Dr. K.S. Gupta is a member of the senior faculty, HAL Management Academy, Bangladore, India. He holds a doctorate in management and master's degrees in electronics and business administration, specializing in HR and marketing. He has thirty years of experience in different capacities in the aeronautical industry in aircraft maintenance, quality assurance and airworthiness, plant maintenance, and international marketing and has served on the faculty of technical and management disciplines as project guide for the master's program in training and consultancy. He has authored twenty papers, both published and unpublished. His interest areas are human resource development, organizational behavior, organization development, restructuring, empowerment, knowledge sharing, transfer of training, and counseling.

EMPOWERMENT INVENTORY

K.S. Gupta

Instructions: The following inventory consists of thirty-seven items reflecting the level of empowerment in your organization. Circle the rating you feel is appropriate for each of the items:

1 = Never   2 = Sometimes   3 = Moderately Often   4 = Often   5 = Very Often

1. My organization is flexible enough to adopt to any change quickly.	1	2	3	4	5
2. My organization encourages innovation.	1	2	3	4	5
3. Top management encourages new ideas and risk taking.	1	2	3	4	5
4. This organization is receptive to new ideas.	1	2	3	4	5
5. This organization facilitates and provides opportunities for individuals to do creative work.	1	2	3	4	5
6. Top management treats people as a vital resource for gaining competitive advantage.	1	2	3	4	5
7. The top management of this organization believes that human resources are extremely important and that people have to be treated humanely.	1	2	3	4	5
8. Problems between departments are generally resolved through mutual effort and understanding.	1	2	3	4	5
9. Everyone has a chance to express opinions on how to do the work.	1	2	3	4	5
10. Communication within this organization is very open.	1	2	3	4	5
11. It is easy to ask for advice from anyone in my organization.	1	2	3	4	5

12. People in my organization solve their
    work-related problems with mutual
    discussions.   1   2   3   4   5

13. I am satisfied with my career progress
    in this organization.   1   2   3   4   5

14. I receive necessary information in time
    to carry out my work efficiently.   1   2   3   4   5

15. I receive regular feedback on my work
    performance.   1   2   3   4   5

16. Any weaknesses are communicated to
    employees in a nonthreatening way.   1   2   3   4   5

17. Employees are sponsored for training on
    the basis of genuine training needs.   1   2   3   4   5

18. People here have an opportunity to
    develop their job skills further.   1   2   3   4   5

19. My organization facilitates employee
    self-improvement.   1   2   3   4   5

20. When important decisions must be made
    regarding any work process, the tendency
    of managers here is to pass the files on to
    somebody else to make decisions.   1   2   3   4   5

21. I make most of the decisions regarding
    my own work and area of responsibility.   1   2   3   4   5

22. I allow my subordinates to make their own
    decisions while carrying out their work.   1   2   3   4   5

23. My boss asks for my views before making
    decisions about my work.   1   2   3   4   5

24. Superiors invite their subordinates for
    informal discussions about their work.   1   2   3   4   5

25. My colleagues share their views before
    any decisions are made on work issues.   1   2   3   4   5

26. Employees returning from training programs are given opportunities to try out what they learned.	1	2	3	4	5
27. Operating procedures are used as guidelines and may not be followed strictly at all times.	1	2	3	4	5
28. Here people are able to do their jobs without much help from their supervisors.	1	2	3	4	5
29. I feel that I am responsible for whatever happens to my organization, whether good or bad.	1	2	3	4	5
30. I care about the growth of this organization.	1	2	3	4	5
31. While away from the job, I often worry that my work is suffering.	1	2	3	4	5
32. I am willing to devote my free time to work.	1	2	3	4	5
33. I am satisfied with the people in my work group.	1	2	3	4	5
34. I am satisfied with my supervisor.	1	2	3	4	5
35. I am satisfied with my job.	1	2	3	4	5
36. I am satisfied with my organization, compared to most other organizations I have heard about or worked for.	1	2	3	4	5
37. I am not always satisfied with my role in this organization.	1	2	3	4	5

EMPOWERMENT INVENTORY SCORING SHEET

Instructions: Use the grid below to calculate your scores for each variable. First, look at each item number and write the score you assigned to that item in the score box. Add the numbers in each score box together and divide by the number of items. The total is the points you assigned for each of the variables and consequences. *Note:* Items 20 and 37 are negatively framed and therefore these scores should be computed as (Score = 6 minus item score).

Empowering Variable	Item Numbers	Average Score
Respect for Team Members (RTM)	23, 24, 25	
Top-Management Attitude Toward Human Resources (TMA)	6, 7	
Open Communication (OC)	8, 9, 10, 11, 12	
Opportunities for Learning Application (OLA)	26	
Organizational Support for Innovation (OSI)	1, 2, 3, 4, 5	
Responsive Superiors (RSR)	20	
Opportunities for Self-Development (OSD)	18, 19	
Degree of Formality (DF)	27	
Performance-Linked Feedback (PLF)	13, 14, 15, 16, 17	
Autonomy (AMY)	21, 22	
Consequences	**Item Numbers**	**Average Score**
Self-Efficacy (SE)	28	
Organizational Commitment (OCT)	29, 30	
Work Environment Satisfaction (WES)	33, 34, 35, 36	
Role Satisfaction (RS)	37	
Job Involvement (JI)	31, 32	

Introduction
to the Presentation and Discussion Resources Section

The Presentation and Discussion Resources Section is a collection of articles of use to every facilitator. The theories, background information, models, and methods will challenge facilitators' thinking, enrich their professional development, and assist their internal and external clients with productive change. These articles may be used as a basis for lecturettes, as handouts in training sessions, or as background reading material.

This section will provide you with a variety of useful ideas, theoretical opinions, teachable models, practical strategies, and proven intervention methods. The articles will add richness and depth to your training and consulting knowledge and skills. They will challenge you to think differently, explore new concepts, and experiment with new interventions. The articles will continue to add a fresh perspective to your work.

The 2002 Annual: Volume 1, Training includes ten articles, in the following categories:

Individual Development: Developing Awareness and Understanding

Hurling Kindness Rather Than Stones, by Marlene Caroselli

Individual Development: Personal Growth

Developing Interpersonal Intelligence in the Workplace, by Mel Silberman

Individual Development: Life/Career Planning

Voluntary Industry Skill Standards: Valuable Tools for Workforce Professionals, by Eleazar O. Velazquez

Communication: Clarity and Precision in Communication

Email Basics: Practical Tips to Improve Communication, by Kristin J. Arnold

Communication: Coaching and Encouraging

The Effective Protégé, by H.B. Karp

Communication: Technology

Implementing E-Learning, by Brooke Broadbent

Problem Solving: Change and Change Agents

The Rhyme and Reason of Improvement and Innovation,
by Mark W. Smith, with comment by George Land

**Consulting: Organizations:
Their Characteristics and How They Function**

Planting the Seeds and Cultivating the New Workforce,
by Harriet Cohen, David B. Johnson, and Debbie Newman

Consulting: Consulting Strategies and Techniques

Action Learning at Finco: A Learning History, by Andy Beaulieu

Facilitating: Techniques and Strategies

Teaching How to Learn Through Online Discussion,
by Zane L. Berge

As with previous *Annuals*, this volume covers a wide variety of topics. The range of articles presented encourages thought-provoking discussion about the present and future of HRD. Other articles on specific subjects can be located by using our comprehensive *Reference Guide to Handbooks and Annuals*. The guide is updated regularly and indexes the contents of all the *Annuals* and the *Handbooks of Structured Experiences*. With each revision, the *Reference Guide* becomes a complete, up-to-date, and easy-to-use resource for selecting appropriate materials from the *Annuals* and *Handbooks*.

Here and in the *Reference Guide*, we have done our best to categorize the articles for easy reference; however, many of the articles encompass a range of topics, disciplines, and applications. If you do not find what you are looking for under one category, check a related category. In some cases we may place an article in the "Training" *Annual* that also has implications for "Consulting," and vice versa. As the field of HRD continues to grow and develop, there is more and more crossover between training and consulting. Explore all the contents of both volumes of the *Annual* in order to realize the full potential for learning and development that each offers.

HURLING KINDNESS RATHER THAN STONES

Marlene Caroselli

Abstract: Sigmund Freud may have been correct in identifying the founder of civilization: The person who hurled an insult instead of a stone. This presentation further promotes civilized behavior by encouraging conflict-reducing behaviors. Although workplace violence is a frightening reality, statistically it impacts very few employees. A great many employees, however, *are* impacted, on a daily basis, by co-workers with difficult personalities. Workplace harmony can be affected by the use of words that defuse conflict before it erupts and by the use of specific strategies that channel conflict toward productive outcomes.

DEALING WITH CONFLICT

Conflict is a normal, natural, to-be-expected, ordinary part of work life. What is *not* normal is the person who deliberately pushes other people around, with or without a reason. It can be a co-worker or a person in authority, but whatever his or her position, we're talking about the individual who enjoys badgering, barging in, browbeating, belittling, or bullying. Workplace bullying—whether it's done verbally or physically—is expensive. When lawsuits are added to lost productivity, higher insurance costs, stress leaves, and workers' compensation claims, the cost to the nation exceeds $36 billion a year (Jossi, 1999).

If you work in a war zone, you can win small and big battles by employing some of the techniques we're about to share. You can learn to jump out of the cauldron of fear the bully has bubbling. For your own safety, security, and peace of mind, you must do something. Remaining in or near the cauldron of negativity will surely lead to physical and/or mental problems. Here are some helpful tips:

- Stand up, stand tall, and ultimately you'll stand out as someone who cannot be bullied. The confrontation need not be hostile. You can simply ask to meet with the individual. Suggest a public place, such as a corner of the cafeteria, so angry words are less likely to be shouted. Try to avoid an adversarial stance. Instead of "you" words, employ "we" words. For example, "There seems to be some 'bad blood' between us. I don't know what's causing it, but I'd like to discuss how we can put an end to it."

- Discuss the situation with several people outside the organization and elicit their feedback. Try out all the possible solutions you hear until you find one that works.

- If you don't have a mentor, find one and discuss the problem with him or her. If you already have one, let the mentor's experience guide you in solving this problem.

- Keep a journal of the instances when you feel you've been treated less than respectfully. There are numerous situations in which this journal may prove to be very valuable to you.

- You can also try to ignore the individual. Maintain a courteous, professional relationship but, basically, try to stay out of his or her way. Don't let this toxic personality poison your outlook or your enjoyment of your job.

Additional Tips

- Seek e-help. Although you'll no doubt find sources of your own, try visiting the website geared for conflict-copers: www.bullybusters.org, where, for example, you'll find strategies successfully employed by those who have survived conflict-ridden situations. Of course, you can also find such help in books, newspapers, and magazines.

- There's strength in numbers. If a group met with the individual, it might help convince him or her of the severity of the problem.

- One seldom-used weapon in the war on conflict is the sharing of a personal experience. Real-life anecdotes can be used to establish trust between two parties and, thus, indirectly lessen the likelihood of acerbic outbreaks. Researchers have repeatedly found story-related content more believable than statistics or policy statements regarding a company's commitment to avoiding layoffs (Martin & Powers, 1982). Apart from credibility, anecdotes help others understand the commonality that binds us. In this way, relationships can be made more harmonious.

AN EXERCISE TO TRY

Replay in your head a workplace conflict situation you've been part of, one you've heard about, or one that you can foresee occurring. Outline the basic stages: What words prompted the conflict? What words accelerated or defused it? What resolution, if any, was achieved?

Now, put the conflict scenario aside. Draw a continuum representing the decades of your life. What one event (sad, funny, frightening, surprising) stands out in your head from each decade? Embellish the details surrounding each one. Then weave one of the anecdotes into the conflict scenario so that it could be used to lessen the tensions surrounding the issue.

The K.I.N.D. Approach

In looking for the right words, realize that you have three choices when it comes to negative workplace situations. You can make them better. You can make them worse. You can leave them as they are. Choosing to improve them is better for your health. When conflicts arise, try the K.I.N.D. approach.

Meet with the person. Begin with a **K**ind statement. Next, **I**nquire: Ask a question that reflects genuine interest or concern. Next, make a **N**ew overture. Suggest a way of working together that you have not tried before. You are creative. You can think of *something* different. Finally, be **D**efinite. Set a time and place for implementing the new approach you have suggested.

The F.E.A.R.-Less Approach

Another technique involves attitudes. It's hard to go a week without encountering someone—inside or outside the workplace—with an attitude so bad you just want to run the other way. And you can. Or you can gather your courage and speak to the person so that you can be F.E.A.R.-less in the future.

Give **F**eedback. Tell the person how his or her actions affect you and others. **E**ducate the person next. Ideally, you can use statistics. For example, a study by ETICON, Inc., reported by Ann Humphries (1999) of Knight Ridder, found that 31 percent of respondents said they would work harder and longer if polite behavior were the norm and not the exception in their work environment. Gather other facts related to the situations you are dealing with. **A**nticipate the arguments or replies the other person is likely to give you. Ask around. Find out what others would say in response to what you are likely to hear. **R**educe the conflict with humor or sincerity or a genuine offer of friendship.

Add Tools to Your Interpersonal Tool Belt

If you're serious about achieving workplace harmony, you can and should undertake a program of continuous interpersonal improvement. Follow these suggestions.

1. Ask a question such as, "What would you like me to do about this?" or "Do you think I did this deliberately?" or "What would *you* be willing to do about this?"

2. If you watch television, make note of statements that worked effectively to defuse hostile situations in various programs. Try them out until you find one that works well. Continue using it.

3. Take notes (if only mentally) during the conflict. Afterward, analyze what worked and what did not.

4. If someone is agitated, do not say, "Calm down."

5. Acknowledge that some of what the other person is saying is true or possibly true.

6. Change the subject in mid-conflict stream.

7. Think of the most "difficult" person with whom you have to interact each day. Then vow to say nothing but kind words to that person for one full day. The next day, vow to do one thoughtful thing for this person. Reward yourself and then set a two-day goal for each action. Continue this cycle until you perceive a change in the way you and this person are interacting.

8. Act as though slights, sarcasm, and/or insults are not intended as such.

9. Engage the difficult person with this request, "Let's each focus on one thing we think prevents us from working together more respectfully."

10. Begin team meetings with a generalized statement about the importance of cooperation.

11. Keep a log of what worked and what did not in each conflict situation. Practice best practices over and over.

12. Do not sink to the level at which some people operate. Acknowledge that you are bigger than the conflict situation, and act accordingly.

13. Set aside one day a month for honoring an actual or self-created ideal such as World Peace Day, Day of Atonement, or Friendship Day. You'll think of others.

14. Know what interpersonal stress can do to your good health. Decide that you will not let others jeopardize your well-being.

15. Study those who seldom have conflict with others. Ask them for their success secrets.

16. List all the hurts and grudges you are harboring. Try to let go of one a month. Congratulate yourself as you do.

17. Be charitable to the fullest extent possible. You simply cannot know what grief other people are carrying. It's possible that personal pain makes them difficult to deal with.

18. If you find yourself close to tears, try these tips: Either push your tongue as hard as you possibly can against the roof of your mouth and/or look up at a bright light as long as you naturally can and widen your eyes as you do so.

PRACTICE SELF-TALK

Self-talk—if you practice it habitually—is a powerful tool in the "fight" against conflict. There are several things you can remember and repeat to yourself when you see or hear trouble brewing, but just one is enough for controlling emotions—yours and the other person's.

"Don't sweat the small stuff" is a good example of a self-talk reminder that will help you avoid plunging into a heated exchange. Identify others that will work to make difficult situations and difficult people less volatile.

REMEMBER THE MARSHMALLOWS

Stress makes nerves raw, tempers short, and responses abrasive. And yet there are those who can concentrate on a goal, seemingly oblivious to the many tensions brewing around them. Perhaps the most famous example of the importance of delaying gratification in order to achieve a goal is the study conducted by psychologist Walter Mischel (1990) forty years ago at a preschool on the Stanford University campus. The children were told they could have one marshmallow immediately or two later, if they could just wait until the researcher returned from an errand.

Not surprisingly, as the children were tracked in this longitudinal study, researchers found that the children who waited were, as adolescents, much better at coping with frustrations. The one-marshmallow subjects were later found to be less flexible, less inclined to be decisive, and more stressed than their counterparts. It's not too late. When you are tempted to respond to a conflict situation in a way that will make you feel good for the moment, re-member the marshmallow research.

When tempted to respond sarcastically or abrasively to a stressful conflict situation, refrain! It might make you feel good for the moment to say exactly what you're thinking, but in the long run it will impair your relationship with the person causing the conflict. Your long-range goal is probably to achieve good working relationships. Delaying the gratifying feeling of "telling someone off" will help you achieve that goal more readily.

NIP CONFLICT IN THE METAPHORIC BUD

You can also anticipate the conflict that is likely to erupt. "Nip it in the bud" by prefacing the exchange with a comment like this: "I know that what I'm about to say will draw some strong reactions from some of you. That's because you will feel as strongly about your viewpoint as I feel about mine. Let me suggest that we listen to each other without interruption. We can take notes, of course, so we won't forget what we want to say in response. Then when each of us has had a chance to voice an opinion, we can lay the issue on the table for further discussion."

By heading off the conflict before it can rear its sometimes-ugly head, you can control it and thereby optimize the encounter.

USE YOUR EARS

It's hard to use the right words if you're not responding to the words that preceded them. Most of us believe we have excellent listening skills, but many of us have spouses who would disagree with our self-assessments. Conflict often arises when one party feels the other has not listened to him or her.

Think about this question: Why do we listen? Then study some of the traits good listeners employ. How would you rate yourself 1 (low) to 5 (high) on these behaviors?

1. Establishes the proper environment;

2. Listens even if the subject is not interesting;

3. Withholds judgment;

4. Does not interrupt;

5. Contains his/her own enthusiasm, which might otherwise lead the conversation away from the speaker;

6. Thinks ahead; evaluates what is being said;

7. Concentrates and follows intricate threads of thought;

8. Periodically checks for understanding;

9. Offers thoughtful feedback; and

10. Uses body language that reflects true listening.

In Conclusion

Our wondrous language makes more than a million words available to us. No matter what situation arises, you have verbal choices to make in response to it. You can choose words that will escalate the tension. You can choose words that are neutral. Or you can choose words that will improve the immediate and long-term situations. Insults may be more civilized than stones, but kind words are best of all.

References

Humphries, A. (1999, July 12). Management issues: Business people see rudeness on the rise. *Rochester (NY) Democrat Chronicle*, p. 5F.

Jossi, F. (1999, February). Workplace violence. *Business & Health*, p. 37.

Martin, J., & Powers, M. (1982). Organizational stories: More vivid and persuasive than quantitative data. In B.M. Staw (Ed.), *Psychological foundations of organizational behavior* (pp. 161–168). Glenview, IL: Scott, Foresman.

Mischel, W., Peake, P.K., & Shoda, Y. (1990, November). Predicting adolescent cognitive and self-regulatory competencies from pre-school delay of gratification. *Developmental Psychology, 26*(6).

Dr. Marlene Caroselli conducts corporate training on a variety of subjects. She also presents motivational keynote addresses and writes—forty-five books to date. View them at her website (http://hometown.aol.com/mccpd) or at Amazon.com.

DEVELOPING INTERPERSONAL INTELLIGENCE IN THE WORKPLACE

Mel Silberman

Abstract: Given the parallel trends of increasing change and globalization in the business world today, it is more important than ever that workers—all workers—develop the skills necessary to communicate and work with others effectively, that is, to be "people smart." In this article, the author describes what it means to be people smart, reviews common barriers to change, and presents a four-step process for developing your interpersonal skills or what the author calls your people quotient (PQ).

This article is adapted from *PeopleSmart: Developing Your Interpersonal Intelligence* (Berrett-Koehler, 2000) by Mel Silberman.

INTRODUCTION

All your employees need to be people smart. No matter what someone's function is, everyone in today's workforce is in the people business! It used to be said that some people were in the business of working with people and some of us were in the business of working with facts, figures, and machinery. But the people business is no longer the domain of the few. It now includes everyone.

WHAT DOES IT MEAN TO BE PEOPLE SMART?

Ask people on the street what it means to be people smart, and you are bound to hear from many who have this picture: "Oh, that's a person who is really a smooth operator . . . a person who knows how to get others to join his side." A different picture you might get is someone who is "personable . . . friendly . . . fun to be with."

Although few people would complain about having those two attributes, they represent a very limited view of what it means to be gifted with people. Being people smart is a multi-faceted competence. It is not limited to our political skills or our social graces, but includes a wide range of abilities.

Howard Gardner (1993), in his highly respected book, *Frames of the Mind: The Theory of Multiple Intelligences,* contends that the ability to manage our inner feelings and our ability to work well with people make up what he calls the "personal intelligences." These abilities are as impressive as our ability to solve math and logic problems (logical-mathematical intelligence), to write effectively (linguistic intelligence), to create music and art (musical and spatial intelligence), and to excel at dance or sports (bodily-kinesthetic intelligence).

Daniel Goleman (1997) takes Gardner's concept of personal intelligence one step further in his best-selling book, *Emotional Intelligence.* Using findings of new brain research, he presents a powerful argument that our intelligence at managing ourselves emotionally and managing our relationships may be among the best predictors of success in life. While our intellectual intelligence might get us hired, our emotional intelligence might get us promoted! That's because how we handle our emotions and collaborate with others is increasingly important in today's team-based organizations. Our emotional intelligence, as Goleman explains, also helps us to think clearly and more creatively. He describes how the brain releases cortical inhibitors that choke the connection between the emotional brain and the thinking brain when we are anxious, frustrated, and angry. When we experience positive emotions, however, the brain releases cortical facilitators that lubricate the connection between the emotional brain and the thinking brain.

People smarts is about that aspect of emotional intelligence that is best called "interpersonal intelligence." Intelligence tests, such as the Wechsler Adult Intelligence Scale, claim to measure "intellectual quotient" or IQ for short. When you consider how important interpersonal effectiveness is, it also makes sense to build the PQ or "people quotient" of your workforce.

What makes up someone's PQ? Consider these questions. Are your employees good at:

- Understanding people?
- Expressing their thoughts and feelings clearly?
- Speaking up when their needs are not being met?
- Asking for feedback from others and giving them quality feedback in return?
- Influencing how others think and act?
- Bringing conflicts to the surface and resolving them?
- Collaborating with others, as opposed to doing things by themselves?
- Shifting gears when relationships are stuck?

How these questions are answered determines someone's PQ. People with high PQs excel in the following eight areas. How do your people stack up?

1. Understanding People

People with high PQs listen actively, empathize with the speaker's feelings, and acknowledge his or her viewpoint. That not only helps them to be appreciated but also works to draw out information they need to figure out what makes the other person tick. They ask questions to clarify what someone is saying when necessary. They also realize that understanding others goes beyond the words they speak. They know how to interpret the unspoken. Finally, they are expert at reading other people's style and motives.

2. Expressing Themselves Clearly

People with high PQs know how to get their message across so that it's understood. When people go on and on to make a point, they simply have no effect on other people. High PQers get to the point when brevity is required, yet give just enough detail so that other people are not confused. They can also sense when the other person has not understood them and can quickly rephrase what they are saying.

3. Asserting Their Needs

High PQers know that they have to be their own people. They have to have limits, and they have to establish those limits. They recognize that, if they try to be all things to all people, they will wind up disappointing at least some people. They also are straightforward with their wishes. Hinting at what one needs from others only leads to disappointment and frustration. Once that happens, one often becomes angry with others and loses the calm and confidence one needs to be at one's best. People with high PQs are able to remain calm and confident, even when others try to provoke them and push their emotional buttons.

4. Seeking and Giving Feedback

High PQ individuals are open about their reactions to others. They are able to give feedback easily and do it in such a way that the other people do not become defensive. They also know that it is smart to be in the habit of asking for feedback themselves. If feedback is withheld, it's as though the person has blinders on. Without feedback, we are always left wondering what the other person is thinking about us.

5. Influencing Others

A high PQ is evidence of someone's ability to motivate others to action. High PQers are also people others come to for advice. They are able to connect with others, unearth their needs, reduce their resistance to new ideas, and persuade effectively.

6. Resolving Conflict

High PQers are exceptional conflict resolvers. They put the subject right out on the table. They figure out what's bothering the other person. They are especially adept at negotiating differences and working out creative resolutions to problems.

7. Being a Team Player

High PQers are team players. They work to advance the group's goals rather than their own. They also know how to complement the styles of others, coordinate the efforts of team members without bossing them around, and build consensus.

8. Shifting Gears When Relationships Are Stuck

Finally, high PQers are flexible and resilient. Although they have an inner core and a predominant style of dealing with people, they also understand that there are different strokes for different folks. They realize that one of the ways they can help a relationship to change is to change the way they behave in it. They know how to get out of old patterns and unfreeze situations that have previously been frozen shut.

RESISTANCE TO CHANGE

Although the kinds of abilities we traditionally associate with IQ are often viewed as fixed and unchangeable, our PQ can be increased beyond our present ability level. That's the good news. However, expect a rocky road! That's because we adults don't change very easily.

Consider these factors:

- Our comfort zones are very well-established. If you don't believe this, do this simple experiment:

  Fold your arms without thinking. Now, fold them the opposite way so that you switch which arm is on top. Feel awkward? You bet. Well, stay that way for a minute. Now, cross your legs without thinking about it. Yep, the upper part of your body is still uncomfortable, but your lower part is nice and comfortable. Now, cross your legs the opposite way. All of you is now out of your comfort zone. So go right back to the way you fold your arms and cross your legs. Feel better now? Yep, that's the real you—comfortable doing something the same way all the time!

- Well, for better or worse, we adults have grown used not only to the ways we fold our arms or cross our legs, but to the ways we relate to other people. And it would be uncomfortable to change our ways.

By the time we are grown up, we have tried a lot of times to change some things in our lives and have not succeeded. Compared to children, we have stopped dreaming and become deeply pessimistic about our ability to change. After all, look at how many times we have failed to lose weight, exercise regularly, spend more quality time with loved ones, donate blood, or do a host of other actions we know are important. Most of us have not kept New Year's resolutions so many times that our failures can't even be counted anymore!

Perhaps the most stubborn source of resistance comes from the fact that, by now, we have highly developed interpersonal styles. The temperament with which we were born, the environments to which we've been exposed, and the relationships we have formed all contribute to the creation of a preferred way to relate to others. This style is so dominant that it will probably not change for the rest of our lives.

Because our styles are somewhat set, no one should expect or desire a complete makeover. But we can look ourselves in the mirror, take pride in our strengths and take stock in our weaknesses, and look for ways to work with and around them.

Think of becoming interpersonally fit just as you would think of becoming physically fit. While your body type, your genetic makeup, and your age place considerable restrictions on what physical prowess you can achieve, you can still become more physically fit than you presently are. The same is true with interpersonal fitness.

FOUR STEPS TO DEVELOPING INTERPERSONAL INTELLIGENCE

In a recent interview, Daniel Goleman was asked whether traditional methods of training are adequate to help people to be personally and interpersonally effective. He replied that the training required to improve these skills cannot be done in a day or weekend workshop. "It's like trying to teach piano by giving someone a single lesson and not have them come back and practice every week. Nothing will happen. The person will have experienced, once, almost playing the piano," he explained. Goleman emphasized that it takes a lot of work, motivation, and support for the emotional brain to be rewired for change.

As you undertake the task of developing PQ in your workforce, consider these four steps as you plan your training. Don't pass over any of them.

1. Get them to "*Want It.*" From the start, your people must be honest with themselves and determine whether they want to develop their PQ. The first thing to do is to have them take stock of their strengths and weaknesses with each of the people smart skills. To assist them with this process, provide them with a short survey that assesses their current ability level in each skill area. Urge them not to rely only on their own perceptions. Push people to find the courage to ask others how they see them as well. Taking a candid look at oneself is a critical step along the road to self-improvement.

   In addition, people can't expect to change without a lot of motivation. Provide them with a list of benefits that they might receive if they improve their people smart skills now. Have them select one or two benefits and use them as their personal inspiration to get out of their comfort zone and do something different. They are also more likely to be motivated if they are aware of when and where they need the skill the most. To help them make this connection, provide them with a list of situations in which they might find the skill in question to be particularly relevant, especially in their immediate jobs.

2. Help them to "*Learn It.*" Interpersonally intelligent people do certain things very well. Invite your people to become familiar with the core skills possessed by people who exemplify each of the eight components of PQ. Although they don't need a whole course in each area to make some changes, it is important to acquire a few basics. Of course, some people may already be familiar with this material. If that describes anyone you know, you should still urge the person to review before taking any action.

3. Ask them to "*Try It.*" Most people make the mistake of going for broke and then fizzle out when results don't come quickly. With each aspect of interpersonal intelligence, encourage your employees to conduct an "experiment in change." You want them to try on a small change in behavior "for size" and see whether they like what happens. Don't kid yourself: They won't persist unless they find that there is something in it for them. By offering them some "experiments in change " for their consideration, you will give them a chance to test their wings and find the initial successes to sustain themselves for further practice.

4. Urge them to "*Live It.*" One of the reasons that changes don't last is that, after people get pumped up about doing something, they try to make it on sheer inspiration and will power. They may have some initial success but then quickly relapse. *Real change* only comes by overcoming obstacles that are in the way in daily life—not by jumping over buildings in leaping

bounds. Help your employees to confront *their* difficulties with each PQ skill. The skill may be difficult for them for reasons that are different than for someone else. If they face the reasons why the skill is difficult for them, they will have a greater chance for incorporating the skill into their lives.

The four steps above can be applied to any area of self-improvement. For example, assume someone wants to lose weight. He or she might begin by taking a good look in the mirror and weighing. The person might ask others (such as their doctor) for an opinion. Even if someone else thinks the person should lose weight, the person himself or herself really has to want to do something about the weight. Therefore, it may prove necessary for the person to become motivated by thinking about the special benefits to be gained through success and to link these benefits to specific situations, such as a forthcoming vacation or an important professional event.

Next, the person might find it helpful to learn about the latest diets, ways to lose calories through exercise, and psychological tips to modify eating behavior. When the person decides to try something different, it will feel like an "experiment in change." If the experiment is successful, then the person may be able to build the approach into his or her lifestyle and start to "live it." Along the way, there will be plenty of obstacles to identify and find ways to overcome. With this approach, the weight loss will last.

These four steps are especially important when someone is seeking changes in interpersonal effectiveness. Before letting someone go forth, one piece of advice: Tell the person not to rush the process. Developing PQ is tough enough. Urge people to be patient and not to skip any of the steps in the process. Remember, they have to *want it, learn it, try it,* and *live it.*

References

Gardner, H. (1993). *Frames of the mind: The theory of multiple intelligences.* New York: Basic.

Goleman, D. (1997). *Emotional intelligence.* New York: Bantam.

Mel Silberman, Ph.D., president of Active Training, is also professor of adult and organizational development at Temple University. He is the author of Active Training, 101 Ways to Make Training Active, 101 Ways to Make Meetings Active, *and* PeopleSmart: Developing Your Interpersonal Intelligence. *Dr. Silberman is also the editor of* 20 Active Training Programs, *Vols. 1, 2, and 3, as well as* The Training and Performance Sourcebook *and* The Team and Organization Development Sourcebook.

VOLUNTARY INDUSTRY SKILL STANDARDS: VALUABLE TOOLS FOR WORKFORCE PROFESSIONALS

Eleazar O. Velazquez

Abstract: As the economy continues to grow and as globalization increases, employers are looking for ways to gain a competitive edge. A better-trained workforce might be one way to increase productivity. But what is the best way to achieve this goal? The author of this article suggests using a national set of standards (1) to ensure that employees have the appropriate skills and knowledge, (2) to assist employers in making effective hiring decisions, and (3) to help educators and trainers to create better and more up-to-date tools and curricula.

This article is based on the material found in the NSSB publication *Built to Work: A Common Framework for Skill Standards* and is adapted with permission. This publication offers valuable information on developing a voluntary skill standards system framework using the NSSB's Common Language Format and general guidance on developing skill standards during this first stage of system building. To obtain a hard copy (subject to availability), please contact the NSSB or download it free by visiting the website at *www.nssb.org* and clicking on the publications link.

INTRODUCTION

The goal of businesses throughout the United States to remain competitive transcends all economic cycles. Whether the economy is growing, slowing down, or contracting, the need for businesses to outperform their competitors is imperative. As U.S. businesses encounter greater competition from abroad, improving worker productivity to remain competitive takes on a critical dimension.

To achieve this goal, many corporate executives and business owners readily turn to professional workforce trainers or available in-house human resource departments for advice and guidance on how to enhance worker productivity or improve workplace processes. Workers in all industries are sent to training programs to learn new technologies, production methods, or ways to improve interpersonal skills. For companies, the investment in training and development that builds on workers' existing knowledge and skills is a small sum to pay to help them remain competitive in an increasingly global marketplace. With the resilient U.S. economy forecast to create fourteen million new jobs by 2008 and the pace of workplace automation continuing unabated, the need for skilled workers will increase (Bureau of Labor Statistics, 2000).

To create a more skilled workforce, businesses, labor unions, educators, and workforce trainers must work together on a national level to communicate their requirements in order to create the tools necessary to maintain momentum in today's dynamic economy. A system of skill standards, assessment, and certification that identifies what a worker needs to know and be able to do to perform his or her job well may hold the answer.

Trainers are in a superb position to help upgrade the skills of the nation's workforce by becoming involved in the groundbreaking work of developing an industry-recognized, voluntary national skill standards system. They have the depth of industry knowledge and the ability to communicate effectively with workers of various industries—useful skills for the development of skill standards for entire industry sectors. Trainers' knowledge of the latest workplace process improvements may assist them in updating standards so that they meet future business demands. Finally, workforce trainers are in a position to enhance the skill standards system framework by contributing their extensive knowledge of assessments. The contributions of workforce trainers will ensure that any skill standards system fulfills its objective.

How Workforce Trainers Might Benefit

In addition to helping *develop* the system, training providers stand to benefit significantly by *using* a national system of skill standards, assessments, and certification, as it would enhance their role as vital links between business and labor. By helping employers improve communications with workers, trainers might use nationally recognized, industry-based skill standards and certifications as guides for aligning or developing curricula. The system would provide them with new tools and resources to use in their work with employees and a common language with which to communicate with workers more effectively. Trainers would also tailor course content to equip program graduates with up-to-date knowledge and skills that meet the employers' actual performance requirements. As a result, student customers would be drawn toward those preparation programs that directly enabled them to obtain, keep, and advance in jobs of their choosing.

By incorporating industry-recognized skill standards into their programs, workforce trainers would enhance the value of their services to prospective clients who support and value the system. In the manufacturing sector alone, more than one hundred leading companies and a number of employer associations representing hundreds of businesses throughout the country have endorsed the concept of skill standards (Emily Brennan, Manufacturing Skill Standards Council, personal communication). Employers who understand the benefits of the proposed national system would likely seek trainers who incorporated skill standards into their programs. Human resource professionals have the opportunity to upgrade their training programs with skill standards that continuously take into account changes in workplace technologies and processes, again enhancing the value of their services.

Finally, skill standards and certifications could be used by providers as the basis of competency-based learning objectives, training practices and procedures, instructional methods, teaching materials, and classroom/work site activities. They may also be used to facilitate improved communication and collaboration among different education and training institutions seeking better articulation with each other and to afford strong foundations for mutually beneficial partnerships with business and industry to enhance area workforce development initiatives with a skilled workforce.

NATIONAL SKILL STANDARDS BOARD

The need for a skilled workforce that meets the demands of today's economy is the reason why the National Skill Standards Board (NSSB) exists today. Created by an Act of Congress (National Skill Standards Act of 1994), the NSSB is charged with building a common framework for a voluntary national system of skill standards, assessments, and certification for front-line workers through first-level supervisors. This system is intended to help U.S. businesses compete more effectively in the global economy; to help workers secure a firmer economic future and achieve higher standards of living; and to help educators and workforce trainers create better and more up-to-date tools and curricula. The National Skill Standards Board provides strategic leadership in the system's development. It is composed of twenty-four representatives from business, labor, education and training, human resources, civil rights, and community-based organizations, plus the Secretaries of Commerce, Education, and Labor as ex-officio members. The work of the Board is carried out by a team of technical experts and research staff.

Representatives from each stakeholder group in this effort have come together for these purposes:

- To identify the requirements of work and the knowledge and skills that workers must possess to succeed in today's high-performance workplace;

- To develop forward-looking standards, which are developed using technically and legally sound methodology, as learning objectives for students and workers to achieve;

- To create assessment tools for students and workers to assess their skills against industry standards and make decisions about jobs and education needed; and

- To implement a certification system recognized by industries nationwide, with certificates that are portable across geographic and industry boundaries to be used as indicators of achievement in education and workforce development programs and systems and by individuals who are making decisions about education and training options or careers.

DEVELOPING SKILL STANDARDS

Given the more than 140 million workers doing thousands of different jobs in hundreds of different industries in the United States, the NSSB divided the U.S. economy into the following fifteen industry sectors—segments of the economy that share similar skill requirements—to facilitate the development of skill standards for each sector.

- Agriculture, Forestry, and Fishing
- Business and Administrative Services
- Construction
- Education and Training
- Finance and Insurance
- Health and Human Services
- Manufacturing, Installation, and Repair
- Mining
- Public Administration, Legal, and Protective Services
- Restaurants, Lodging, Hospitality and Tourism, and Amusement and Recreation
- Retail Trade, Wholesale Trade, Real Estate, and Personal Services
- Scientific and Technical Services
- Telecommunications, Computers, Art and Entertainment, and Information
- Transportation
- Utilities, Environmental, and Waste Management

The development of skill standards around industry sectors will equip workers with "portable" skills and certifications that they can use to transition within an industry sector or into other industry sectors. These will help enhance career opportunities and protect individuals against dislocation in the event of an economic downturn.

Industry sectors group industries with similar skill requirements for the purposes of developing skill standards. In this way, individuals who acquire these skills will be equipped to work in a number of different industries in which many of the same skill needs are evident. In addition, developing sector-wide standards also gives employers a large pool of qualified workers to fulfill their employment demands—demands that call for front-line workers to carry out a broad range of responsibilities to assist their organizations in responding more effectively to customer needs.

To promote this kind of portability across industries, the NSSB is establishing industry coalitions called "voluntary partnerships" to develop skill standards for the industry sectors listed earlier. Industry coalitions comprise representatives from business, labor, education and training organizations, and community-based and civil rights organizations. Skill standards development has been underway since 1998, with the development of assessments by several voluntary partnerships to begin shortly.

Core, Concentration, and Specialty Standards

As opposed to developing standards for each front-line position in an industry sector, the common framework calls for the development of three types of skill standards within an industry sector:

- *Core Standards:* The knowledge, skills, and job requirements that are common and critical to all front-line jobs within an industry sector. Mastery of the core standards will offer individuals a broad-based introduction to work across the sector.

- *Concentration Standards:* The knowledge, skills, and job requirements that are needed for major areas of front-line responsibility, typically covering families of related jobs and occupations. The NSSB Common Framework calls for the identification of up to six concentrations within each industry sector. As an example, the manufacturing industry sector has identified the following six concentrations:

    Manufacturing production process development

    Logistics and inventory control

    Production

    Production quality assurance

    Health, safety, and environmental assurance

    Maintenance, installation, and repair

- *Specialty Standards:* The knowledge, skills, and job requirements that are unique to a particular job or occupation, to an individual industry, or to a specific company. Specialty standards will be developed by outside organizations, such as trade associations and professional groups. The NSSB will work with these groups to develop linkages between specialty standards and the broader national skill standards framework.

Once the standards have been identified for core and concentration skills, the voluntary partnerships will employ a number of assessment tools to evaluate the level of workers' knowledge and skills. Individuals who fail their assessments will receive performance feedback, and they will be afforded the opportunity to retest following additional training. Those who pass will be awarded industry-recognized skills certificates.

The NSSB will offer Core Plus Certificates, which will certify an individual's mastery of a core skill standard plus that of at least one concentration. Specialty certificates will be awarded by the outside organizations that developed those standards. The NSSB will recognize specialty certifications that are aligned with the national framework.

A Common Format and Language for Skill Standards

Now that the organizational framework for the development of a skill standards system has been identified, it becomes necessary to understand the skill standards—the building blocks of the entire system. A skill standard—as defined by the NSSB—is composed of the following two elements:

- A *work-oriented* component, which describes the relevant work requirements; and
- A *worker-oriented* component, which describes the requisite knowledge and skills to perform that job.

Together, the work-oriented and worker-oriented components of the skill standards provide individuals with a comprehensive picture of the knowledge, skills, and job requirements for success in today's workplace.

The Work-Oriented Component

The work-oriented component identifies what workers need to be able to do on the job. This component is made up of the following three elements:

- *Critical Work Functions (CWF):* The major responsibilities of work covered by a concentration. Most concentrations can be characterized by fewer than fifteen critical work functions, which serve as the building blocks for the development of all other aspects of the standards.

- *Key Activities (KA):* The major duties or tasks involved in carrying out a critical work function. Most critical work functions can be described by three to six key activities.

- *Performance Indicators (PI):* Measurements of an individual's performance of each key activity. Three to six performance indicators typically describe effective performance of key activities. Performance indicators are benchmarks that accurately measure competent performance.

The following partial example describes a critical work function and two of five key activities and their corresponding performance indicators in the Manufacturing, Installation, and Repair industry sector:

Critical Work Function: Produce product to meet customer needs.
Key Activity: Establish and verify that resources, such as materials, tools, and equipment, are available for the production process.
Performance Indicators:

- Raw materials are checked against work order.
- Tools and equipment are checked against work order.
- Inventory discrepancies are communicated to the proper parties.
- Necessary resources are at work station when required.
- Workers with appropriate skills are scheduled according to production needs.

Key Activity: Identify customer needs.
Performance Indicators:

- The needs of internal and external customers are recognized.
- Customer contact about product aspects and printed specifications is maintained to ensure understanding of needs.
- Customer needs are reviewed on a regular basis.
- Customer specifications are up-to-date.
- Customer needs are communicated effectively to others, including shift-to-shift, co-workers, and managers.
- Issues preventing customer needs from being met are addressed proactively.

The Worker-Oriented Component

Each work-oriented component is complemented with a worker-oriented component that identifies the requisite knowledge and skills to perform competently. The NSSB Common Framework divides knowledge and skills into three categories:

- *Academic Knowledge and Skills:* Knowledge and skills associated with the academic disciplines of reading, writing, mathematics, and science.

- *Employability Knowledge and Skills:* Applied knowledge and skills used to perform effectively across a broad range of occupations, such as teamwork, decision making, and problem solving.

- *Occupational and Technical Knowledge and Skills:* The specific technical and occupational knowledge and skills needed for the work, such as engine repair, knowledge of sales methods, or database programming.

The NSSB has established a common language for describing the academic and employability knowledge and skills that transcend subindustries within a sector. Individual voluntary partnerships are responsible for the development of occupational and technical knowledge and skills, which are largely specific to each industry sector.

A Common Language for Knowledge and Skills

The NSSB has identified a common framework for academic and employability knowledge and skills that transcend all concentrations.

1. Academic Knowledge and Skills

The following is a list of the categories of academic knowledge and skills that are part of the NSSB Common Framework:

- Reading
- Writing
- Mathematics
- Science

2. Employability Knowledge and Skills

The following is a list of the categories of employability knowledge and skills that are part of the NSSB Common Framework:

- Listening
- Speaking
- Using information and communications technology

- Gathering and analyzing information
- Analyzing and solving problems
- Making decisions and judgments
- Organizing and planning
- Using social skills
- Adaptability
- Working in teams
- Leading others
- Building consensus
- Self- and career development

3. Occupational and Technical Knowledge and Skills

Occupational and technical knowledge and skills include such things as the use or operation of tools, machines, and equipment. They encompass knowledge of methods or theories, particular products or services, and languages other than English. Occupational and technical knowledge may also include other elements, such as knowledge of computer software programs and applications, general business and industry knowledge, and an understanding of workplace systems, culture, and policies.

Occupational and technical knowledge and skills identified for core and concentration skill standards should apply across all the industries that make up an industry sector. For example, knowledge of safety regulations for the manufacturing industry sector should cover knowledge of safety regulations that are relevant to all industries within the sector (for example, rules that would apply to food manufacturing, automobile manufacturing, and the other manufacturing industries that make up the sector). Knowledge of safety regulations that are unique to food manufacturing, for example, might be covered by the occupational and technical knowledge and skills developed for the specialty skill standards.

Linking the Knowledge and Skills to Critical Work Functions

Using these descriptions of the academic, employability, and occupational and technical knowledge and skills, the voluntary partnerships identify the knowledge and skills needed to perform each critical work function (along with its key activities and performance indicators) in a concentration.

The 2002 Annual: Volume 1, Training/© 2002 John Wiley & Sons, Inc.

To accomplish this objective for each critical work function, the following must be addressed:

- Which of the academic knowledge and skills are needed to perform this critical work function?
- Which of the employability knowledge and skills are needed to perform this critical work function?
- Which of the occupational and technical knowledge and skills are needed to perform this critical work function?

Linking the knowledge and skills at the critical work function level will help users of the skill standards, such as educators, trainers, and those developing assessments based on the standards.

Finally, to enhance the value of the skill standards, the worker-oriented components will provide information on the level of complexity required for each knowledge or skill, along with examples of work that illustrate the different levels. Voluntary partnerships determine the levels of complexity for each critical work function.

SKILL STANDARDS: A TOTAL PACKAGE

National voluntary skill standards offer a rare and powerful combination of information. They describe what an individual needs to know about requirements of the workplace (the work-oriented component), and they describe the knowledge and skills needed to perform competently (the worker-oriented component). Skill standards include both worker- and work-oriented components that enable different groups to use the standards for different purposes. However, the real power of skill standards is the synthesis of both the work-oriented and worker-oriented components.

With work changing so rapidly, employers often need a way to communicate fast-changing business goals and objectives to employees in a way that will result in better performance. Although many companies can clearly articulate their business goals and strategies, they rarely have the tools they need to explain exactly what workers need to be able to do to achieve these goals. Workforce trainers are often called on to communicate employer goals and objectives to workers. Industry skill standards will equip trainers with powerful tools for communicating what employers expect workers to be able to do on the job and link that with the knowledge and skills they will need to meet those expectations.

Workforce trainers have an opportunity to enhance the value of a national skill standards system by bridging the gap between employer demands and worker competencies. Their industry knowledge and ability to communicate with workers will help in upgrading employees' skills and knowledge effectively. Their ability to conduct assessments will aid in the development of comprehensive tools to test workers' knowledge and skills. In return, workforce trainers who incorporate industry-recognized skill standards into their programs will find that employers and workers will utilize their value-added services. In addition, trainers will increase their visibility by helping to lay the foundation for productive partnerships with business and industry in furthering workforce development initiatives throughout the country.

The development of a voluntary national skill standards system will help the U.S. workforce keep pace with today's changing workplace. Workforce trainers have an essential role to perform, helping business and labor come together to realize their goals. Their investment of time and resources through active participation in helping to develop the system, along with those of employers, employees, and educators, will yield beneficial returns to themselves and to the nation.

Reference

Bureau of Labor Statistics. (2000). *Occupational outlook handbook, 2000–01.* Washington, DC: Author.

Eleazar O. Velazquez is a communications specialist with the National Skill Standards Board in Washington, D.C. He provides primary support for the organization's outreach activities and plays a major role in executing its strategic communications plan. Mr. Velazquez holds a master's degree in European studies from the George Washington University in Washington, D.C., and a bachelor's degree in international relations from Claremont McKenna College in Claremont, California.

EMAIL BASICS:
PRACTICAL TIPS TO IMPROVE COMMUNICATION

Kristin J. Arnold

Abstract: Email has the enormous potential for enabling, as well as complicating, the ways we communicate. Lisa Kimball, a pioneer of the virtual team concept, calls email the "pigeon of technology. It's everywhere." Whether you are two feet away or two continents away, email is quickly becoming the standard method for business communication. Whether we share information, query employees, explore possibilities, bounce ideas off of others, or update action items, email is emerging as the prime vehicle for teams to communicate.

Interestingly enough, most companies have not established common "ground rules" to ensure that email is used productively within their organizations, much less when communicating with the outside world. This article is intended to help HR professionals and internal/external consultants set the proper example to use and manage email.

Basic Ground Rules

As you begin to set some standards within your organization, first discuss some of the ground rules for using email, many of which are listed below, as a team. Your team may wholeheartedly agree, violently disagree, agree with reservations, or have its own ground rules to add. The value is in the discussion and the team members' agreement to follow its own email ground rules.

Frequency.   Agree on how often team members will check messages. For example, "If in the office, we agree to check our in-box first thing in the morning, at lunch, and before we leave for the day. While traveling, we agree to check our email at least once a day." Also agree on a reasonable time to respond to incoming email—typically within one working day.

Technological Limitations.   Know each other's technical limitations and capabilities. Some have high-speed access and instant email notification. Others, especially those emailing from home, may have technical limitations that affect how quickly they can receive or respond.

Tolerance.   Be tolerant of your teammates' mistakes. Some are new to using email correctly, so be gracious. Coach them. Support them. Give helpful feedback and suggestions. On the other hand, don't be shy either. Ask others for help, and learn how to use email to its fullest and best potential.

Keyboarding.   Increase your ease with the keyboard. Learn how to type at least fifty words per minute using inexpensive typing tutor programs such as *Mavis Beacon Teaches Typing*. Learn your software's speed keys to navigate quickly through your email program.

Chat Time.   Chatting by email is acceptable as long as both team members agree it's okay *and* it's not against company policies. Agree whether or not instant messaging is okay. Identify specific times to "gather," for example, between 2 and 4 p.m. EST. Otherwise, pick up the phone or go get a cup of coffee to chat.

The 2002 Annual: Volume 1, Training/© 2002 John Wiley & Sons, Inc.

Mix It Up.   Nurture the personal touch that fosters the spirit of teamwork. Send great email along with an occasional hand-written note, a fax, a personal thanks, a phone call, etc. Mix up your media.

Traffic.   Avoid back-and-forth replies such as "thank you" and "okay." You don't have to acknowledge each and every email.

Timely Response.   Get back to teammates when you say you will. Team members will assume the worst if they don't hear from you. Prevent their imaginations from conjuring up wild stories by letting them know you received the email and are still working on it.

Format.   Agree on when it is appropriate to send a "paper copy" versus an email. Do not send a paper copy *and* an email. Agree on how to pass along critical information. Sometimes, email is *not* the preferred medium. Do not hide behind email to say something you should say face-to-face.

Confidential Information.   Agree on what is acceptable and unacceptable information to be passed by email. If you must email confidential information, agree to write "confidential" in the subject line. Otherwise, after multiple replies, the confidentiality will be long-lost or forgotten.

Flaming.   Flame wars destroy teamwork. Don't "flame" another teammate (write a strongly worded, emotionally charged opinion), and avoid *pit-bull* phrases such as "That's a stupid idea" (opinionated declarations); "I'm not about to . . ." (heated denials); and "Why is everyone . . ?" (paranoid remarks). Don't respond to incoming flames by email; otherwise, you will be entering into an "email flame war" where no one emerges victorious. Instead, go face-to-face or pick up the phone.

Urban Legends.   Stop "urban legends" at your desk. These requests to forward letters to help a dying child, save the planet, or support the cause of the day are often unknowingly forwarded by kind-hearted, politically conscious team members. Don't be fooled into thinking it's safe because you know the person sending it. Check out its validity at www.urbanlegend.com.

Policies.   Review your company policy on email and Internet use. Understand that email is about as private as a postcard. You have no right to privacy. Your email lives on long after you have hit the delete button.

Abbreviations.   Agree on common abbreviations (or acronyms), such as *as soon as possible* (ASAP), *for your information* (FYI), *close of business* (COB), *by the way* (BTW), and *in my opinion* (IMO). A good rule of thumb is to only use acronyms common to the English language, your industry, your team product/project, or your organizational culture.

Emoticons.   Emoticons or "smileys" haven't hit mainstream email yet; however, they can help team members distinguish the tone of a message. Discuss the advantages and disadvantages of using emoticons and agree on when and how they should be used effectively.

Distribution Lists.   Ask your system administrator to set up a team distribution list—a "global address" that anyone can use that will automatically send a message to a predetermined list of people.

Attachments.   Agree on attachment specifications such as type and version of software. Include any compression software and settings, if applicable.

Moratoriums.   Periodically, have an "Email Moratorium Day" where team members can use any other medium *except* email for the day. At the end of the day, debrief the process and discuss what worked and what did not. Discover better ways to communicate with one another.

Easy Reading.   Be considerate of others when communicating by email. When writing an email, remember that your email is *one of many other emails* that land in the person's in-box. Make it easy for others to read and respond to your message quickly.

CREATE COGENT MESSAGES

This section gives some pointers on drafting the text; editing the text; attaching a file; addressing the message; and sending the message.

Draft the Text

Write with your teammates in mind. Before you start typing, ask yourself, "What is the purpose of this message?" Anticipate your teammates' questions: Who needs to do what? By when? How will they do it? and Where do they

The 2002 Annual: Volume 1, Training/© 2002 John Wiley & Sons, Inc.

need to be in order to be successful? Be clear about what you want. Be specific. Be brief and concise without being abrupt. Email wasn't intended for carrying on long conversations.

Multiple issues to cover? Write multiple messages. Focus on one subject per message to make it easier for your teammates to respond to each issue and to file the information when done.

Create a specific, concise subject line that will quickly identify the purpose of your email, prioritize the actions needed, and motivate another to open your message. If appropriate, develop standard prefixes for the subject line, for example: *action; FYI; confidential; reply ASAP.* Develop standard subject lines for routine items such as "Team Meeting Fri 12/5 from 3 to 5 in Board Room."

Do not repeat your subject line as the first sentence of the text or anywhere else in the message. Put requests for information, deadlines, and meeting dates at the beginning of your message. Then give the details, explanations, and reasons for your request.

Be polite. Start with the person's name, as you would if you were addressing him or her in person. No need to be formal and start with Sir or Madam. If, on the other hand, you are sending a message to everyone on the team, just start the message. Alternatively, you can begin with "Hi Everyone!" "Hi Folks!" or "Hi Y'All!"

Make it easy for your teammates to answer your email quickly, for example:

1. Write questions and number them for ease of response and

2. Leave blanks for your teammates to respond directly on your original message.

When addressing information or action items to more than one person, start each section with the team member(s)' name(s) followed by the information/tasking *or* identify who is responsible for each action to be taken in bold-face type or capital letters. Otherwise, teammates will assume someone else is taking care of the action.

When emailing an agenda for a meeting, state your purpose, desired outcomes and/or deliverables, location, and start and end times. Provide instructions on what your teammates should bring, what "homework" they should do, and the format for delivery (for example, handouts, transparencies, presentations). Enable your team to be prepared for the team meeting.

End the message with your name or signature line. Don't assume everyone knows you. Your reply address might not clearly identify you. Include the best way to contact you for immediate response or discussion. Add "Thanks" if you're asking for something or just want to say thanks! There is no need for a formal closing, such as "Sincerely."

Once you have established a working relationship, it's okay to simply sign off with your name, for example, "Kristin." No need to keep putting your signature line on every reply—it's probably already in the "thread" of the email conversation.

Keep your signature line simple. Include your email address and the best way to contact you. Don't clog up the system with enormous signature files with motivational quotes, commercials, cartoons, or graphics. A good rule of thumb is no more than four lines of text.

Ideally, an email message should be no longer than the visible screen. If it's longer than a screen, you risk it being skimmed. Don't want to be skimmed? Then edit your message for brevity and clarity.

Edit the Text

After you have drafted your message, reread what you have written. Edit your stream of consciousness prose to make your points clear and concise. The convenience of email does not give you an excuse for poor writing. Pay attention to grammar, punctuation, and spelling.

Make your email easy on the eyeballs. Select a simple, universal font such as Times New Roman or Arial. Avoid cursive fonts. Use a font size everyone can read such as 12 point. UNLOCK YOUR CAPS. DON'T SHOUT AT YOUR TEAMMATES! Only use upper-case words when trying to make a point (the way I just did).

Keep your formatting simple. Just because your software can add colorful backgrounds doesn't mean you have to use them. Special formats add to the message file size and may not look as good on other computer monitors or software systems.

Divide long paragraphs into shorter ones—three to six lines of type. Leave a white space between paragraphs. When listing up to three items, consider creating a "horizontal" list: (1) point one; (2) point two; (3) point three. When listing three or more items, create a "vertical" list:

1. Use numbers (or letters) to enumerate your points.

2. Start with the same word form, such as all verbs (use, start, insert).

3. Insert white space between points.

If you must send a lengthy message, separate sections by using bold-faced or capitalized paragraph headlines or number the sections in separate paragraphs.

Condense your information. Use bullets rather than sentences. Delete irrelevant text. Use one word instead of two or three to express the same idea. Delete parenthetical comments ~~(unless you can't help yourself)~~ and exclamatory comments. ~~Can you believe people actually do that!!!!~~

Make sure the most important information is at the beginning of your message. Summarize the information that will follow in the message.

Stay away from "business speak" clichés, such as "Let's harvest the low-hanging fruit" or "We're not trying to boil the ocean here."

Use active voice rather than passive voice. Use positive words. Avoid *not, no, none, never*. Personalize your messages by using first names and the words *you, your, yours, our, me, my, us, I, we,* etc. When sending a message to the entire team, avoid third-person references, such as *team, them, they*.

Don't rely on your teammates' abilities to tell the difference between serious statements, satire, sarcasm, or double entendres. Avoid using satire and sarcasm altogether *or* use an "emoticon" or "smiley" to convey a specific tone of voice. Use emoticons and acronyms sparingly. Unless everyone on the team is an email junkie, acronyms and smiley faces can be extremely annoying : -).

Be positive. Emphasize what you can do versus what you cannot or are unwilling to do.

Keep the overall message size to under one megabyte (1MB). Should your teammates want more information, put the details in an attachment, post it on a shared hard drive, or embed a link to a website. When sending a website address, always type in the full URL address, such as *http://qpcteam .com*. Most email programs allow the user to click on the URL address and link immediately to the site.

Attach a File

Once you have written your message, you may want to put the details in an attachment or attach relevant documents. In the body of your message, let your teammates know what is in your attachments. It's their choice to open them (or not). Also, it's a nice touch to mention what type and version of software you used to create the attachment.

Try saving your document under a slightly different name. The "old" file has lots of changes, edits, pastes, and adjustments that take up space. When you "save as" to a brand new file, the "new" file is often significantly smaller and faster to send.

Send large attachments with discretion. Everyone may not have a high-speed connection. Consider making large (over 100kB) documents "small" by using alternative file formats, such as Adobe Acrobat® or WinZip®. Call your teammate before sending anything over 500kB, or, as a last resort, fax or mail lengthy documents.

Just because you sent an attachment doesn't mean your teammates were able to open it or that they actually read it. Some people either cannot (or will not) open file attachments. Consider pasting the information directly onto the message after your signature line.

Routinely and frequently scan your system for viruses, especially when receiving or downloading files from other systems. It's damaging (and embarrassing) to send a virus to a teammate.

Address the Message

You have written and edited your message and attached any necessary files. Now it is time to address your message to your teammates as well as others who need to know the information or take action.

■ Send email to *(to:)* those who must take action. Courtesy/carbon copy *(cc:)* those who need to know the information, but don't need to take action or reply. Blind courtesy/carbon copy *(bcc:)* those who need to know the information, don't need to take action, and don't want (or need) anyone else to know that you shared the information with them!

■ Be careful with bcc's. Depending on your email system, those who receive a bcc may not know it was supposed to be blind. On the receivers' end, it appears that the message was sent *to* them. Bcc's should not be used to "get around" others. For example, don't send an email to the team leader's boss asking if you can talk to the team leader about a particular point with a bcc for the team leader!

Send the Message

When you want to send an email to an expanded list (team, department, division, etc.), send the email to yourself and bcc everybody else (this prevents the recipients from seeing—and having to print out—a long list of recipients) *or* consider setting up an email distribution list with all your team members' addresses. Simply send the email *to* the distribution list. Rather than sending bucket loads of information to everybody, ask, "I have this. Do you want it?"

If you aren't sure whether you need to keep everyone informed, add a note at the end of your message: "If you don't want to receive messages on this subject, please let me know."

Follow chain of command procedures for corresponding "up the food chain." Don't send a complaint via email directly to the top just because you can.

Never assume a team member you cc'd actually read and understood your message. If you want to know whether your teammates got the message, include a personal statement asking them to let you know whether they received it or not. Or you can ask for a computerized confirmation by using the "Return Receipt Requested" option. Use this function *only* if you genuinely need to know whether the person received the message. Return receipts bug people for lots of reasons, including email system compatibility and personal privacy issues. So use them sparingly.

Not everyone has email. Make sure those who don't are still kept in the communications loop. Electronically fax the email, or remind yourself to fax/mail them a copy.

Remember where your teammates are physically located. If you send a message, the other person might be home asleep when it arrives.

Help others triage their in-boxes by using the high, normal, low priority feature appropriately. Send messages marked "urgent" or "high priority" sparingly. You don't want to fall into the "boy who cried wolf" syndrome. If it is really urgent, pick up the phone. Most messages should be sent "normal" priority.

Before you hit the "send" button, ask yourself whether you would mind having this email published in the company newsletter or your local newspaper. If your answer is yes, don't send it.

Email also serves as legal documentation. Say only what you mean to say. Would your attorney be able to defend you from your own words?

Use a spelling, punctuation, and grammar checker before you hit the "send" button. Set up a system default to run your "spell checker" when you hit "send." Before you blindly accept "change all," take a look at what you are accepting. Do not rely completely on your spell checker.

Before you hit the "send" button, take one last good look at your message addresses, text, and attachments.

Manage Your In-Box

The typical corporate email user receives over thirty messages a day and spends between one and two hours dealing with these messages. Learn to manage your in-box efficiently so you can realize the benefits of email: It's less formal, quicker, easier, more convenient, and more cost-effective than other forms of communication.

Quit fiddling with email throughout the day. Check your email regularly (perhaps first thing in the morning and right after lunch). Do not allow email to interrupt your day. You don't need to know every single time you've got mail. Control your email; don't let it control you!

Turn off your noisy email alarm. It drives your office mates crazy.

Before you open messages, check your email subject lines while in your in-box/browser. Delete the junk mail. It's the equivalent of standing by the trash can as you go through your "snail mail."

Save a tree. Only print out those emails for which you absolutely need to have a hard copy. When printing out emails for office use only, try "recycling" the unprinted side of used paper.

Handle emails only once. Discipline yourself to DRAFS as many messages as you can: delete; reply; act; forward; save.

Delete

Delete spam, unwanted messages, and incoming "free offers." Nothing is free. Email is a great way for companies to collect information and leave "cookies" (little pieces of software) on your computer.

Delete those messages you won't read or don't have time to read.

If you don't want to receive jokes, chain letters, or other types of "junk" email, politely tell your teammates to delete your name from their distribution lists.

Create a "rule" or "filter" that will automatically delete unwanted email from your in-box.

Reply

Reply within your agreed-on times, even if a brief acknowledgment is all you can manage. Ignoring or postponing responding to a teammate's message is downright rude. When you know your teammates are expecting a reply, but you need more time, send a short "what's happening" message to let others know when you will get back to them.

You are not expected to reply to an FYI or copy to/cc message.

Use threads (a string of responses to a single message) by setting up the "reply" function. You can set up your system to include the sender's message at the beginning or at the end of your reply—usually a matter of preference. Don't forget to edit excess forwarding information that does not relate to the content of the message.

Don't reply to a point in a prior email message without quoting or paraphrasing what you're responding to and who said it. When replying to just one point of a long email, clip and paste the pertinent paragraph only. ">" inserted before text means "you wrote." Try using a different color and size font so that your answers stand out from the original message. Let others know, for example, "See my response in blue."

You can use the "reply all" feature to "brainstorm" a topic, allowing everyone on the team to participate. However, be cautious about using reply all. Do all of the people from the incoming to: and cc: lines need to know?

Unless the matter is really urgent, don't try to reply to a message as soon as it comes in. Generally speaking, people who respond to *every* message within five or ten minutes are paying more attention to their email than to their jobs.

When email has been lobbed back and forth (like a tennis ball) for more than three volleys, it's time to pick up the phone or go face-to-face.

Act

Take immediate action on items that will take less than two minutes, or if they'll take longer than that but you have the time, deal with them on the spot.

Group all messages that will take longer than two minutes into an "action folder." Clean out your action folder when you have time to deal with it appropriately (usually once per day).

Flag your email messages for follow-up actions.

Stop procrastinating. Just take action.

Forward

Forward misdirected emails to the correct address. Don't ever forward spam or chain letter email. Not only are chain letters against the law, but it's tacky to perpetuate them.

When forwarding messages, put your comments at the top of the message.

Email gives us an illusion of privacy, but your email could be forwarded to *anyone*. Do not forward your fellow teammates' mail without permission (or tacit understanding), especially if it may embarrass them. It is all too easy to forward a personal letter to the entire team, division, or company.

When forwarding email, set your email client character width to 70 characters. This keeps your text from getting pushed off the screen with older software that does not have a "word wrap" feature.

Fwd:Fwd:Fwd:Fwd—No one likes to scroll through the numerous names and files to get to the body of the message. More than three "forwards" and you're out!

Save

Develop an orderly filing system for those email messages you wish to save. Create file folders to save your messages. Create subfolders for each process, project, or program your team works on. When saving your messages, re-name them with descriptive titles under a specific subject folder so you can find them later.

Only save messages you think you will need to retrieve at a later date. After all, how many paper files have you ever gone back to?

Create a shared drive or website to post and save team information.

Keep messages remaining in your electronic mailbox to a minimum. If you don't know what to do with it, or don't have time to deal with it, save it to a "temp" folder. Clean out your temp folder at least once a week.

OTHER EMAIL ISSUES

If you can't understand what you're reading, read it again. If you still can't understand the message, pick up the phone and call to clarify.

If a message generates emotions, look again. At first glance, the message might appear offensive. Upon rereading it, you may discover that the sender just used a poor choice of words.

Accept the fact that communication errors are inevitable. When there is a misunderstanding, take the blame. Apologize. Say what you meant more clearly. Then put the incident behind you.

Follow up important email communications with a face-to-face meeting or with a telephone call/conference call with all team members. Sometimes you can explain something better verbally.

When you're away, send an "auto response" message indicating when you will return, or ask a teammate to read your mail for you and respond accordingly (give them a temporary password), or "auto forward" your email to a teammate.

Never give your user ID or password to another person, and don't leave your email account open when you leave your computer. Anyone could sit down at your keyboard and send out a libelous/offensive/embarrassing message under your name.

If managing your email is taking up too much time, bring it up within the team. Review and/or revise your ground rules.

SUMMARY

As you put these techniques into practice, you'll find your email communication will be much more crisp and meaningful. You will be able to respond promptly and with ease, as well as keep your in-box clutter-free.

Kristin J. Arnold, M.B.A., specializes in coaching executives and their leadership, management, and employee teams, particularly in the areas of strategic and business planning, process improvement, decision making, and collaborative problem solving. An accomplished author and editor of several professional articles and books, as well as a featured columnist in The Daily Press, *a Tribune Publishing newspaper, Ms. Arnold is regarded as an expert in team development and process-improvement techniques. With building extraordinary teams as her signature service, she has provided process facilitation, training, and coaching support to both public- and private-sector initiatives.*

THE EFFECTIVE PROTÉGÉ

H.B. Karp

Abstract: Mentoring is fast becoming one of the most useful processes for supporting individual development in the organizational setting. Large amounts of time and organizational resources are being invested in assisting mentors in becoming more effective. Protégés also need some orientation and training as well in order to maximize their abilities to learn and take an active part in the mentor-protégé relationship.

This article presents a training approach that assists the protégé in becoming more proactive in the mentor-protégé working relationship. The need for protégé training is presented, along with a process that supports the protégé's role. Setting objectives, defining roles and responsibilities, and basic skill development are all presented and placed within a suggested training format.

OVERVIEW

The process of mentoring is fast becoming one of the most effective and widely used strategies in the fold of individual development. There are many reasons for this, including the rising costs for traditional training; the untapped wealth of managerial experience that exists outside the formal training function in most organizations; and finally, the Generation X preference for individual attention. These and other changes in organizational life all make mentoring increasingly more relevant.

Mentoring itself has become the focus of a great deal of training. Programs ranging from several hours of orientation to several days of instruction are growing in number as mentoring continues to increase in popularity. Unfortunately, there is a built-in problem that comes with the territory. The relationship between mentor and protégé is, by definition, one of unequal status. Stereotypically, the mentor is the one who is older, wiser, more experienced, more effective, better connected, and the more active partner in the relationship. The protégé is traditionally seen as being young, inexperienced, ambitious, somewhat naive, and mostly passive. It is the mentor who actively leads and teaches, and it is the protégé who passively follows and learns.

There is probably a lot of truth in this stereotype, and there is nothing wrong with this, to some extent. The point is that the more dominant the mentor becomes and the more passively the protégé reacts, the less likelihood there is that the relationship will result in the development of the protégé. This process tends to produce clones, rather than strong, self-confident, individual leaders, which is what the mentoring process is all about.

There is no question that those people who are generous and willing enough to become mentors usually require some training. It is one thing to have the requisite talent, skill, and political savvy needed to be organizationally effective. It is quite another to have the awareness and communication skills needed to be able to pass them along to the colleague whom the mentor has agreed to take under his or her wing. This is mostly what mentor training is about. The more skilled and self-confident the mentor becomes, the greater the likelihood that the protégé will become even more awestruck and passive.

One way to build more equity and interactivity into the mentor-protégé relationship is to provide some training for the protégé as well as for the mentor. The more the protégé can increase his or her activity in the relationship, the higher the probability that the desired outcomes will occur.

PROTÉGÉ TRAINING

An effective protégé-training program has five characteristics:

1. It Is Based on the Mentor Training Program That Is Currently Being Utilized. The goal of the training program is to develop a stronger, more effective relationship between the protégé and the mentor. The easiest way to facilitate this is to provide as much of the content from the mentor's program as feasible, but from the protégé's perspective. For example, if the mentor's program highlights the various roles that a mentor can take, the protégé should also be aware of these so that he or she is more aware of what might be available. Although the mentor is traditionally seen as a giver of sage advice, the role is not merely limited to that. The mentor can also take on the role of trainer, sounding board, coach, counselor, and/or political advisor.

2. It Focuses on the Protégé's Role in the Process. The standard view of the mentor-protégé relationship is that the mentor does all the giving and the protégé does all the receiving. This does not reflect reality because, as in any ongoing, long-term relationship, one person never does all the giving while the other does all the receiving. Furthermore, it provides a poor model for what to expect in forming other relationships as one moves up in the organization.

In the mentor-protégé relationship, the mentor provides the protégé with planned professional development activities, an increased likelihood of success, a better match of the protégé's abilities with the organization's needs, unconditional positive support, and a friend in high places. The protégé, on the other hand, is also in a position to provide the mentor with professional assistance on work projects, an ear in other parts of the organization, and a perspective on the differences in values and perspectives between the mentor's age group and the protégé's.

3. It Provides Training in the Skills Needed to Maximize the Developmental Opportunities in the Relationship. Just as the mentor needs to know how to be a more effective communicator and supporter of individual development, the protégé also has to master certain specific skills needed to facilitate his or her own growth, as well. The most important skill that a protégé needs is that of active listening. Unless the protégé takes an active listening stance, the mentor has no way of knowing whether the guidance being given is understood or even relevant to the protégé. The protégé must not only be willing to listen actively but must know how to do so as well. Specific listening techniques such as attuning, encouraging, restating, reflecting, clarifying, and summarizing are the responsibility of the protégé and are essential to the communication process.

Another set of skills that the protégé needs is understanding the nature and need for political awareness in the organizational setting. Every system has a political structure embedded in its culture. Many organizationally naive people view politics as a sleazy way of getting things done or moving up the organizational ladder. A protégé training program that introduces politics as a positive force and an organizational reality will go a long way in laying the groundwork for the mentor to provide specific information and techniques designed to increase the protégé's effectiveness in the organization.

4. It Forces the Protégé to Become Proactive in His or Her Own Judgment.
The training program gives the protégé the opportunity of viewing his or her role before there is any contact between the protégé and the mentor. It is much more advantageous for the protégé to know what he or she wants before entering the mentoring relationship than it is to simply defer to the views of the mentor. Any differences between their respective viewpoints about what's in the best interest of the protégé can easily be negotiated at the start of the relationship. There is a much higher probability of an authentic collaborative effort when the final objective is negotiated than when it is merely acceded to by the protégé.

One way to increase the probability of this happening is to have the protégé training begin with the "What do I want?" exercise. Step One would be to ask the protégé to write down, in clear, specific terms, three things he or she would like in the short term (within the next three months to six months); three things he or she would like in the intermediate term (six months to a year); and three things he or she would like in the long term (one to three years). Then ask the protégé to write down a list of blocks or personal barriers that are getting in the way of achieving these objectives. Step Two is to ask the protégé to list what additional skills, perspectives, and capacities he or she would need to overcome the blocks and personal barriers.

At the beginning of the relationship, the protégé can share the list of objectives with the mentor to see to what extent they are feasible and attainable. Once objectives are mutually agreed on, finding ways to overcome the list of blocks and personal barriers becomes the basis for setting up a developmental program for the protégé that is highly individualized.

5. It Provides a Boundary Between the Mentor and the Protégé. One of the major objectives of any mentoring program is to have the protégé emerge as a strong, capable, self-confident individual. One risk to this, as alluded to earlier, is that the protégé will try to become like the mentor, rather than seeing the mentor as a separate individual who is willing to provide some guidance. The irony in this is that, the more effective the mentor is, the more likely this is to happen. One way of minimizing this risk is to encourage the mentor and the protégé to negotiate a contract between them at the outset of the relationship. The purpose of the contract, which is composed of the following seven elements, is to define the relationship.

- *The objectives of the mentoring process.* Before any progress can be made, both the mentor and the protégé must be in agreement about what is to be accomplished. Information from the "What do I want?" exercise will be invaluable to this process. The objectives need to be stated as specifically as possible in time-bounded, results-oriented terms. This is the place to check each objective for feasibility and availability. It is also necessary to build in milestones for each objective so that progress can be measured along the way. Finally, once the objectives are clear and agreed on, the mentor and protégé can more realistically state what they would like and what they need from one another in the process of pursuing the objectives.

- *What each person wants from the relationship.* Each party to the relationship has a potential for gain, which needs to be stated in specific terms when possible. For example, the protégé may want guidance, someone he or she can turn to when confused, or the opportunity to make his or her own mistakes when that seems appropriate. The mentor might want to learn specific technical skills that the protégé has or to hear a different view from someone who is younger or has access to different parts of the system. Being clear about what the protégé might be able to do for the mentor helps make the relationship stronger and less disparate in status.

- *Acceptable and unacceptable behaviors.* It is a lot easier to avoid unwanted behaviors than it is to correct them, particularly if they have been repeated. Being clear about what is and what is not wanted from the outset creates a much safer environment for the protégé and alleviates the risk of the protégé offending the mentor and having to be told after the fact. Inappropriate protégé behaviors could include calling the mentor off the job when it is not a clear emergency, dropping in on the mentor unannounced, or "dropping" the mentor's name injudiciously. Some inappropriate mentor behaviors might include insisting that the protégé follow specific advice or inadvertently "gossiping" about the protégé's issues. It is probably more appropriate for the mentor to raise these issues and assure the protégé that they will not occur than it is for the protégé to raise them, given the protégé's lower status position.

- *Handling questions and/or differences of opinion.* A good mentor-protégé relationship is based on questioning. Sometimes the protégé doesn't know how far to take this aspect of the relationship or where the line lies between being seen as an eager learner versus a defiant wise guy. The contract is an excellent place for the mentor to be sure that the protégé knows that differences of opinion between them are healthy and natural and that questioning is welcome at all times. If this is not the case, it becomes *vitally* important for the protégé to know exactly where the line lies.

- *Who is responsible for what.* This concern is probably the most crucial one in getting the mentor-protégé relationship off to a productive start. The first, and most important, aspect is to establish the expectation that the protégé is 100 percent responsible for the choices he or she makes and the mentor is 100 percent responsible for making contact, for example, "You contact me if and when you want guidance; I'll contact you when I want to know how you are progressing." Both parties must sit down at the outset and determine what specific responsibilities are unique to *their* particular relationship.

- *Termination.* All relationships come to an end, and that includes the mentoring relationship. The mentor may feel that he or she can no longer be of assistance to the protégé, and/or the protégé may feel the same way. Either may feel that the protégé is now ready to fly solo or needs mentoring from someone else with different skills. Either may feel that the other has somehow betrayed the relationship or has done something that makes it politically necessary to end the relationship as soon as possible. For whatever reason, there has to be a clear understanding, at the beginning, that the relationship can have a "no fault" termination. It is also wise to establish that the termination will be openly discussed, regardless of who initiates it, so that both parties understand and agree that it is a timely and wise decision.

- *The contract is always negotiable.* This has to be the final codicil of any mentor-protégé relationship. As the protégé becomes more effective, the role of the mentor may change. There has to be open discussion and mutual agreement so that the relationship stays focused on what is happening in the "here and now." The contracting process can be as formal or informal as the mentor desires. The most important thing to keep in mind is that each mentor-protégé working relationship is absolutely unique. There are no contracts that will meet the needs of more than those people who are negotiating it.

ASSUMPTIONS ABOUT THE RELATIONSHIP

Here are a few things to keep in mind about effective mentor-protégé relationships:

- The relationship between the mentor and the protégé is a matter of mutual give-and-take.
- The mentor does not always know what is right or best.
- The protégé takes full responsibility for all decisions that he or she makes.
- The mentor needs to be shown by the protégé how to mentor effectively.
- The mentor's primary role is to help surface options, not make decisions.
- No mentor-protégé relationship is forever.
- The best mentors are not in the protégé's direct chain of command.
- Both roles must be voluntary.
- The mentor's effectiveness is, in part, measured by the protégé's performance.

RISKS AND PITFALLS FOR THE PROTÉGÉ

Being a protégé, like anything else, has a certain number of risks associated with it. It is important that new protégés be aware of things that can go wrong so that, when they do, there won't be any surprises. The following list is a representative sample. These unfortunate results are not destined to happen, by any means, but they could occur—and it is best to be prepared in case they do.

- *Being the object of gossip or jealousy.* There is often a cost that comes with being in a favored position. Being selected to be a protégé may, in some organizations, be perceived as being in a preferred position and therefore be a mark of status. There is little likelihood that peers of the protégé will feel secure or supportive of the individual who is in a preferred situation. This is particularly so among those who are presently not being mentored themselves or among those whose mentor may seem to be less influential.

- *Having a mentor who does not keep commitments.* Even with the best of intentions or the most enthusiastic of beginnings, some mentors are going to be less committed to the mentoring process than others. There is always the risk that the mentor will, over time, allow new priorities to get in the way of the mentoring process. The protégé has to take the responsibility to make sure that his or her needs are being met and, if not, must take the initiative to correct the situation or to find another mentor.

- *Having unreal expectations for promotion.* While being mentored often indicates that a protégé is on the fast track, it rarely implies that he or she is on the "inside" track. Being clear about the difference between being sponsored for a promotion and being mentored is critical in establishing a long-term, mutually supportive relationship. This perspective should definitely be included in any protégé training! Too often, protégés think that a promotion is the next step in the mentoring process, or that promotion is the whole objective to the mentoring process itself, when this is rarely the case.

- *Hitching your wagon to a boulder.* Sometimes a mentor will run afoul of the political system. This can happen in any one of several ways: A mentor can make a mistake that causes his or her boss or the organization embarrassment; a new CEO takes over with his or her own personal favorites; or the "in" group has now suddenly become the "out" group. Regardless of the cause, if the mentor falls into disfavor, there is a reasonably high likelihood that the protégé will also lose favor through association. There is no question that a protégé owes his or her mentor a reasonable degree of loyalty, but there is no implied agreement that the protégé is obligated to "go down with the ship." Loyalty is a reciprocal thing. Should the mentor discover that he or she is experiencing a loss of influence, the ethical move is to cut the protégé loose as soon as possible. Should the mentor fail to do this, the protégé must find a tactful and respectable way to disengage.

SAMPLE FORMAT FOR A MENTORING WORKSHOP*

A brief outline of a four-hour protégé program designed to assist new protégés in working with their respective mentors is presented here. This sample protégé workshop is as much an orientation to the process as it is an attempt to teach skills. In almost all cases, the program will take less time and can accommodate more participants than does a mentor's program.

I. Introduction (35 minutes total)

  A. Ground Rules for Today's Program (15 minutes)
    1. Purpose and objectives of the training
    2. Questions and interruptions are welcome
    3. Shared responsibility for the outcome
    4. The need for active participation
    5. Nuts and bolts (e.g., starting and ending times, etc.)

  B. What Do I Want as a Protégé? (20 minutes)
    1. Exercise: List what is wanted
    2. Exercise: List skills, knowledge, etc., that are needed
    3. Make the point that protégé is not a passive role. The clearer you are about what you want, the easier it is to get it

II. Roles (40 minutes total)

  A. Definitions of Supportive Roles* (10 minutes)

  B. Mentor's Functions (10 minutes)
    1. Trainer
    2. Sounding board
    3. Coach
    4. Counselor
    5. Political advisor
    6. Ask whether participants can think of additional roles.

  C. Protégé's (10 minutes)
    1. Benefits*
    2. Pitfalls

  D. Eight Assumptions About the Mentor-Protégé Relationship*
    (10 minutes)

---

*This article is a follow-up to the author's previous piece, "A Pragmatic Primer for Mentoring," which appeared in the *2000 Annual, Volume 1: Training*. The starred items in this workshop format are discussed in greater length in that previous paper.

III. Skills (1 hour and 15 minutes total)

A. Listening (45 minutes)
1. Input or training film on listening skills
2. Input on active listening
3. Active listening exercise
4. Exercise: Have I Been Listening to You?
   a. Place a "Yes" or a "No" on the flip chart or overhead projector.
   b. Ask participants to identify *specific* behaviors that indicate when you have, or have not, been listening to them

B. Political Awareness (30 minutes)
1. Input on what organizational politics are and the role they play
2. Avoid political pitfalls (exercise optional)

IV. Selecting the Mentor (1 hour and 5 minutes total)

A. What to Look For (20 minutes)
1. Refer back to the "What do I want?" exercises to develop a list of specific areas for support
2. Develop a list of individuals who can mentor you in these areas, or list the areas of expertise that a mentor must have to be a best resource to you

B. Establish a Contract (45 minutes)
1. Why a contract is important
2. The steps in developing a contract
3. Have participants develop a contract

V. Debriefing (15 minutes)

A. Final Questions, Evaluation, and Good-Byes

H.B. Karp, Ph.D., *is presently on the faculty of management of Christopher Newport University in Newport News, Virginia. He also is the owner of Personal Growth Systems, a management-consulting firm in Chesapeake, Virginia. He consults with a variety of Fortune 500 and governmental organizations in the areas of leadership development, team building, conflict management, and executive coaching. He specializes in applying Gestalt theory to issues of individual growth and organizational effectiveness. He is the author of many articles,* Personal Power: An Unorthodox Guide to Success *(Gardner Press, 1995), and* The Change Leader: Using a Gestalt Approach with Work Groups *(Jossey-Bass/ Pfeiffer, 1996), and is a co-author of* The Boomer–Xer Gap: Creating Authentic Teams for High Performance at Work *(Davies Black, in press).*

IMPLEMENTING E-LEARNING

Brooke Broadbent

Abstract: In this article, the author draws from his experience as an e-learning consultant to suggest seventeen steps that are involved in implementing e-learning, defined as using digitized technology in education, training, coaching, and informal learning. E-learning includes self-study, instructor-led, performance support, and informal learning.

INTRODUCTION

Continued growth is forecast for e-learning worldwide, because it offers the advantages of being available at any time, at any place, and on almost any subject. Pundit Brandon Hall predicts it could constitute 50 percent of all training at some point.[1] Forecasters in Europe predict that the use of multimedia training will explode over the next few years, with industry estimates pointing to a major growth in the market to over $13 billion U.S. by 2005.[2] Canadians, who for years have been world leaders in the development of communications technology and distance education, are also catching the e-learning bug. The Conference Board of Canada estimates that 30 percent of Canadians will use learning technologies by 2003, up from the current level of 14 percent.[3]

Money is flowing into e-learning. Investment promoters such as Michael Milken have entered the fray as one of the high-flying co-founders of the Knowledge Universe and unext.com. Spokespersons such as Milken and Hall tell us that the $2 trillion international training and education industry will become a major area of investment. Investors are targeting e-learning worldwide, including Australia.[4] Some entrepreneurs have taken a philanthropic approach. High-tech billionaire Michael Saylor has donated $100 million to start a free online university that he promises will be as good as Harvard.[5] Time will tell where worldwide entrepreneurial and philanthropic drivers will guide e-learning. It will be interesting to watch from the sidelines or, even better, from the middle of the battle. Will you be joining the thousands of other instructors, developers, and managers who embrace e-learning?

---

[1]See *New Research Trends in the E-learning Industry* at www.oracle.com/ebusinessnetwork/elearning_report.html.
[2]Information provided by Ros Sutton of PricewaterhouseCoopers' European Client Training Group.
[3]See *Training Report Newsletter,* April 2000, p. 6.
[4]See http://e-newsletters.internet.com/australia.html.
[5]See "Online Education to Be Free: N. Va. Billionaire Envisions Cyber-U" by Cindy Loose. *Washington Post,* March 15, 2000, page A01.

THREE MAIN DRIVING FORCES

There are three main reasons for the current interest in e-learning:

- The bottom-line focus of modern school and business administrators leads college administrators and training managers to reduce training and education program costs. E-learning costs more to develop initially, but saves on delivery and overhead by reducing capital expenditure for buildings and the costs of travel and accommodation for business training.

- The expanding numbers of mature learners in schools and business are motivated, independent, and focused. They know they must keep learning or they will fall behind. Many are computer literate and ready for the independent study mode of e-learning. Mature students with busy schedules and family responsibilities appreciate the opportunity to study at home or at the office.

- Entrepreneurs look at the forecasts indicating that there will be substantial growth in online learning. E-learning is touted as a gold mine for the entrepreneur with the right product. They want to jump on the bandwagon if it will produce profit for investors.

> It is a luxury to get together in class and see people face-to-face. Especially in my case, because I live four hundred miles from my school. So I love e-learning. With it I can study at home and at the same time be in touch with classmates. —Dave, a doctoral student

WHAT TO DO ABOUT THE PREDICTED GROWTH OF E-LEARNING

Organizations face difficult questions, be they public, private, or not-for-profit. Are you personally ready to be a pioneer who develops, uses, or manages e-learning? What can you, as a learner, instructional designer, instructor, or administrator do to reap the advantages of learning innovations? Are you ready to help open the new frontier?

When organizations are faced with a decision about whether or not to use e-learning, how do they decide? What drives their decisions? Senior management fiat? Or perhaps an influential decision maker read about the latest high-tech equipment or saw an ad in a trade publication and became convinced that all learning materials should be converted to e-learning immediately. Let's hope not! E-learning may not be the right option.

If it does makes sense for your organization to embrace e-learning, you also must decide what type to use: informal, self-paced, instructor led, or knowledge management/performance support tools.

- *Informal* learning typically involves finding relevant information on a website or through an online discussion hosted by a community of practice.

- *Self-paced* learning is typically computer-based training (CBT) or web-based training (WBT), where the learner selects a *time* to learn as well as *what* to learn.

- *Instructor-led* learning may be delivered in any of three ways:

    - An instructor may facilitate an Internet-based discussion;

    - An instructor may speak live to learners over the web; or

    - Content from instructors may be delivered to learners through online videos.

- *Performance support tools* are software programs that are used to help learners perform a task. The "wizards" in software are a form of performance support tool.

Perhaps the best solution to most organizations' needs is a combination of e-learning and classroom learning, a "blended" approach. Whether you are an instructional designer, consultant, instructor, or manager, you can begin to make sound decisions about e-learning for your organization.

Although e-learning has become such a hot topic in the training world, early adopters are finding that it can upset the learning framework that has been established previously. Thus, implementing e-learning can be challenging. Learners have to use new technology. Instructors must learn new approaches. Developers must acquire new tricks of the trade. Managers must acquire new management tools.

Organizations that have successfully implemented e-learning are often eager to talk about the challenges they faced. You can learn from their experiences by attending conference presentations, by reading journal articles, and by reading books. Some of the themes include:

- Implementing e-learning is complex.
- Most organizations are still experimenting with e-learning.
- Organizations are using a variety of approaches for implementing e-learning.
- Implementing e-learning means far more than subscribing to the courses of a service provider.
- Implementing e-learning is about project management, change management, and risk management.

Seventeen elements that must be considered when developing and designing e-learning are listed, with their necessary actions, in the tables below. The items are arranged by order of priority, with the idea that Number 1 must be done before Number 2, and so on. Implementing e-learning won't rival the adrenaline rush of starting a relay race, but there are some similarities: first comes strategy, and then the starter shouts, "On your mark, get ready, get set, go."

RACING STRATEGY

Follow the actions listed in the tables to manage e-learning effectively—and win the race! Before you start, plan for hurdles along the way: perhaps some branches that may trip you, other racers who will slow you down, or a change in the weather. Remain nimble, sharp, and fleet of foot. The seventeen steps are not a rigorous road map through a perilous jungle. Rather, they are meant as a way to adapt to your particular situation. In this race, you can change lanes if necessary.

On Your Mark

Do your homework before launching an e-learning program. Prepare. Clarify the management structures, grasp the context, identify how people learn best, and plug yourself into the latest research about e-learning.

Element	Actions
1. Management	Define structure of coordinating body (i.e., empowered stake-holders who can influence decisions about the implementation of e-learning). Articulate roles and responsibilities. Select champions (i.e., business leaders who are knowledgeable enough about e-learning to explain it to others). Explain management framework to all stakeholders.
2. Context	Identify driving and restraining forces for the acceptance of e-learning. Identify steps needed to attenuate the restraining forces. Explain findings to main stakeholders.
3. Learners	Determine how they learn best. Identify their performance gaps, experiences, and expectations.
4. Research on e-learning	Explore research and anecdotal information to determine how to implement e-learning in your environment successfully. (You can begin your research at http://www.elearninghub.com/resources.html.) Explain findings to main stakeholders.

Get Ready

Do some serious thinking about technology, business case, business model, and evaluation.

Element	Actions
5. Technology	Identify what technology is available, what technology will be needed, and the role of standards such as SCORM (Shareable Courseware Object Reference Model, a set of technical specifications that enables the reuse of e-learning content across multiple environments and products). Develop a relationship with your technical advisors.
6. Business case	Identify the why, what, and how of implementing e-learning in business terms. Provide estimated costs and cost savings. Obtain approval for a phased project.
7. Business model	Select the best model or models: integrated/decentralized, minimal/optimal, make/buy, independent/co-operative, national/international.
8. Evaluation	Develop an evaluation strategy, instruments, and reports. Determine how evaluation results will be used with each step.

Get Set

As you slip into the starting blocks, concentrate on communication, administration, content, and methodologies.

Element	Actions
9. Communication	Identify who communicates to whom, how, what, and when. Identify what questions people have about e-learning. Build a change management strategy to answer people's questions about the new initiative.
10. Administration	Decide how participants will select, sign up, and pay for their courses. Decide whether a learning management system (LMS) is required to manage the training; if so, select the best one for your needs.
11. Content	Identify what needs to be taught and developed internally and externally.
12. Methodologies	Based on information collected above, select training methodologies. Identify extent of blending of conventional and e-learning. Select from four types of e-learning (informal, self-directed, instructor-led, and performance support tools).

Go

Bang! The race has started. You still have important work to do associated with human resources, selecting a starting point, implementing, evaluating, and constantly re-jigging your approaches.

Element	Actions
13. Human resources	Identify roles of instructors, developers, and administrators. Select and train them.
14. Starting point	Identify which topics are best to teach at the beginning in order to foster high levels of usage, understanding, and buy-in. There is an opportunity here to do something innovative. Follow the pain; find a topic that is not taught now and that can be learned successfully with e-learning.
15. Implement	Launch cautiously. Communicate extensively with all users: learners, supervisors, instructors, and administrators.

Table continued on next page

Element	Actions
16. Evaluate	Conduct an evaluation with solid data and soft data from stories.
17. Re-jig	Continually review progress and revise items above as required.

Winning

If you are competent, healthy, and mentally prepared, you will run a good race. Watch for hazards. Keep your concentration. Pace yourself. Remember, you are running a relay race. You are not alone. Be careful about passing the baton. Collaborate carefully. Foster partnerships. Support your teammates before, during, and after the race.

CONCLUSION

For the next few years, it looks as though many of us will be like Dorothy in the *Wizard of Oz,* trying to follow the yellow brick road to e-learning. The reward at the end of the road should be learning—for individual development, for better job performance, and for the common good. Learning propels us forward as workers, societies, and humanity. Emerald City does not hold the answer. Wizards won't help us find learning's Holy Grail either. We need people who take learners and e-learning back to Kansas, to simple things. To the nurturing of Auntie Em. The fun of Toto. The caring of the farm hands. The determination, honesty, and good sense of Dorothy. Learners, instructors, developers, and administrators need to work to make e-learning effective. Like the Straw Man, the Tin Man, and the Lion, we must rediscover our brains, our hearts, and our courage: brains to think critically about e-learning; hearts to seek the right approach to e-learning; courage to take a stand for the right thing. I hope the seventeen steps help you find Kansas—and happiness—in your own back yard.

Brooke Broadbent is the founder of e-LearningHub. He is a frequent contributor to training publications and a popular conference speaker.

THE RHYME AND REASON
OF IMPROVEMENT AND INNOVATION

Mark W. Smith, with comment by George Land

Abstract: Improvement or innovation? Both are types of change, but which is better? The authors argue in this article that the issue is not which is better, but when each is most appropriate. Using Land and Jarman's (1992) Breakpoint Theory and Deming's (1986) Four Cornerstones of Quality, the authors endeavor to show that recognizing where your organization is in its development is key to determining the appropriate type of change.

Innovation and improvement. One is a part of the other. One is better than the other. They're both the same thing. You can't do both. You must do both.

In the immortal words of Charlie Brown, "AAUUGGHHH!!!"

CHOOSING IMPROVEMENT OR INNOVATION

As is the case with many of the concepts in the realm of quality, clarity and confusion often reside side by side. In the early days of the introduction of quality principles in most industries, two key concepts emerged as important activities: improvement and innovation. Both were said to be important, but they were also said to be distinctly different. Most dictionaries define "improvement" as some degree of betterment of the existing state or method, while "innovation" is said to be a wholesale reinvention—the introduction of something brand new.

Many organizations have struggled with the issue of how to hold these two concepts together in such a way as to complement one another, rather than one being "better" than the other. It is our feeling that it is, in fact, a fallacy to say that innovation is better than improvement. Such an unconditional statement causes more harm than good and is simply not true. The point is not *which* approach is better—it is *when* one is better or, more correctly, more appropriate than the other.

It may be an overly simplistic way of framing the issue, but the premise of this article is to provide a model of organizational change that answers the question, "When should we improve, and when should we innovate?"

Which Is What?

The idea of innovation is not new. Dr. W. Edwards Deming spoke to the need to move beyond merely improving existing processes in the 1950s. In his early model, The Four Cornerstones of Quality (Deming, 1986), he presented the following four elements related to quality:

1. Improvement of product.

2. Improvement of process.

3. Innovation of product.

4. Innovation of process.

If an organization were truly to be about the business of continuous quality improvement, according to Deming it ought to be focused on all of these activities. He presented the model as a hierarchy, with the last activity being the most powerful, but not necessarily the most important. That is, the activities aimed at improvement are necessary, but not sufficient. They could be said to be the foundations upon which innovation occurs. By viewing this model as a hierarchy, one can see the point of the phrase, "Not just doing things better, but doing better things." Paraphrasing Dr. Deming, "It is not enough to merely improve. A satisfied customer may switch. He who innovates will capture the market." Again, without meaning to be redundant, it is not about which activity is better or more important than the other. The issue really is about *when* one is more appropriate than the other.

For the purposes of this article, "improvement" will mean the incremental increase in performance of the existing methods of doing work; the fundamental design elements (or assumptions) are not challenged. "Innovation" will be defined as the complete reinvention of the work without regard to the existing present. Perhaps a concrete example will help.

FROM THE PONY EXPRESS FORWARD

For many years, if one wanted to send a letter or document across the country, one relied on first the Pony Express and, more recently, the U.S. Postal Service. The Postal Service actually still does the *exact same thing* as the Pony Express: It physically moves your letter to its intended recipient. Technology has progressed, obviously, and planes and trucks have replaced horses and riders, but it is still essentially the same process with the same basic assumption: Physically transporting the document itself is what is required.

In the early 1970s a small enterprise sprang up in Memphis that moved the delivery process further still. FedEx took the methods of the Postal Service to an even higher level of performance, and even though some of the ideas that came up were themselves radical in nature, *the fundamental assumption was not challenged*. Despite the fact that they do it faster, FedEx (and every other overnight delivery service) still does the same thing that the Postal Service does: They physically transport your document or parcel to its intended recipient.

The innovation in document delivery came about only when someone challenged the fundamental assumption regarding physical transportation. Once it became clear that physically moving the paper was not really what the customer wanted, all things became possible. Once it became clear that the *information* on the paper was what the customer truly needed, entirely new ways of meeting the need became possible. Thus, the birth of the facsimile machine. But the process of evolution didn't stop there. Compare the fax technology available today to that of the earliest models and look at the vast improvement in almost all aspects of the device! And today, as the pace of change continues to accelerate, email has all but eclipsed the fax machine as a primary mode of information delivery.

Looking back from the fax to the Pony Express, you can see a clear journey. It was a journey of improvement and innovation coupled together, each building on the past successes of the other. Ask yourself this: What would have happened if, at the birth of the fax machine, its inventor(s) did not settle down with their newfound product, but rather discarded the idea and kept on experimenting? We would not have had the chance to improve and expand the technology, and the worldwide impact of fax technology might never have been made. The point is this: There ought to be—and there is—a rhyme and reason of improvement and innovation. We have learned a way of understanding when to improve an existing design and when it's best to seek radical reinvention. In order to explain these ideas, a little background information on the change process itself is necessary.

BREAKPOINT CHANGE

Over forty years of empirical research into general systems, planning, and the natural sciences has revealed that there is, in fact, an ordered process of change itself. Once thought to be random, chaotic, and perhaps unnatural, we now know that change itself is a natural process that has followed the same pattern literally since the dawn of time. This theory of change, called the Breakpoint or Transformation Life-Cycle Theory of Change (Land & Jarman, 1992), has been found to operate in all systems, whether they be organic ecosystems or manmade businesses. Understanding how this change process operates and determining where your organization is in the process is key for untangling the "improve versus innovate" dilemma. Briefly, the theory describes the change process as one with three distinct phases: forming, extending, and fulfilling (see Figure 1).

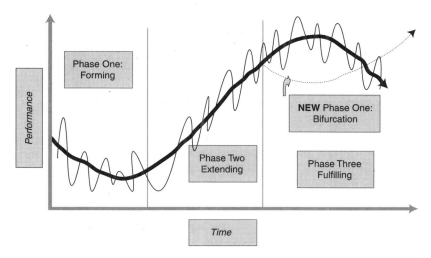

Phase One:
Forming

NEW Phase One:
Bifurcation

Phase Two
Extending

Phase Three
Fulfilling

Performance

Time

Figure 1.   The Rhyme and Reason of Improvement and Innovation

The *forming* phase is literally that—the birth of a new system. For a business, this is analogous to the classic start-up phase. When a new business is formed, the successful leaders experiment with all manner of ideas, imaginatively probing the environment, trying to learn everything possible. Failures are frequent, but not dwelt on. The *only* aim is to *find what works.* It may be in terms of an internal process, or customer demands, or market expectations, but it is always about "what works."

Phase One is a terrifying and exhilarating time, and the key to navigating this phase successfully is to be focused on rapid experimentation and innovation. The key to understanding all the experimentation and innovation is to focus on the future. Guided by its own compelling vision of success, the successful Phase One organization, if persistent, eventually finds its pattern—what works. At this point—what we call a break point—the rules governing success literally shift 180 degrees.

Extending the pattern is the challenge in Phase Two; in other words, the organization now must move from finding what works to *using what works.* To be successful in Phase Two, believe it or not, the wild experimentation and creative innovation must cease! This may sound crazy, but think about it: If you found the pattern, found what works, and instead of putting it to work, you discarded it and kept on experimenting, what would happen? While it may not lead to complete failure, the chances of success seem rather small.

Go back to the example of the fax machine and look at the improvements layered on the original innovation itself. That's what we mean by shifting 180 degrees: The emphasis shifts from innovating to improving. The successful strategies in a Phase Two business are those that protect the pattern, find ways to improve it, and reduce variation around the best methods that are found to work. This is sometimes referred to as "growth through limitation." Creative and imaginative ideas aren't necessarily discouraged, but the wild and divergent innovations for innovation's sake are not sought. Incremental improvements and refinements can and must continue. As was said before, it's a matter of emphasis. In Phase Two, success flows to those who seek incremental improvement.

The second phase breakpoint occurs when the pattern exhausts itself. In nature, this means the fuel needed to continue the pattern may literally be exhausted. In business, it may mean that advances in technology, or changing customer needs, or a competitor's offerings translate to less and less market share for your offerings. What once worked will work no longer—or at least won't work as well or, to put it differently, you must remember that "Nothing fails like success!" Another fundamental shift is required to move to Phase Three.

In the *fulfilling* phase, the innovation so prevalent in Phase One returns. What was once excluded is now tried anew: The system is "opened up" to the new and different. Creative ideas are actively sought, and experimentation is again emphasized. The challenge in Phase Three is to *find what works better*. Incremental improvements to the basic pattern will no longer be sufficient and, if followed, might well lead to gradual deterioration and death. The only way to keep the pattern alive is to emphasize innovation. The technology behind the fax machine may well be at this phase, and the next generation of computing technology, for example, email, has already all but replaced the fax machine.

Another type of innovation occurs in Phase Three, and even though this article is not about the theory itself, a brief amount of attention is needed here in order to completely apply this way of thinking to the improve versus innovate question. Referring again to Figure 1, note a separate curve forming in Phase Three. This is called *bifurcation*. Recalling that bifurcation is simply a fancy word for a split, in business this phenomenon represents an entirely new product line emerging, separate from the original pattern. It may be a new delivery method or entirely new approaches to financing. Whatever the case, the bifurcation represents a *new* Phase One, which will necessarily lead to Phase Two, and Phase Three, and so on. And in this bifurcation, the Phase One rules for success reappear and then shift to

Phase Two. And so on. And so on. In this model, then, there doesn't have to be a "death" of any product or service or business. By understanding the bifurcation as a chance for reinvention, a system can be reborn again and again. To apply the power of both improvement and innovation successfully, these shifts must be understood. It is analogous to learning how to navigate a four-way intersection with a traffic light. When the light shines green, you go. When it's red, you stop. Mix your responses to the environment, and you invite disaster. Improvement and innovation are no different. It's a matter of understanding where you are in the organization's life cycle and responding accordingly.

STEPPING BACK FOR THE BROADER VIEW

Change is a natural evolutionary process. The big question for organizations is "What kind of change?" Are we creating a new pattern, improving an existing pattern, or integrating something very new and different? The first two kinds of change are understood relatively well; the third kind—innovating—is less understood. It requires a profound understanding of the fundamental purpose of the enterprise. In the example used here, this understanding led to seeing the need to convey information, not necessarily documents, and led to many new possibilities. Just as railroads did not examine their deep purpose, many organizations become locked into perceptual boxes—invisible straightjackets that limit their futures. Probe, probe, probe. If necessary, exhume the original purpose that drove the business at the beginning and examine it under the light of today. Is the issue "better soap" or possibly "clean clothes"?

The health care "business," for example, may require fundamental rethinking. What is "health"? Is it defined differently today than previously? Does it mean longer life or perhaps a higher or different quality of life? What do customers really desire from those who would be their trusted advisors serving their health needs? Is it simply physical and/or mental? Or might it include family and relationship life, social life, and spiritual life? Certainly "wellness" concepts represented an improvement in the old pattern of health care, but the innovation difference will only be seen in those who dig down to unearth the deepest needs of total health. The same challenges are faced by all industries at some point in their life cycles. Today, what business are oil companies really in? Oil? Or energy in general? What about banks? Are they merely places to stash your cash?

Given the constant change that is now commonplace in the business world, it is more important than ever that organizations take a hard look at their products and processes to ensure that they can continue to survive in the future.

References

Deming, W.E. (1986). *Out of the crisis.* Cambridge, MA: MIT Press.

Land, G., & Jarman, B. (1992). *Breakpoint and beyond.* New York: Harper Business.

Mark W. Smith *is the founder and president of Helix Associates and an associate partner with Leadership 2000. In this role he collaborates often with Dr. Land and the Leadership 2000 network of associate partners around the world in their efforts to facilitate creative change and strategic thinking.*

George Land, D.Sc., Ph.D., *the CEO of Leadership 2000, is a general systems scientist and the originator of the Transformation Life-Cycle Theory of Change. He has served as an advisor to over two hundred major organizations in the United States and abroad. He invented the first computer-assisted group creative collaboration systems now in use worldwide. He is listed in* Who's Who in America *and* Who's Who in the World.

PLANTING THE SEEDS AND CULTIVATING THE NEW WORKFORCE

Harriet Cohen, David B. Johnson, and Debbie Newman

Abstract: How can employers attract enthusiastic workers, create a highly motivated and well-performing workforce, develop service-minded and technologically savvy applicant pools, and improve their organizations' presence in the community? In an effort to retain their competitive edge in the global marketplace, the Los Angeles World Airports (LAWA) created the GATEWAYS Model by forming strategic alliances with external consultants, corporate partners, educators, and students to achieve these outcomes and more. GATEWAYS created a model to facilitate business access to a qualified applicant pool for entry-level jobs that provide interns with good career and growth potential.

Introduction

To quote the poet Robert Frost: "Two roads diverged in a wood and I took the one less traveled by and that has made all the difference."

Many businesses at Los Angeles World Airports (LAWA) have chosen to take the road less traveled. Are they being purely altruistic when they agree to partner with educators as part of the GATEWAYS collaborative partnership? Or have they recognized that to have the well-trained workers they need they must actively sow the seeds that will produce those workers?

LAWA'S local, national, and international businesses partner with consultants and educators to identify the performance objectives they deem necessary to produce highly qualified new employees. Then educators refine their programs to incorporate these performance objectives, recognizing that, as new employees develop, they need a combination of knowledge and skills. As plants need water and nutrients, so too do new workers need a performance-based education and on-the-job training. As plants grow and flourish, at harvest their growth is benchmarked and measured. Students too grow their skills, which are benchmarked and measured using real-time performance standards and guidelines.

After the first six months of performance-based education, students are ready to be assessed against performance objectives and criteria used by many LAWA employers for entry-level workers. LAWA employers have been trained to work with interns using performance measures. Periodic evaluations are completed, and the on-the-job training and classroom instruction are adjusted to reflect what the interns need. Finally, it is time to harvest what has been sown.

Working with educators to teach skills and behaviors that are desired by employers, as in the GATEWAYS Model, produces a harvest of new employees who can make a strong contribution to the workplace. When businesses choose the road that leads to partnering with schools to grow interns, they may discover this road yields a crop of better qualified applicants.

This article will describe how employers and educators can create their own collaborative for workforce development.

Background of the GATEWAYS Model

Los Angeles World Airports (LAWA) is a municipal department of the City of Los Angeles, responsible for managing the Los Angeles International Airport (LAX), which is unquestionably one of the most significant economic forces in the Southern California region. With an estimated annual financial impact of $43.5 billion, LAX is the gateway to over sixty-one million annual passengers from the Pacific Rim and other world regions. Direct employment at LAX includes approximately 59,000 employees at LAX, with an additional 150,000 jobs generated in the City of Los Angeles and neighboring cities. One in twenty jobs in Southern California is related to LAX operations.

It is projected that by the year 2015 an additional 60,000 airport-related jobs will be developed. These activities require the training of a workforce able to provide the leadership and technical skills necessary to maintain and grow LAX's economic promise.

The GATEWAYS Internship Program was developed as one of several approaches to address the current and projected demand for qualified employees to fill positions at LAX. The pilot for the program was launched in July 1998 as a collaborative initiative among LAX employers and local school districts. GATEWAYS can serve as a model for other communities to help today's youth find employment and to help employers find qualified and motivated employees.

There are three primary roles necessary to establish a successful collaborative: industry leader, educator, and employer.

Industry Leader. In the GATEWAYS Model, LAWA is strategically positioned to act as a sponsoring employer. It serves as the liaison between participating employers and educators and provides overall project management and coordination. While LAWA underwrites the GATEWAYS internships, it is not necessary for the industry leader to provide this kind of funding for such a model to be successful.

The program manager should have experience with issues including recruitment, interviewing for employment, skills development, training, and other staffing activities in the workplace. Human resources professionals may be well-suited for overseeing this type of project.

Ideally, an employer will act as a sponsoring agency, but there are other options. For example, federally funded Workforce Investment Boards may be able to manage job development and training programs like GATEWAYS. Most major cities have applied for federal funds and have established agencies for workforce development. The GATEWAYS program brings together several federal- and state-funded agencies in the Los Angeles area to assist with implementation and coordination. However, using these agencies as the primary sponsor may place additional restrictions on the criteria and methods used to measure outcomes due to government-imposed guidelines. These guidelines may be adversely restrictive and limit program accessibility to the majority of students.

Because the GATEWAYS Model is independently funded, it permits employers to determine measurable outcomes to meet "real world" employment needs and to determine eligibility requirements for student participation.

Educator. The involvement of local schools is critical. They have primary access to potential program participants and may already have established business curriculums. Leveraging resources from existing school programs minimizes the amount of fund raising needed and may improve access to qualified instructors. Schools also have school-to-career counselors assigned to develop job opportunities for students. A GATEWAYS-type program could help them satisfy their placement goals by providing opportunities and resources. Educators receive a curriculum guide that identifies performance objectives of participating employers; they use the guide to develop classroom training.

School curriculum should be developed with the following goals in mind:

- To train students/interns to perform to employer industry standards;
- To relate and apply academic learning to the world of work; and
- To develop training that has outcomes that are behavioral.

Employer. The employer is, of course, a key component to the collaboration. Employers will provide the jobs and the on-the-job training. The goal of a GATEWAYS-type program is to create opportunities for students to become aware of viable career paths. Employers are encouraged to consider interns for regular employment by the end of their internships.

Do's and Don'ts of Establishing a Collaborative Partnership

Table 1 shows a summary of lessons learned during the first three years of the GATEWAYS program.

Do's	Don'ts
DO focus your purpose and interview potential stakeholders to form a vision and mission.	DON'T pre-establish methods to accomplish your purpose without input from fellow stakeholders.
DO identify organizations with similar goals. They are likely to have funds targeted toward these types of projects and funding for events, materials, and staffing. Overall project implementation is less likely to become an issue.	DON'T define organizations as competitors.
DO meet with organizations individually to explain your purpose and concept. This will give you a feel for how each organization can benefit from participating in your program. It will also allow you to identify good partners for a strong collaboration that works in a cooperative manner.	DON'T limit your resources by geography or try to rewrite an organization's mission by over-selling them on the idea that they should participate. This will only come back to haunt you if and when the going gets tough. Each organization should be trusted to know whether this type of program is in line with its goals.
DO form a collaboration of organizations willing to participate and commit resources to the project.	DON'T establish an elitist group of non-worker bees. Implementers, not just decision makers, should be included in the collaboration.
DO identify roles and responsibilities in collaborative partner meetings to obtain buy-in from implementers. Implementers will define the methods to accomplish the goals.	DON'T start with too many stakeholders. This can slow the process of achieving consensus.
DO continually identify ways to participate in each organization's events, programs, boards, or associations. Share information and resources that benefit collaborative partner clients.	DON'T hide resources from collaborative partners. This will only embitter your partners and they will give less and less to the project.

GATEWAYS IN ACTION

Table 2 is an example of a possible implementation timetable.

Time Frame	Training Component	Delivery Resources
February to June '01	Pre-employment activities: • Tests of Adult Basic Education (TABE) Assessment/ Secretary's Commission on Achieving Necessary Skills (SCANS) Employability Skills Testing • Classroom training for resume writing, interviewing, career search, and basic intern skills in customer service and administration	• Junior Achievement • Community-based agencies • Work experience • Workforce Investment Act programs • Educational institutions
July '01	• Students are interviewed and hired as interns	• Internships with participating employers
July–August '01	• On-the-job training (paid employment up to 400 full-time work hours) • Supplemental classroom training regarding career exploration and skill development	• Employers • Educators
September–June '02	• On-the-job training (paid employment up to 20 part-time work hours per week) supplemented with concurrent classroom and on-the-job training and performance appraisals • Classroom training regarding career exploration and skill development	• Employers • Educators

The 2002 Annual: Volume 1, Training/© 2002 John Wiley & Sons, Inc.

WHO IS THIS NEW WORKFORCE?

More than likely, a first-time worker entering the marketplace through a GATEWAYS-type program will be between 16 and 21 years of age. If that 16-to-21 year old was born between 1980 and 1985, this young person will probably not know how to make popcorn without a microwave, consider a pager or cell phone "basic equipment," and has never known life without MTV, AIDS, legal abortion, Disneyland, fax machines, answering machines, copy machines, and personal computers.

Members of this generation have probably never used a manual type-writer, a mimeograph machine, carbon paper, a record player, or a card-based library index system. They have probably never had a polio shot, played Pac Man, seen an 8-track tape player, or paid less than 32 cents for a postage stamp. For this generation, TV sets have always had more than thirteen channels, have always been in color, have always been controlled by a remote, and have always had cable. Roller skating has always been "in line," and Jay Leno has always hosted the *Tonight Show.*

This so-called "Nexter" generation grew up with *Sesame Street,* Barney, and the Teenage Mutant Ninja Turtles. They consider the Kennedy years, Watergate, and the Vietnam War as "ancient" as WWI, Abraham Lincoln, and George Washington. This generation was prepubescent when the Berlin Wall came tumbling down, when the Exxon Valdez spilled oil, during the Persian Gulf War, and at the time of the Challenger space disaster. On the other hand, they are all too familiar with the Columbine High School massacre, the Oklahoma City bombing, the Clinton/Lewinsky scandal, and "pregnant chads."

This is a generation of young people who have been dealing with issues of diversity, hate crimes, drugs, and violence since elementary school. They are likely to have been raised in blended, single-parent, multi-cultural families, and many were latchkey kids who learned to "supervise" themselves at a very early age. This is a generation characterized by self-reliance and instant gratification.

WHAT EMPLOYERS SHOULD EXPECT FROM FIRST-TIME WORKERS

Developmentally speaking, most young people between the ages of 16 and 20 are working through identity issues. They are appropriately attempting to transition from childhood to young adulthood and are generally concerned with how they appear in the eyes of their peers.

Most young people are preoccupied with dating, school events, learning to drive, working, and preparing for college and the "real world." They want to be taken seriously and seek to express their own individuality. They are reactive to peer pressure and are struggling with their desire for the privileges of adulthood and accepting appropriate responsibility for their own choices.

In unfamiliar environments, like any new employee in the workplace, a young person is likely to need to work through issues of basic trust, autonomy, doubt, initiative, and self-confidence. Throughout these struggles, most young people work hard to "appear" competent and capable, even when they feel confused and unsure.

In the face of all this "growing up," it is important for the astute employer to find ways to provide direction without squelching new workers' creativity, to provide feedback without destroying new workers' confidence, and to provide training without humiliating or shaming new workers.

BUILDING AN EFFECTIVE EMPLOYER/EMPLOYEE RELATIONSHIP WITH A FIRST-TIME WORKER

Understanding, coaching, mentoring, training, clear direction, timely feedback, loads of encouragement, and patience are all requirements of the employer/employee relationship. Without providing all of the aforementioned "services" to the new employee, supervisors of first-time workers should not expect young people to be confident, to be appropriately assertive, to act within limits of authority, to take the initiative, or to assume reasonable responsibility for their choices. "Fitting in" to the workplace culture is likely to be punctuated with many episodes of culture shock and misunderstanding. The adult's world of work is very different from the child's world of school; employers should not "assume" the first-time worker "knows better."

TOOLS TO HELP SUPERVISORS CO-CREATE SUCCESS

Two documents will be of particular value when co-creating a successful first-time work experience for both the employee and the employer—the learning commitment (performance plan) and the report card (performance appraisal).

The Learning Commitment (aka Performance Plan). Exhibit 1 is a sample of a learning commitment used in the GATEWAYS program. This successful program is based on the assumption that first-time workers succeed in internship programs when there are collective contributions by educators, curriculum developers, supervisors, etc. In the example, the respective commitments of primary stakeholders are documented, and the new worker is able to see that success is a "group" project and that he or she is not in it alone.

Internship Program
Stakeholder Commitment
(The Keys to Success)

The purpose of this document is to record the commitments of stakeholders to the Gateways Internship Program (the Program) to prepare interns to achieve on-the-job performance expectations as defined in the attached *Classroom Curriculum Development Guide for Aviation Industry Performance Objectives* (the Guide).

Stakeholder Commitment	*Approved and Agreed*
The Curriculum Developer will:	
⊘	*Date:* _____
⊘	*Signature:* _____
⊘	*Print Name:* _____
The Educator will:	
⊘	*Date:* _____
⊘	*Signature:* _____
⊘	*Print Name:* _____
The Program Supervisor will:	
⊘	*Date:* _____
⊘	*Signature:* _____
⊘	*Print Name:* _____
The Intern will:	
⊘	*Date:* _____
⊘	*Signature:* _____
⊘	*Print Name:* _____

Exhibit 1. Sample Learning Commitment

The Report Card (aka Performance Appraisal). Feedback should be directly linked to the performance requirements included in a learning commitment. Feedback should be delivered frequently during the first year on the job. Ideally, for a first-time worker, feedback meetings should be completed every week for the first four to six weeks, then every month for the next three to six months, and quarterly thereafter.

By the way, feedback needs to go both ways. The first-time worker should be given the opportunity to assess his or her own performance against measurable behavioral criteria. In addition, the worker should be asked to assess the performance of the other stakeholders who have committed themselves to assist in the worker's on-the-job success.

It is not the purpose of this article to focus on the theory and practice of performance management, nor is it the purpose of this article to debate the pros and cons of the performance appraisal process and its efficacy in performance improvement in the workplace. Suffice it to say that, for many reasons, employer and employee alike often dread appraisals of performance. When it comes to assessing performance of a first-time worker, it is very important to make every effort to understand the worker's performance from the worker's own perspective and to gather input from stakeholders as defined in the learning commitment. Only after understanding how the worker sees his or her performance can the supervisor respectfully clarify and refine expectations of workplace behavior, mobilize resources to assure continued worker success, and, most important of all, build worker morale and confidence.

FROM KNOWLEDGE-BASED TO PERFORMANCE-BASED CURRICULUM

Over the years, managers and supervisors have expressed disappointment and concern about the lack of job readiness of entry-level employees. Now, in the current economy, there are fewer qualified applicants. To grow a larger qualified applicant pool, employers essentially have two choices: (1) They can hire an underqualified worker and rely on the services of educational management organizations (EMO) to train the new worker, or (2) they can proactively work directly with the schools to grow qualified applicants. The GATEWAYS program promotes working with schools in the community to shift from a knowledge-based curriculum to a performance-based curriculum.

GATEWAYS created a win-win situation by identifying behaviors and developing skills that are necessary in the workplace. By design, success in classroom performance results in paid internships—a real incentive for students. Through their proactive efforts, employers save time and money by leveraging community resources to develop a well-trained pool of applicants.

Shifting from a knowledge-based curriculum to a performance-based curriculum requires several specific steps. The first step is recognizing that performance must be measurable and realistic in terms of the performer and the situation.

Employers identify the core competencies they want new employees to bring to the job. These competencies must be described in specific and objective terms to enable teachers to teach to employer-defined objectives and to assure that the students will perform adequately. A typical example involves customer service. The importance of "good customer service" is promoted at all levels of business education, but what does it mean in performance terms? For the GATEWAYS partners, it means that employees will answer all phone calls before the third ring, will identify their own business unit, will state their own names, will deliver a greeting, and will ask the caller how they can be of assistance. This example illustrates clearly defined and measurable performance competencies. An employer could use such competency descriptions to evaluate a worker's performance objectively.

Additional steps in moving from a knowledge-based to a performance-based curriculum are shown in Table 3.

Step	Example
1. Employers identify performance expectations.	The employee will demonstrate exemplary telephone etiquette.
2. Performance expectations are broken down into measurable task components.	The employee will: • Answer all phone calls before the third ring, • Identify his or her own business unit, • Identify him- or herself, • Deliver a greeting, and • Ask the caller how he or she can be of assistance.
3. Task components are analyzed and described in the most basic and fundamental terms.	The employee is able to: • Hear the ringing phone, • Count the number of rings, • Pick up the receiver, and • Verbally respond to the call.
4. Classroom curricula and on-the-job training are designed to prepare students to acquire the knowledge and skills to achieve the performance-based expectations and successfully perform their assigned job.	Materials might include: • Leader/participant guides • Pre-tests • Post-tests • Job aids

CONCLUSION

The GATEWAYS Model facilitates preparation of first-time workers for success in the workplace by partnering employers with educators to prepare students for on-the-job success while providing employers with a qualified applicant pool. This type of innovative collaboration is good for our communities, businesses, and next generation of workers because it proactively cultivates a bumper crop of qualified applicants. Employers are pleased to find cost-effective solutions to staffing shortages. Students earn entry to the world of work and gain on-the-job experience, which promises opportunities for career growth and inspires greater motivation for scholastic achievement. Community-based agencies and educational institutions have access to additional resources produced by collaboration with employers and are better positioned to report higher levels of academic excellence and curriculum efficacy. Properly managed, a GATEWAYS-type collaboration can result in win-win rewards for all stakeholders.

Harriet Cohen, president of Training Solutions, a firm that provides expert outsourced resources, has over twenty years of experience in team dynamics, performance management, strategic planning, marketing, and customer-driven quality. Ms. Cohen has first-hand knowledge of business strategies and procedures that, combined with corporate training and K-12 teaching experience, offer the practical and theoretical information to excel in today's marketplace. A local and national ASTD leader, she was the 1995 ASTD-LA president and the National ASTD West Coast field consultant.

David B. Johnson, a senior manager with Los Angeles World Airports, leads the Jobs and Education Connection Unit for the Small Business and Job Opportunities Division. He holds a bachelor's degree in political science with an emphasis in constitutional law and has played a key role in developing programs for youth and young adults, including the L.A. Youth at Work Limited Internship program, the L.A. Bridges program, and the LAWA GATEWAYS Workforce Development programs.

Debbie Newman, ASTD-LA's 2001 chapter president, is a respected facilitator and diagnostician who helps clients assess and resolve work-related conflict, stress, and derailment. She established Working Relationships, an individual and organizational consulting, coaching, and counseling practice, to help people work better together. An accomplished instructional designer, facilitator, and performance consultant, Ms. Newman's specialties include interventions to promote effective teaming and respectful communication. She designs/implements performance evaluation approaches that honor individuals and inspire performance excellence at work.

ACTION LEARNING AT FINCO: A LEARNING HISTORY

Andy Beaulieu

Abstract: This article details the experiences of an action learning team at a real firm in the financial services industry. The format presents a first-hand account using the actual words of participants, alongside an outsider's commentary about the meaning and implications of the various comments. Called a "learning history," this format helps to guide the reader to the essential learning points, while at the same time encouraging the reader to look closely for additional implications. This article can be used for its content—to learn more about action learning—or for its format—as a tool to document, assess, and explore a critical incident in a firm's history.

INTRODUCTION

Contained on the following pages is a *learning history* about an *action learning team* at FinCo, an actual but disguised leading financial services firm. It is intended for two primary uses:

1. It can be consumed by organizations undergoing or considering an action learning program as a way to encourage dialogue leading to program acceptance and/or adaptation. A suggested process for disseminating the FinCo learning history is outlined below.

2. It can be used as an example of a format for capturing and disseminating learning on any topic in an organization.

Before proceeding, let us define the two terms above that may be new to some readers.

Learning History.   According to its creators, Art Kleiner and MIT's George Roth, a learning history is "a retrospective history of significant events in a company's recent past, described in the voices of people who took part in them" [www.learninghistories.com/what.html#what]. Its purpose is to "create a record that allows people to recognize their own blinders and to see their own point of view in the context of a larger, shared understanding" [www.learninghistories.com/what.html#what]. So, in a way, a learning history is like a case study, but, as its creators point out, with its roots in the "theories, techniques, and skills from social science research, theater, anthropology, oral history, process consultation, and journalism" [www.learninghistories.com/Background.html]. Thus the learning history is well-stocked with anecdotes and actual dialogue.

Another innovation that will be immediately apparent to the reader is the use of a two-column format where the right side documents the participants' views and experience while the left column presents "objective comments" from nonparticipants. These comments are intended to help the reader see some of the themes, issues, and conflicts emerging in the text to the right. They also help the reader to reflect and draw conclusions.

Admittedly, this particular learning history falls short of the 50 to 150 pages suggested by its creators. However, it provides a tool that can be more easily adopted in situations in which resources and potential value are more limited. The process used to generate this particular learning history (data collection and writing) is reviewed below. The process developed by its creators can be learned through manuals and training courses described on the website of Roth and Kleiner's firm, Reflection Learning Associates: www. learninghistories.com.

Action Learning. This term has been applied, often erroneously, to a wide variety of training techniques. Therefore, we offer our own definition: A planned approach to generate learning by placing the learner in nearly the same situation for which the skills are needed. For example, an action learning approach to project management would require the learner to *manage an actual project*. This is distinguished from simulations, which create a "lifelike" situation, and some versions of "experiential learning," which may use an out-of-context experience such as a ropes course to generate learnings to be transferred back to the real-world situation.

DATA COLLECTION

The data for this particular learning history was collected in a variety of ways:

- *First-hand observation.* The author of this learning history was also the program manager and facilitator for action learning at FinCo. While this may arguably place the author in a less-than-objective position, it did provide a first-hand view of the project. This dual role may also reflect the reality of the resource constraints under which learning "mini-histories" may be generated.

- *Program documentation.* The action learning program's launch workshop is fairly well developed, providing such documentation as a participant binder and facilitator notes.

- *Project deliverables.* The launch of an action learning team produces a couple of key artifacts, including a project charter and project plan. The team's final deliverable to management included a presentation and supporting document. Together these provided the "technical/logistical data" that is cited on occasion.

- *Debriefing.* A few weeks after the conclusion of the action learning project, the author conducted a forty-five-minute "lessons learned" debriefing with all project members, using the following three question sets to guide the discussion, capturing the data in summary format on flip charts:

- How would you rate the results (both business and learning results) you achieved on this project? Why did you give it this rating?
- What contributed to your success?
- What may have impeded your success? What would you try differently next time?

- *Additional debriefing.* A few weeks after the debriefing, the author asked whether the team would be willing to take the process a bit further. When they agreed, a two-step process was adopted:

  - Team members all responded to a brief survey instrument consisting of seven questions (some of them with multiple parts). The survey was conducted via email; thus the data were immediately available electronically.

  - Six of the eight team members met a couple of days later for one final discussion of about seventy-five minutes, with four together in one location and the other two on a speaker phone. The session was tape recorded and transcribed.

- *Sponsor interviews.* A day later, the author interviewed the two sponsors of the action learning team. The one-hour interview was captured by the author in long-hand notes.

WRITING THE LEARNING HISTORY

As with many writing tasks, the production of this document took much longer than anticipated. The process is reviewed below.

- *Structuring the sections.* A basic structure was adopted that divided the experience chronologically into phases. At the end, two sections were included to address the two primary objectives of the action learning program: business results and professional development.

- *Approach to writing.* To complete the right-side column, the text of the interviews and survey was literally dumped into the sections described above. After that, the author rearranged text to improve the flow and reduced some (but, intentionally, not all) of the redundant and less relevant commentary. Looking back, a better process would have been to generate a separate "index card" for each data point (a participant comment/quote) and then use a technique such as "affinity diagramming" to create groupings and order from the data. To complete the left-side column, comments were added by the author throughout the process.

- *Time to create final product.* The following times are estimates, and are probably slightly understated.

    - Generate the data: about thirty hours (includes participants and author)

    - Transcribe second debriefing: about twelve hours

    - Compile and edit the document: about fifty hours

    - Second-party editing: about two hours

USING THE LEARNING HISTORY

Depending on one's objectives and the environment, a variety of uses of this learning history may be appropriate:

- Action learning champions may use the document as a basis for a dialogue within the organization about the merits of such a program.

- Action learning program designers may read the document before adapting the approach for their own use.

- New action learning teams may read the document and discuss it during their initial meeting as a way to accelerate their own learning.

- Sponsors of action learning teams may read the document to identify some of the critical success factors they can influence.

- Champions of organizational learning and improvement may use the document as an example of a technique that might help their own organization with its reflection and development.

BACKGROUND

FinCo is a real firm in the financial services industry.* An active "action learning" program at FinCo spawned the team that is profiled below. The program is a part of one FinCo division's management development program. Its key components follow:

- Real business projects to be worked on—part-time—by participants over about a fourteen-week timeframe;

- Project goals stated as bottom-line results actually achieved by the team by implementing its own ideas and changes within the allotted time frame;

- Two or three projects run in parallel, with six to eight team members on each;

- Senior line managers as sponsors for each action learning project;

- A "launch workshop" lead by two facilitators to kick off the project teams;

- Professional development accomplished via individual development objectives selected out of 360-degree feedback delivered at the beginning of the launch workshop and woven into the business project;

- Limited "process coaching" of the project teams by the program facilitators; and

- A "closing workshop" wherein final project presentations are delivered to top management and the program is debriefed.

Although this team was successful in many ways, other action learning teams at FinCo have generated impressive business results (including even higher dollar-value benefits) and substantial professional development for their members.

This document is a somewhat abridged adaptation of the "learning history" format devised by Art Kleiner and George Roth. Their manuscript, *Field Manual for a Historian* (Reflection Learning Associates, 1996) should be considered the definitive source of guidance for producing and using a learning history. A learning history is noted for the following features that will be apparent to the reader:

---

*To maintain anonymity, the name of the firm is disguised as "FinCo," and team members' last names are omitted in favor of descriptive titles: Team Member Mark, Co-Sponsor Kathleen, etc.

- The narrative is divided into a number of sections or "short stories," each introduced with a bold "headline."

- Beneath each headline is an overview of the situation addressed in that section.

- The remainder of the section is presented in two columns. The right-hand column presents the "story line," including detailed anecdotes and quotes from the perspectives of various participants in the event.

- The left-hand column presents objective commentary and questions to help the reader reflect on the narrative, find meaning, and draw conclusions.

- At the end of some of the sections is a chart showing the sequence of activities included in that phase.

Encore

Although a current round of "action learning" at FinCo was already underway, the vice president who had been the program's biggest supporter called in a favor. He wanted to conduct an abbreviated launch workshop (1½ days versus the normal 2½) with just one team (versus two teams in each of the previous three rounds). Facilitator Andy set to work helping Co-Sponsors Don and Kathleen and the selected Action Learning Team Leader, Barb, to prepare by:

- Selecting a date for the launch workshop;

- Selecting team members;

- Refining the charter of the business project to be tackled by the team; and

- Streamlining the launch workshop without losing the essence of the program.

As a result, a team of eight was selected from across two departments and also from across three locations in the United States.

Just prior to the launch workshop used to kick off the project, participants were informed that they had been selected for the program. Below, the participants discuss hearing about being selected and making preparations for attending the launch workshop.

This communication to participants has always presented challenges, with some hearing the news through inadvertent sources, others finding out prior to their own manager knowing, etc.

[Team Member Ann] I was asked to participate because the person who was initially going to participate moved to another department. So I found out a week or so before and really had no idea that it was an action learning team, but thought it was some kind of task force.

The days before the launch meeting were hectic, my team was experiencing a lot of turnover, and I had taken on more people and accounts. I really didn't have time to think about the days ahead.

[Team Member Cristina] I was excited to be a part of the team, as I knew it was a much-needed group just from dealing with many difficult situations myself in CSC that I felt could be improved on. At the same time, I was also a little nervous because of my work load and other projects, teams, et cetera, that I had going on at the time. I had heard some feedback from others on action learning teams who said they had to devote a lot of time to the project and that it was sometimes difficult to do that. Above all, though, I was excited to meet everyone and work on the team.

A second person verifies: There's never a good time for development.

More communication glitches.

[Team Member Peter] I actually found out by surprise when my manager announced I would be a part of it during our quarterly staff meeting. I was unsure of what it was all about, and figured that it would probably be a good opportunity to network with Operations associates.

[Team Member Kanan] I didn't know what to expect and what it was or what it involved. I'd just had major changes to my group; another group was merged with ours and transition issues as well as process changes were ongoing.

The 2002 Annual: Volume 1, Training/© 2002 John Wiley & Sons, Inc.

FinCo has something of a legacy of analysis projects that don't always lead to change.

[Team Leader Barb] Early on, I thought this would just be another effort focused on the same issues we have been tackling for years. However, as I learned more about the program, such as the sponsorship, authority granted to the group, and senior-level endorsement, I knew this is what we needed to get things done.

[Team Member Jon] Honestly, I felt pretty overwhelmed when I was presented with the opportunity. I had a demanding boss at the time, and it created additional short-term stress. Plus, I spoke to other [action learning "alumni"], and two of them said something like, "Well, you are not going to have a lot of time to do your regular job; you are really going to be stuck doing this a lot of your time; you know you have to do a lot of travel" and this and that. At the same time, however, I did feel pretty good about being considered for such an important team. Action learning teams are revered in my satellite location, so an opportunity like this one was a good one.

One participant does a little digging and gets the inside scoop.

[Team Member Mark] My Business Operations Manager asked me if I would be interested in joining the team. Both he and my manager described the team as being very important and very visible. As a result, I was very excited about the team. The launch was coming at a good time because I was looking forward to something new to work on.

Good timing??!!

[Team Leader Barb] The conference call [prior to the launch workshop] helped introduce everyone and help us get to know the facilitator [Andy]. He helped us relax a bit, as he was the only one who had been through this before.

Sequence of Activities During this Phase	
When*	**Activity**
−8 weeks	Decide to launch action learning team(s)
−8 weeks	Select project(s) and sponsor(s)
−7 weeks	Select team leader
−7 weeks	Identify prospective team members
−6 weeks	Communicate/negotiate with direct managers of prospective team members
−6 weeks	Communicate to team members
−5 weeks	Schedule Action Learning Launch Workshop
−5 weeks	Initiate 360-degree feedback process with team leader and members**
−4 weeks	Develop and refine project charter and goal
−2 weeks	Provide charter to team
−2 weeks	Facilitator conducts meeting/conference call with team members
−1 week	Facilitator conducts conference call with managers of team members**
−1 week	Facilitator prepares for launch workshop

*Relative to the launch workshop; thus −3 weeks means three weeks *prior* to launch
**Activities noted with this symbol did *not* occur in this abbreviated round of action learning

The Day Arrives

Before anyone was ready, the day of the launch workshop arrived. The normal 2-½-day launch breaks down to about 60 percent of the time spent on understanding, planning, and negotiating the business project and 40 percent spent on understanding, sharing, and planning the development objectives of the individuals. This abridged launch workshop, lasting 1½ days, consisted of about 80 percent of the time spent on the project and 20 percent on individual development. Below, the team members describe their impressions of the launch workshop.

The 2002 Annual: Volume 1, Training/© 2002 John Wiley & Sons, Inc.

This team included participants from both sides of an interdepartmental issue—thus the initial anxiety and discomfort.

[Team Member Ann] It felt a little uncomfortable at first because everyone came in the room one at a time, and we were all looking at each other and saying "Hi," but I could tell everyone was feeling the same way. No one really knew one another well—or at all in some cases. Throughout the launch workshop, everyone warmed up to one another and it became pretty comfortable. The hands-on approach to teamwork allowed this bond to be established early on.

[Team Member Peter] A bit of tension—maybe out of nervousness, but also the fact that CSC and Operations were in the same room together to discuss "issues." We weren't sure how our protective boundaries would be broken down to work together.

[Team Member Jon] Once I met the group, I felt much better about our team. I had no idea of everyone's backgrounds other than Barb, Cristina, and Peter, so I was tentative coming in. I also had no background or prior meetings with the Operations side of the business, so I wasn't sure what to expect.

"Us . . ."

[Team Member Mark] What stood out for me was how quickly the team came together. I was expecting to have to do a lot of negotiating with the people who had CSC backgrounds.

". . . Them."
Some possible trust issues.

[Team Member Cristina] The launch workshop was interesting. I sometimes felt unsure of some of the things being discussed, possibly stemming from the short time I had been in the department and not really knowing a whole lot about the Operations side at the time.

[Team Member Kanan] A whole lot of information fitted in the short time. Well-organized—a sense of direction throughout the launch as to where the meeting was headed, even though I did not comprehend the whole project.

Cautious. Did not want to step on any toes. Wanted to know the group. I felt drained at times, enthusiastic at others.

[Team Leader Barb] I felt a little apprehensive on the first day. On the second day, the apprehension somewhat faded and was replaced by confidence and enthusiasm. It was such an intense and overwhelming project; however, the facilitator was very calm from the beginning, which set the tone for the whole group.

[Co-Sponsor Don] [Team Leader] Barb was clearly prepared to hit the ground running. Next time I will spend more time with the team leader beforehand so that he or she can be as ready as Barb was.

[Team Member Jon] Because I had little formal project planning background, I remember feeling frustrated when we were covering basics and planning in the first day. I wanted to really dive in and get started and not pay attention to the small details. I had never taken a large project like this and put together a Gantt chart or operated along specific project plan guidelines in the past. I experienced a lot of humility in the first day.

The application of project planning techniques seems to have affected the group's confidence, sense of organization, and teamwork.

[Team Member Peter] The planning was key. At first we had no clue as to what we were responsible for and how. Then, as we started to brainstorm the different opportunities, excitement grew. All of the team-building activities were also key. This helped us understand each other as people, but also as employees and the many hats we all wear.

The president of the division stopping in "unannounced" to emphasize the importance of the program and the project

[Team Member Mark] The launch was a little intimidating with [President] Charlie stopping in.

[Co-Sponsor Don] Going forward, we should always have the president of the division come in at the launch.

and to encourage the team seems to have made a lasting impression.

One of the program's design principles clearly had its desired effect. Projects are supposed to require that the changes actually be implemented and the impact be measured.

[Team Member Jon] When [President] Charlie came and kicked it off, we all knew walking out of there, boy, we really had to get the job done. Charlie basically came and said, "Look, you guys not only need to find what is wrong, but you guys need to fix 20 percent of it." That put us in a completely different mindset.

[From the team's charter] Team's business objective:

> *Implement recommendations that will decrease the time spent on handoffs [between CSC and Operations] by 20 percent (either through eliminating or streamlining the handoff).*

Out of the Frying Pan . . .

After such an intense launch workshop, one could imagine feeling satisfied with the experience and ready to move on to other things. But in this program, the learning is just beginning as the team has about fourteen weeks to complete the project and report back to senior management. And, unlike during the launch workshop itself, the team does not generally receive additional facilitation support. If the facilitator does attend one of the team's meetings, it is to provide "process consulting" and feedback only. As shown below, the team came together against its challenge, but not without significant test of character.

Once again, the requirement to implement generated the need for perseverance—and a great developmental experience.

[Team Member Mark] I think that we got off to a great start. We really had a lot of momentum after the launch. I think that our highlights were collecting data and communicating our efforts. Some low points appeared when we came up with solutions. Many of our solutions were difficult or impossible to implement.

[Team Member Jon] I remember feeling the overwhelming size of this project in the next few weeks. After the communication piece, which went along smoothly, we moved to data collection. That was when we started to see the magnitude of this project. I remember speaking with several of the team members and each of us was like, "Whoa, what are we getting into?" At the same time, it really forced all of us to come together and chip in. We knew there could be no "sitting on the sidelines" and letting others carry the work.

[Co-Sponsor Don] One thing this team did extremely well was implement partial solutions as soon as possible. By implementing as they went, the team members found they could make incremental progress and get early results. They gained confidence, as did the groups they touched. This is one thing I would coach future teams to do: Get through the analysis piece as quickly as possible and start to implement. You learn more from implementing than you do by continuing to gather data and study the situation.

[Team Member Ann] Those of us in Operations were swamped, and the turnover was at a high. Management was tightening procedures, and everyone was taking on more. Some days it was hard to leave my desk, and I found it was hard to work on some of the "to do's" outside of our meetings. The bond between us all became stronger throughout this time frame because we all relied on one another at times for expertise, support, and to maintain sanity.

[Team Member Kanan] We kept attacking issues we came up against and just kept going. I never realized the extent of work accomplished until the end, and I still can't believe

Sponsor Don, a quintessential "Ops guy," has sent four teams into the action learning program. His bias for action shows in this statement.

By design, the action learning project should take about 20 percent of participants' time over the fourteen weeks. However, few participants actually try to free up this capacity in advance.

One convention introduced at the launch workshop is a "check in": Team members take a minute at the beginning of each meeting to describe the things going on in their personal and professional lives. This team maintained that convention throughout their project.

This new team member got help entering the team, even though it was well past its own "forming" stage.

This piece of the sponsor role—influencing for cooperation—is not always well-implemented.

it. We dug in and covered for each other when needed because of just knowing little things about each other.

[Team Member Cristina] I think the team developed rather well. Everyone seemed to get to know each other on somewhat of a personal level, which helped build camaraderie among the group. I think everyone was good about pitching in and helping, but the more we got into it, the more I felt overwhelmed at all we had to do.

[Co-Sponsor Don] The team communicated very well, and team members always clearly explained the implications of their changes: "You gave us feedback about x, so we did y. That means you no longer have to do z." Very effective.

[Team Member Kelly] Because the team was really developed prior to me coming on board [four weeks into the project], I didn't have much input. I must say that everyone was more than helpful in bringing me up to speed on how the group dynamics worked and could not have been any nicer.

[Team Member Ann] I think we thought we were going to have some closed-minded people. We were surprised that it worked out.

[Team Member Jon] Right. It was almost as if some of the people we knew traditionally had been pretty resistant to change had kind of been coached, "Hey look, you need to keep a more open mind; these people are trying to solve your problems." Obviously [President] Charlie and [Co-Sponsors] Kathleen and Don had gotten word out to their respective organizations and said, "Look, we are backing these people. Let's try to find them some

solutions." I do not recall ever having to go around anybody to get anything done.

[Team Leader Barb] I think that it is even more than the sponsors going out, because I think the direct managers went to their groups to say, [Team Member] "Kanan is on this team, we need to represent her, we need to help her and solve some of their problems as they are solving our problems." So I think even the managers took it upon themselves to get out for us in their groups.

[Co-Sponsor Kathleen] The team used us less than I had expected. On the whole, team members came to me after things were already being implemented. I often found out what was going on through the communications they sent to the whole division. We did tell them that they didn't need to run everything by us.

[Co-Sponsor Don] The team members were doing so much communication to the division that they got their guidance from their audience. This kept them from having to run things by us all the time.

But was it really the sponsors' doing—
or perhaps the team's own confidence—
that melted resistance?

	Sequence of Activities During this Phase	
When*	**Activity**	
1 to 3 weeks	Facilitator follows up with participants about their 360-degree feedback**	
1 to 5 weeks	Facilitator attends some of team's meetings as a process coach	
1 to 7 weeks	Team executes first half of project plan	
Periodically	Team updates sponsor(s)	
7 weeks	Mid-project working session (often two days)	

*Relative to the launch workshop; thus 3 weeks means three weeks *following* the launch
**Activities noted with this symbol did *not* occur in this abbreviated round of action learning

Into the Home Stretch

During the last couple of weeks before the final presentation to management, an action learning team can be simply cleaning things up and preparing the final presentation or scrambling to fit in all of its implementation. This team was somewhere in between: Although it had been implementing all along, the measurements needed to understand its bottom-line impact were developing more slowly. Either way, the 20 percent time allotment is generally out the window at this point, with at least some of the team members working overtime to pull things together.

[Team Member Ann] I think everyone felt a lot of pressure. We didn't really know for sure where we stood with meeting our goal. We knew we had to do it, but were nervous while we were putting all the results together. Once we did, we all felt a huge sense of accomplishment because we had no idea we went above and beyond our set target.

Team members were feeling the pressure to be ready in time.

[Team Member Cristina] Nervous is right. There was a lot of work to do, and as time grew closer and closer, I got more and more nervous. Once I traveled out to headquarters for the final presentation and preparation, I felt like I could get more of a handle on what we were planning and so forth. It was hard being in a remote site and trying to work and stay in touch with the rest of the team.

Outside events continued to provide additional stress.

[Team Member Kelly] Things were very hectic in my location, as we had a lot of turnover and chaos. I was feeling pretty overwhelmed, but I knew we would be able to pull the presentation off with all of the hard work we had done.

[Team Member Mark] I was completely swamped before the presentation. I had just been promoted and had many new responsibilities. I had the feeling that the team felt the same

way, and we were really looking forward to wrapping up our work.

[Co-Sponsor Kathleen] I had some concerns about the amount of stress they might have incurred, as there were a lot of personal and professional changes going on during this project. This was a very dedicated group.

[Team Member Peter] I think we spent too much time on minute details, rather than our larger scores and preparing the presentation. A few key players took on the majority responsibility of creating the presentation, binders, hand-outs, et cetera. I saw us staying late, while others didn't volunteer. This was challenging because you didn't want to say anything, but felt like you should. In addition, I had just assumed a promotional role and those respon-sibilities were mounting up as well.

[Team Member Kanan] We were scrambling to get things done. I felt exhausted, but at the same time elated.

[Team Leader Barb] I felt that we had done a lot of work and we had to distill the pertinent pieces to share the results with management. I was feeling like this was the "make or break" of the effort, as I knew we had done every-thing we were challenged to do (and more). I felt a sense of overwhelming strength and determination. My goal was to give our very best shot at the presentation. I knew how hard the team had worked for the results, and I was determined to have them feel a sense of achievement after this period.

[Team Member Jon] A lot of things came to-gether in the last several weeks. Mostly, we were trying to figure out the best way to mea-sure our successes from the projects. We were also wrapping up some loose ends on some

This team may not have developed a full capacity for candor and feedback. This "holding back" very much replicates the larger culture of FinCo.

Here the team leader describes why she felt so committed, and admits to "carrying" things a bit in the final days.

The action learning projects are scoped to be

addressable by a team using 20 percent of its time at work. Clearly, that standard was exceeded during the final days before the management presentation, as this team scrambled to pull everything together.

This team really seemed to laugh together. Besides these, numerous funny stories had to be omitted from the write-up. It was clearly a feature of this team. Could this be just a by-product, or perhaps a more significant contributor? If so, is there any way to replicate this feature by intent?

outstanding fixes. This was where I feel [Team Leader] Barb really stepped in and took over. All of us were pretty frantic as far as how to report, to put the presentation together, and to put the finishing touches on everything. I remember feeling a great sense of relief in one of our last meetings before the presentation when Barb showed how we were summing everything up. Her leadership here was exceptional.

[Team Member Peter] [Team Leader] Barb did a really good job keeping the tone of the meetings light where possible. She brought in badminton rackets or we did fun icebreakers, so it kind of de-stressed the situation a bit. And the outside dinners and the karaoke events definitely helped us bond a little bit more and get to know each other on a personal basis, as well as the business side.

[Team Leader Barb] One piece that I remember—I just have a real visual of this—when we had that two-day session in June and we were in that little conference room in Building Four and [Team Member] Kanan literally looked dazed, and we started laughing. We had been working on this for hours and all of us had that glazed look; she actually crawled out of the room.

[Team Member Peter] And the squeaky crabs. They were provided at the initial meeting, and they kind of stuck through the entire time. It was kind of a good way to bring out a laugh when we really needed it. [Team Member] Jon would take out the squeaky crab.

[Team Leader Barb] Any time you met with this group, you knew you were going to have fun. You looked forward to the meetings—it was a diverse outlet, a relief—and you knew the time away from work would be productive.

What they don't teach you in business school.

[Team Member Peter] I think that you have to find a way to build trust within each other as well. We all trusted and respected everybody's ability; we had to trust them as persons as well so that we could be open and honest and talk bluntly about what was frustrating and what was not frustrating, and I think that is where the team building came in. You had to make that a part of it so that people would feel comfortable with each other as people, which then carries over to the business side as well. Whether that is inside the office or outside the office, just having some sort of icebreaker or debriefing session really helped.

Sequence of Activities During this Phase	
When*	**Activity**
7 to 14 weeks	Team executes second half of project plan
Periodically	Team updates sponsor(s)
9 weeks	Team completes Team Effectiveness Survey to assess/address teamwork**
11 weeks	Team members complete Peer Feedback forms to generate individual feedback**
13 weeks	Team generally "crams" for its final presentation to management

*Relative to the Launch Workshop; thus, 3 weeks means three weeks *following* the launch
**Activities noted with this symbol did *not* occur in this "abbreviated" round of action learning

Pick Your Poison: Implement Change or Present to Top Management?

Although there may be little that is more challenging than implementing organizational change, the prospect of presenting to top management garners a more acute anxiety. Below, the team members describe their feelings about this unforgettable activity.

[Team Member Kelly] I think the presentation went better than I expected. I felt like we really got the point about our improvements across, and the response from [Co-Sponsor] Kathleen and the rest of the group was really positive.

[Team Member Jon] I think it went as planned. We were working up to the deadline the night before (who doesn't?), but not too late. We all had speaking portions—some large, some small—depending on the presentation strengths of the group. I remember feeling when it was all over that our sponsors really got what we had done and were happy with the result.

[Team Leader Barb] I recall thinking how much fun the presentation actually turned out to be and realizing that we brought the group's energy to whatever setting we were in, whether a team meeting, dessert session, or a final presentation to senior management.

[Team Member Mark] I think the presentation went better than expected. We were ready for all questions, and we did a very good job of communicating our results. It was great to see the importance the effort had with upper management.

A hint of the nervousness the team must have felt.

[Team Member Ann] The presentation did go as planned. We were all nervous with timing, how much detail to include, et cetera, but we got through it.

But far more emphasis on their sense of accomplishment.

[Team Member Cristina] Yes, it went as we had planned and practiced. What stood out for me the most was the delight I could see in the other team members' faces and also the managers we were presenting to. I felt as though everyone on both sides was very satisfied with the outcome.

Some had selected pre-
sentation skills as their
developmental objective;
coaching from other team
members is part of the
process.

[Team Member Peter] A lot of nervous anticipation, but I felt very confident going in. I think,
for the most part, all went as planned and expected. I enjoyed trying to build confidence in
those who were not comfortable presenting.
What stood out most was seeing some of the
managers' reactions during the presentation
and the fact that they were impressed with the
amount of work we had done. Very rewarding.

Normally the final presentation to management is followed by a "closing
workshop" in which the feedback reports, as referenced above, are distributed and the team debriefs its final presentation and overall project.
Because this round of action learning was somewhat abridged, and also
because the facilitator was unavailable for the final presentation, this
closing was omitted.

The "Action" Side—Business Results

By design, the business results of an action learning
project should be evident at the time of final presentation to management, just fourteen weeks or so
after the initial launch. That's because the team
should be reporting the results of its implementation efforts, rather than presenting recommendations for consideration. Still, results can be subject
to perception, like anything else; below, the participants discuss the results they were able to achieve.

[Team Member Cristina] I think the project
made some very good changes, as well as identified a lot of issues that needed to be brought
to the surface and worked on.

[Team Leader Barb] We achieved the business
challenge of reducing time spent on handoffs
between CSC and Operations. We calculated
that the equivalent of sixteen jobs were being
spent in handoffs between the two groups.
By reducing this number by 47.2 percent, we

saved the firm over $415,000 annually in direct labor.

[Co-Sponsor Kathleen] The team was more successful than I had hoped. We pulled the 20 percent goal out of the air, and they more than doubled it.

[Team Member Kelly] I think the project was a *huge* success. All of the improvements that we made helped both Operations and CSC improve the efficiency of their jobs.

The same requirement that initially produced dismay ("You mean we have to implement?") is now cited with pride.

[Team Member Jon] Our project yielded tangible results, as opposed to "findings." We now have a ton of new business solutions that are more cost-efficient, effective, and accurate than before. That would be how I would define a business success.

[Team Member Ann] It was a success because we were able to gain the confidence of the associates in all different levels and departments. We were able to bring Operations and CSC together in one room to have an open discussion of what works and what doesn't work and to work on solutions together. This has never really happened before and is definitely needed now and in the future for FinCo. I really wish the team did not have to end.

Benefits beyond the financial results.

[Team Member Peter] We saved over $400,000 in associate manpower by streamlining procedures. But we also brought a better understanding of roles and responsibilities to both departments. Another good result of our project, which you cannot really measure, is the improved relationship between the two sites, the empowerment. I truly think associate satisfaction is on the rise due to some of our changes.

[Team Leader Barb] I agree. We recognized a clear underlying need to have stronger com-

munication and awareness between both units and focused a lot of time on this effort (through dessert sessions, video-conferencing, focus groups). Although this was not spelled out as an objective, it was an even greater win, as we were building the partnership between the two areas, which is a prerequisite in building an effective operation.

And the "Learning" Side— Professional Development

In addition to achieving a business goal, remember that the objective of the program was to develop managers along a number of dimensions. Below, the team members discuss the kinds of skills they were able to hone via the project.

Probably not a development goal at the outset— but a great outcome nonetheless.

[Team Member Mark] From a personal perspective, the project was a great success. I was promoted to a leadership role, and working on the action team was a big part of that. I really enjoyed working with the people on the team, and I consider them my friends.

[Team Member Jon] This experience did teach me patience and trust. I had to rely, for the most part, on others to get tasks done, sell ideas, et cetera, since most of the things getting done had to be done at headquarters.

Skills around delegation, influence, and trust show up in these two discussions.

[Team Leader Barb] I was able to work on my own leadership development: Utilizing more delegation and realizing ways I can add value without doing all the work. Equally, a number of times we were challenged to think of some creative solutions for new problems. I enjoyed stretching myself in that way. I also felt that I was able to identify the different learning styles [among team members] and tailor my approach to each individual.

A number of the members mention the exposure they received to the workforce and to upper management.

[Team Member Kanan] It gave me a lot of exposure with the department because it was a high-profile project.

[Team Member Peter] This was the best thing I have been involved with since being employed at FinCo. The personal rewards came from implementing so many new things and from receiving gratitude from the associates and exposure to upper management. I think I got all that I could have out of the project and look forward to working on another one.

[Team Member Cristina] Overall, I was pleased with the team's success and think we all got something out of it. I learned more about Operations, which was one of my key objectives, and I was satisfied with that.

Problem solving

[Team Member Kelly] Personally, I really learned a lot from the CSC group, and I found it very challenging to come up with solutions to big problems. I wish that I could have been involved in the program from the beginning.

Presentation skills

[Team Member Ann] The team did allow me to grow personally, specifically with regard to presentation skills and being able to present to larger groups of audiences at all levels. Also, it felt good to establish relationships with people I didn't really know and to see us grow together and work together as a strong team. I left the team feeling like I would never again get that sense of strong team spirit, but I knew I could take it back and apply it to my area.

Teamwork skills are mentioned here, along with presentation skills.

[Team Member Peter] I wish we would have videotaped the presentation so we could reflect on all we did, as well as show those who were uncomfortable presenting how well they really did.

[Team Member Jon] I think the way it was set up, with us coming up with the 20 percent

improvement and having the project kicked off at such a high level and having such high sponsorship, really set the stage for us in a lot of ways. We did not have a lot of choice; we really had to persevere in a lot of things. The stage was definitely set in the beginning that we were going to have to persevere and get results, as opposed to the more typical "go out and find some data, tell us what you think is wrong, and present us with recommendations."

Probably one of the most critical management skills of late—"driving for results"—is apparent in these statements.

[*Team Member Mark*] I think that I am definitely more organized, more resourceful, and a better planner probably. And what I am really happy about from the whole experience is just the resources I was able to pick up over in CSC and how these contacts kind of branched out to other people I have met. When we first started the launch, it was helpful to go through all that beginning process and not just jump right in. If I have another problem or project that comes up, I will make sure to do that.

The rigor of planning and organizing was not just a "classroom exercise," but seems to have made an impression.

[*Team Member Jon*] I agree. I don't think I ever formally understood how to put an entire project together from beginning to end. I think it was a really good exercise—just put the brakes on and teach everybody about the basics of putting a project plan together and how everything should start, work in the middle, and wrap up. So I thought that was an extraordinary piece that I have already passed on to others around me.

[*Team Member Peter*] Maybe what I got out of this project is that I learned more about what being responsible for a project is. Whereas before I probably would have gone and done half this work on my own, I think I learned better how to get results out of my reps. Instead of me going out and sitting in with reps

Key lessons in delegation.

and tracking calls, I got the reps tracking themselves and trusted them to give me that information.

[Team Member Ann] We were all there for one another no matter what throughout the entire process beginning to end. I thought this was key to our success—to work together as an on-going team and to pull together in times of need.

... and a teamwork experience the members will undoubtedly use to gauge future experiences.

[Co-Sponsor Kathleen] The team members really bonded and came to care for one another. They involved lots of others in their effort, and they developed broader perspectives about the business. The changes they made showed they were really empowered.

A learning experience for all involved.

[Co-Sponsor Don] They motivated me as a sponsor to continue with the [action learning] program.

After It All

The project is over, the tape recorder switched off, the right-hand column empty. But the reflections, the learning, the growth continue.

Can you make all projects action projects, with implementation goals rather than analysis goals, and firm, short-term deadlines established up-front?

Can you engage top management in all projects using sponsorship and executive presentations?

How can you weave professional development into your business activities,

even if your organization
does not have an "official"
action learning program?

References

Reflection Learning Associates, Inc. (1996). *Field manual for a learning historian*. Unpublished manuscript.

Roth, G., & Kleiner, A. (1997, September-October). How to make experience your company's best teacher. *Harvard Business Review, 75*(5), 172–177.

Roth, G., & Kleiner, A. (1998, Autumn). Developing organizational memory through learning histories. *Organizational Dynamics*, pp. 43–60.

Senge, P., Roth, G., Roberts, C., Ross, R., Smith, B., & Kleiner, A. (1999). *The dance of change: The challenges to sustaining momentum in learning organizations*. New York: Doubleday Currency.

Andy Beaulieu *has contributed to the* Annual *each year since 1998. An organization effectiveness consultant with over fifteen years of experience, Mr. Beaulieu has consulted to clients such as NASDAQ, American Airlines, British Petroleum, Veterans Administration Hospitals, SAFELITE AutoGlass, World Bank, and Showtime Networks.*

TEACHING HOW TO LEARN
THROUGH ONLINE DISCUSSION

Zane L. Berge

Abstract: During the last decade, the pace of technological change has accelerated, and efforts to keep
up can be exhausting and confusing. Trainers are
responding to this by changing what they teach and
the way they teach it. Learners, caught in the same
struggle, are becoming aware that lifelong learning
and the willingness to learn are their keys to economic survival.

Generally, an individual learns in two ways—
passively and actively. When instructors promote a
passive learning approach, by lecturing or demonstrating to learners, students do nothing more than
listen and take notes. On the other hand, instructors
who focus on active learning demand whenever possible that the learners organize information, engage
in activities that involve skills learning, and reflect
on all they have learned and done (Malaguti & Rudnick, 1998/1999). Discussion has also been identified as an active learning strategy (Brookfield, 1986;
Brookfield & Preskill, 1999) especially suited to adult
learning. In this article, the author explores the training and preparation necessary for successful discussions, as well as those issues specifically raised by the
emergence of online discussion.

Purposes of Discussion

Given adequate student preparation, teaching through discussion is most successful when used to develop higher-level thinking skills—critical thinking, analysis, synthesis, and evaluation (Malaguti & Rudnick, 1998, 1999). They define the terms as follows:

- *Critical thinking* is the ability to interpret and make informed judgments about facts, arguments, and conclusions.

- *Analysis* is breaking a concept into its parts, explaining the interrelationships between the parts, and distinguishing relevant from irrelevant material.

- *Synthesis* is putting concepts together to form a scheme and solve problems creatively.

- *Evaluation* is using a set of criteria to come to a reasoned judgment.

Why Discussion Teaching Can Fail

Instructors cannot assume that instruction based on discussion will automatically be useful to students or that they will necessarily like it. Discussion activities, and the questions that generate them, must be carefully planned. The instructor (1) not being prepared to engage in discussions, (2) not having made explicit the ground rules for discussion, and (3) failing to model democratic participation in discussion are the main reasons why discussion fails to meet both learners' and instructors' expectations (Brookfield & Preskill, 1999). Learners need to have practice and training in using discussion methods to be successful. This is especially true when technology is used for teaching and learning (Galusha, 1997).

Technical Training

It is difficult to find a corporate or campus information technology plan that does not include training in the use of both software and hardware. It is even becoming easy to find *organizational* strategic plans, outside of information technology, that include such technical training, especially in organizations in which distance and distributed learning are important enterprise-wide.

But even successful technology training is not sufficient preparation for distance learning—especially for persons who are novice to computer systems or to the delivery of distance education. Like teamwork, discussion is ubiquitous in the workplace and in higher education classes—yet I would suggest that its processes are little understood by students or faculty! Teaching through discussion is one of the most common methods used in classrooms that are completely online or in classes that are mixed with both in-person and online delivery (Berge, 1997).

Training for Technology

Much of distance education and training involves adult learners, who may not be well-versed in the use of computer and communication systems nor the Internet. These shortcomings are compounded when a learner does not have very good communication skills, especially in written expression, given the text-based nature of computer-mediated communication. As Galusha (1997) pointed out, using electronic media in distance learning can inadvertently exclude students who lack computer or writing skills. Students will typically be offered volumes of electronic-based information, which will be a problem for some nontechnical students, as they must be taught how to manage not only their study time, but the materials and method of learning. If students are undertaking distance learning courses that require knowledge of computers, then the students must be taught, at a minimum, the fundamentals of operating the system of choice of the distance-taught course. Technical barriers must not be an issue.

Commonly, learner preparation includes instruction in connecting to remote computers at the organization, using modems, and the use of dial-in procedures and conferencing software. Learners are also given practice in using other electronic tools and services, such as email and web browser(s). Also, both instructors and learners must be trained to access technical support within their particular learning environment. A successful electronic learning environment also assumes that learners have access to and are trained in the use of information manipulation tools, such as word processing, web browsers, email, spreadsheets, etc.

Problems with the hardware or software, or even having to devote a great deal of thought to using the technology, are distracting to learners. The learner's interface with technological tools should be made as intuitive and easy as possible to overcome some of the frustration and discouragement learners (and instructors!) feel when they are not as technically literate as others (Hartley & Collins-Brown, 1999). The goal is to have a seamless interface with technology so that students can focus on the discussion at hand. Such training in the use of the technology in advance of the learning activities is best. The learner-interface interaction will also improve, as will learner and instructor confidence and sense of competence, over time and with practice.

Training for Discussion Learning and Teaching

All the technology training mentioned above is *necessary training* but *not sufficient training* for successful online discussion. Vacc (1993) said, "Learning through participation in discussions does not develop naturally; it requires the teacher's guidance" (p. 226).

Learners can be resistant to using discussion and undermine an instructor's efforts to do so, especially when they have learned from prior experience that "discussions are often a thin veneer for maintaining traditional teacher power through nontraditional means" (Brookfield & Preskill, 1999, p. 43). Learners need encouragement and guidance to (1) seek clarification when the discussion is unclear to them, (2) talk about their own ideas, (3) listen and respond to other students' ideas, (4) build on other students' ideas, which often helps them to increase their understanding and motivation, (5) be sensitive to others' feelings, and (6) regularly evaluate the discussion's effectiveness (NCTM, n.d.). NCTM goes on to state that learners can be assisted in using effective discussion when instructors:

- Encourage the development of listening skills by having one learner paraphrase what another learner has said before giving a response;
- Reward group performance during a discussion, rather than recognize individual participation;
- Help learners recognize that such feelings as rejection, frustration, and dependence may affect others' participation in the discussion;

- Reserve time at the end of a lesson to share learners' perceptions of the benefits derived from the discussion or areas of concern; and

- Use evaluative comments at the end of a lesson to initiate future discussions.

TEACHING ONLINE WRITING SKILLS

Winiecki (1999) suggested that learners should be taught online writing skills that will help everyone better understand the discussion. Some of those specific skills include the following:

- *Use Strategic Snipping:* Learners and instructors should include short excerpts of the exact portions of the original message to which they are responding. Embed these "snips" in the message, then respond to each one in turn. This creates a turn-taking conversational pattern.

- *Begin with a Synopsis:* Persons involved in online discussions should briefly summarize the conversational thread that has preceded the current message. Include contributors' names and the ideas that provide a logical lead-in to the message being contributed. This brings other participants up to speed, even if they have missed reading all the prior messages in the thread.

- *Weaving:* A summary of all the major points and contributions to the discussion should be made periodically. The ideas of all of the participants should be synthesized, and the conversation should be refocused if needed. An appropriate time for weaving is when the discussion begins to lag and therefore needs to be re-energized or when the discussion is moving off target. Weaving can be done by the facilitator or by the participants.

DEVELOPING QUESTIONS FOR ONLINE DISCUSSION

Forethought and planning are needed to develop and moderate an online discussion effectively. When questions to precipitate discussion are written, the "avenues of thought" those questions will trigger need careful consideration (Hunkins, 1972). Responding to such questions can focus student attention on essential elements of the learning experience or take the discussion participants in divergent directions. Follow-up questions can be used to request elaboration of points made or be used to refocus wandering attention.

Beaudin's (1999) survey research revealed that, for the 135 online instructors who responded, the number-one technique used to keep conversations on topic was to design questions that specifically elicited on-topic discussion. There is no point in attempting to create a rigid discussion plan that leads inexorably through the course content, but potential outcomes should at least be carefully thought through. (For a more complete discussion of how to write effective questions for a variety of online discussion formats, see Eisley, 1999, and also Muilenburg & Berge, 2000.)

CONCLUSIONS

Developing one's skill in constructing questions ahead of time is more likely to allow students to practice critical thinking, analysis, synthesis, and evaluation and to stay focused on the content and goals of the online learning experience.

Moving training and learning to distance learning settings, where much of the process is dependent on the sharing and building of knowledge through structured, written conversation, is an excellent opportunity to make the necessary preparation that must be undertaken by both instructors and learners explicit.

References

Beaudin, B.P. (1999). Keeping online asynchronous discussions on topic. *Journal of Asynchronous Learning Networks* [On-line], *3*(2). Available: www.aln.org/alnweb/journal/Vol3_issue2/beaudin.htm [last accessed 4/24/01]

Berge, Z.L. (1997). Characteristics of online teaching in post-secondary, formal education. *Educational Technology, 37*(3), 35–47.

Brookfield, S.D. (1986). *Understanding and facilitating adult learning.* San Francisco, CA: Jossey-Bass.

Brookfield, S.D., & Preskill, S. (1999). *Discussion as a way of teaching: Tools and techniques for democratic classrooms.* San Francisco, CA: Jossey-Bass.

Eisley, M.E. (1999). Guidelines for conducting instructional discussions on a computer conference. *DEOSNEWS* [On-line], *2*(1). Available: www.ed.psu.edu/acsde/deos/deosnews/deosnews2–1.asp [last accessed 4/24/01]

Galusha, J.M. (1997, December). Barriers to learning in distance education. *Interpersonal Computing and Technology: An Electronic Journal for the 21st Century*

[On-line], 5(3–4), 6–14. Available: www.emoderators.com/ipct-j/1997/n4/galusha.html [last accessed 4/24/01]

Hartley, J.R., & Collins-Brown, E. (1999). Effective pedagogies for managing collaborative learning in online learning environments. *Educational Technology & Society* [On-line], 2(2). Available: www.ifets.ieee.org/periodical/vol_2_99/formal_discussion_0399.html [last accessed 4/24/01]

Hunkins, F.P. (1972). *Questioning strategies and techniques.* Boston, MA: Allyn & Bacon.

Malaguti, P.M., & Rudnick, C.R. (1998/99, Fall/Spring) The excellence in law teaching project. Discussion teaching: An introduction to MSL's suggested method of "discussion teaching," with tips and examples. [On-line]. Available: www.mslaw.edu/Excellence%20(Articles1).htm [last accessed 4/24/01]

Muilenburg, L., & Berge, Z.L. (2000). A framework for designing questions for online learning. *DEOSNEWS* [On-line], 10(2). Available: www.emoderators.com/moderators/muilenburg.html

NCTM (National Council of Teachers of Mathematics). (n.d.). *Implementing the professional standards for teaching mathematics* [On-line]. Available: www.carson.enc.org/reform/jouranls/104917/nf_4917.htm [last accessed 4/21/01]

Vacc, N.N. (1993, December). Implementing the professional standards for teaching mathematics: Teaching and learning mathematics through classroom discussion. *Arithmetic Teacher* [On-line], 41(4), 225–227. Available: www.carson.enc.org/reform/journals/104917/nf_4917.htm [last accessed 4/24/01]

Winiecki, D.J. (1999). Keeping the thread: Adapting conversational practice to help distance students and instructors manage discussions in an asynchronous learning network. *DEOSNEWS* [On-line], 9(2). Available: www.ed.psu.edu/acsde/deos/deosnews/deosnews9_2.asp [last accessed 4/24/01]

Zane L. Berge *is currently director of training systems and of the instructional systems development graduate program at the University of Maryland, Baltimore. His scholarship in the field of computer-mediated communication and distance education includes numerous articles, chapters, workshops, and presentations. Most notable are a three-volume set,* Computer-Mediated Communication and the Online Classroom, *that encompasses higher and distance education, and a four-volume set,* Wired Together: Computer-Mediated Communication in the K-12 Classroom, *co-edited with Mauri Collins. More recently, he co-edited* Distance Training *(1998) with Deborah Schreiber. Dr. Berge's newest book is* Sustaining Distance Training *(Jossey-Bass, 2000). He consults internationally in distance education.*

Contributors

Lynne Andia
1800 Chautauqua Trail
Malvern, PA 19355
  (610) 983–9603
  fax: (610) 983–9604
  email: Lynne.Andia@airgas.com

Kristin J. Arnold, MBA, CPCM
Quality Process Consultants, Inc.
48 West Queens Way
Hampton, VA 23669
  (757) 728–0191 or (800) 589–4733
  fax: (757) 728–0192
  email: karnold@qpcteam.com

Dee Dee Aspell, M.A.
Aspell Empowerment Enterprises, Inc.
P.O. Box 460688
San Antonio, TX 78246–0688
  (210) 930–4664
  fax: (210) 828–0965
  email: deedee@aspell.com

Patrick J. Aspell, Ph.D.
Aspell Empowerment Enterprises, Inc.
P.O. Box 460688
San Antonio, TX 78246–0688
  (210) 930–4664
  fax: (210) 828–0965
  email: pat@aspell.com

Andy Beaulieu
Results for a Change
13036 Mimosa Farm Court
Rockville, MD 20850
  (301) 762–9141
  email: andy_beaulieu@troweprice
  .com

Zane L. Berge
University of Maryland—Baltimore
  Campus
1000 Hilltop Circle
Baltimore, MD 21250
  email: berge@umbc.edu

Robert Alan Black, Ph.D.
Cre8ng People, Places & Possibilities
P.O. Box 5805
Athens, GA 30604–5805
  (706) 353–3387
  email: alan@cre8ng.com
  URL: www.cre8ng.com

Brooke Broadbent
e-LearningHub
207 Bank Street, Suite 177
Ottawa, Ontario
Canada K2P 2N2
  (613) 837–6472
  fax: (613) 233–1056
  email: brooke.broadbent@ottawa
  .com
  URL: www.e-learninghub.com

Marlene Caroselli, Ed.D.
Center for Professional Development
324 Latona Road, Suite 1600
Rochester, NY 14626
  (716) 227–6512
  fax: (509) 696–5405
  email: mccpd@aol.com
  URL: hometown.aol.com/mccpd

Harriet Cohen, M.Ed.
Training Solutions
P.O. Box 984
Agoura, CA 91376–0984
　(818) 991–8116
　fax: (818) 991–2007
　email: Tsolutions@prodigy.net

John E. Fernandes
General Superintendent of
　Fuel and Ash
Southern Energy Mid-Atlantic
Morgantown Generating Station
12620 Crain Highway
Newburg, MD 20664
　(301) 843–4524
　fax: (301) 843–4640
　email: john.fernandes@
　　southernenergy.com

Adrian F. Furnham
Department of Psychology
University College London
26 Bedford Way
London WC1 0AP
England
　011 44 171 504 5395
　fax: 011 44 171 436 4276
　email: ucjtsaf@ucl.ac.uk

Diane M. Gayeski, Ph.D.
Gayeski Analytics, LLC
407 Coddington Road
Ithaca, NY 14850
　(607) 272–7700
　email: diane@dgayeski.com

Izzy Gesell, M.Ed., CSP
Wide Angle Humor
P.O. Box 962
Northampton, MA 01061
　(413) 586–2634
　fax: (413) 585–0407
　email: izzy@izzyg.com

K.S. Gupta
Senior Faculty
HAL Staff College
Vimanapura, Bangalore 560017
India
　080–5233133
　email: ksgupta37@hotmail.com

Lois B. Hart, Ed.D.
President, Leadership Dynamics
Director, Women's Leadership
　Institute
10951 Isabelle Road
Lafayette, CO 80026
　(303) 666–4046
　fax: (303) 666–4074
　email: lhart@seqnet.net

Cher Holton, Ph.D.
The Holton Consulting Group, Inc.
4704 Little Falls Drive, Suite 300
Raleigh, NC 27609
　(919) 783–7088 or (800) 336–3940
　fax: (919) 781–2218
　email: DrCher@aol.com

David B. Johnson
Los Angeles World Airports
7301 World Way West, 9th Floor
Los Angeles, CA 90045
　(310) 535–6692
　fax: (310) 649–3489
　email: djohnson@airports.ci.la.ca.us

H.B. Karp
Personal Growth Systems
4932 Barn Swallow Drive
Chesapeake, VA 23321
(757) 488–3536
email: pgshank@aol.com

George Land
Chief Scientist
Leadership 2000, a division of SAIC
3333 North 44th Street
Phoenix, AZ 85018
(602) 852–0223
fax: (602) 852–0232
email: George@L2000.com

Anne M. McMahon, Ph.D.
Professor of Management
Youngstown State University
One University Plaza
Youngstown, OH 44555
(330) 742–2350
fax: (330) 742–1459
email: ammcmaho@cc.ysu.edu

Carol Mikanowicz, Ph.D.
Professor of Health Professions
Youngstown State University
One University Plaza
Youngstown, OH 44555
(330) 742–3658
fax: (330) 742–2921
email: ckmikano@cc.ysu.edu

Debbie Newman, MA, MFT
Working Relationships
16055 Ventura Boulevard, Suite 717
Encino, CA 91436
(818) 385–0550
fax: (818) 891–2926
email: WorkingRel@aol.com

John E. Oliver, Ph.D.
Valdosta State University
Department of Management
Valdosta, GA 31698
(912) 245–2233
email: joliver@valdosta.edu

Robert C. Preziosi, D.P.A.
Professor of Management
Wayne Huizenga Graduate School of
　Business
Nova Southwestern University
3100 SW 9th Avenue
Fort Lauderdale, FL 33315
(954) 262–5111
fax: (954) 262–3965
email: preziosi@huizenga.nova.edu

Linda Raudenbush
7201 Kindler Road
Columbia, MD 21046
(410) 381-2747
fax:(410) 381-0472

C. Louise Sellaro, D.B.A.
Professor of Management
Youngstown State University
One University Plaza
Youngstown, OH 44555
(330) 742–1893
fax: (330) 742–1459
email: clsellar@cc.ysu.edu

Mel Silberman
President
Active Training
26 Linden Lane
Princeton, NJ 08540
(609) 924–8157
email: mel@activetraining.com
URL: www.activetraining.com

Mark W. Smith
Helix Associates, LLC
2176 Hillsboro Road, Suite 120
Franklin, TN 37069
  (615) 595–9129
  fax: (615) 595–9128
  email: smithmw@bellsouth.net

Saundra Stroope
WorldCom
2400 North Glenville
Dept/Loc 9836/107
Richardson, TX 75082
  (972) 729–6689
  fax: (972) 729–7347
  email: Saundra.Stroope@wcom.com

Steve Sugar
The Game Group
10320 Kettledrum Court
Ellicott City, MD 21042
  (410) 418-4930
  email: ssugar@erols.com
  URL: www.thegamegroup.com

Eleazar O. Velazquez
Communications Specialist
National Skill Standards Board
1441 L Street NW, Suite 9000
Washington, DC 20005
  (877) THE-NSSB OR (877)
  843–6772
  direct: (202) 254–8628
  fax: (202) 254–8646
  email: information@nssb.org
  URL: www.nssb.org

Homer Warren, D.B.A.
Associate Professor of Marketing
Youngstown State University
One University Plaza
Youngstown, OH 44555
  (330) 742–1816
  fax: (330) 742–1459
  email: hbwarren@cc.ysu.edu

Janet Winchester-Silbaugh
Senior Consultant
Change Management Resources
51 Pinon Heights
Sandia Park, NM 87047
  (505) 286–2210
  fax: (505) 286–2211
  email: Silbaugh@silicon-desert.com

Contents of the Companion Volume, The 2002 Annual: Volume 2, Consulting

---

*See Experiential Learning Activities Categories, p. 6, for an explanation of the numbering system.